16

D1252558

DOCTOR WHO

BBC

THE EIGHTH DOCTOR

VOL 1: A MATTER OF LIFE AND DEATH

"George Mann easily matches Steven Moffat as a writer... and the art by Emma Vieceli is a delight."

MY GEEKY GEEKY WAYS

"The adventures of the Eighth Doctor are a welcome addition to Titan's line... they give us an ideal opportunity to learn more about this Doctor... there's plenty here to discover, and with art as strong as Vieceli's, it's an adventure well worth joining!"

COMIC BUZZ

"What George Mann has delivered is simply fascinating... he's managed to embrace the spirit of the Eighth Doctor beautifully. I find myself elated with the artwork; it helped bring this tale to life, with the emotion oozing off the page."

SNAP POW

"An exciting spectacle... a fun little comic and a great beginning for the Eighth Doctor and Josie's travels in the TARDIS."

BLOGTOR WHO

"Mann doesn't disappoint his reader, giving an authentic McGann-voiced Doctor his reins and letting him New Who it up a little. The artwork embraces the grand spirit of adventure of Who in general and this Doctor in particular... You'll find yourself returning, time and time again!"

FLICKERING MYTH

"Yet another top notch book from Titan. Any Eighth Doctor fans out there will find more than enough to enjoy, and hopefully he'll gain some new fans as well!"

NERDS UNCHAINED

TITAN COMICS

EDITOR
Andrew James

ASSISTANT EDITORS
Jessica Burton
Gabriela Houston

COLLECTION DESIGNER
Rob Farmer

SENIOR EDITOR
Steve White

TITAN COMICS EDITORIAL
Lizzie Kaye, Tom Williams

PRODUCTION SUPERVISORS
Maria Pearson,
Jackie Flook

PRODUCTION MANAGER
Obi Onuora

STUDIO MANAGER
Emma Smith

SENIOR SALES MANAGER
Steve Tothill

SENIOR MARKETING & PRESS OFFICER
Owen Johnson

DIRECT SALES & MARKETING MANAGER
Ricky Claydon

COMMERCIAL MANAGER
Michelle Fairlamb

PUBLISHING MANAGER
Darryl Tothill

PUBLISHING DIRECTOR
Chris Teather

OPERATIONS DIRECTOR
Leigh Baulch

EXECUTIVE DIRECTOR
Vivian Cheung

PUBLISHER
Nick Landau

Special thanks to Steven Moffat, Brian Minchin, Mandy Thwaites, Matt Nicholls, James Dudley, Edward Russell, Derek Ritchie, Scott Handcock, Kirsty Mullan, Kate Bush, Julia Nocciolino, and Ed Casey, for their invaluable assistance.

DOCTOR WHO: THE EIGHTH DOCTOR VOL 1: A MATTER OF LIFE AND DEATH
HB ISBN: 9781782767534 SB ISBN: 9781785852855
Published by Titan Comics, a division of Titan Publishing Group, Ltd. 144 Southwark Street, London, SE1 0UP.

A CIP catalogue record for this title is available from the British Library.
First edition: July 2016.

10 9 8 7 6 5 4 3 2 1

Printed in China. TC0936

BBC WORLDWIDE

DIRECTOR OF EDITORIAL GOVERNANCE
Nicolas Brett

DIRECTOR OF CONSUMER PRODUCTS AND PUBLISHING
Andrew Moultrie

HEAD OF UK PUBLISHING
Chris Kerwin

PUBLISHER
Mandy Thwaites

PUBLISHING CO-ORDINATOR
Eva Abramik

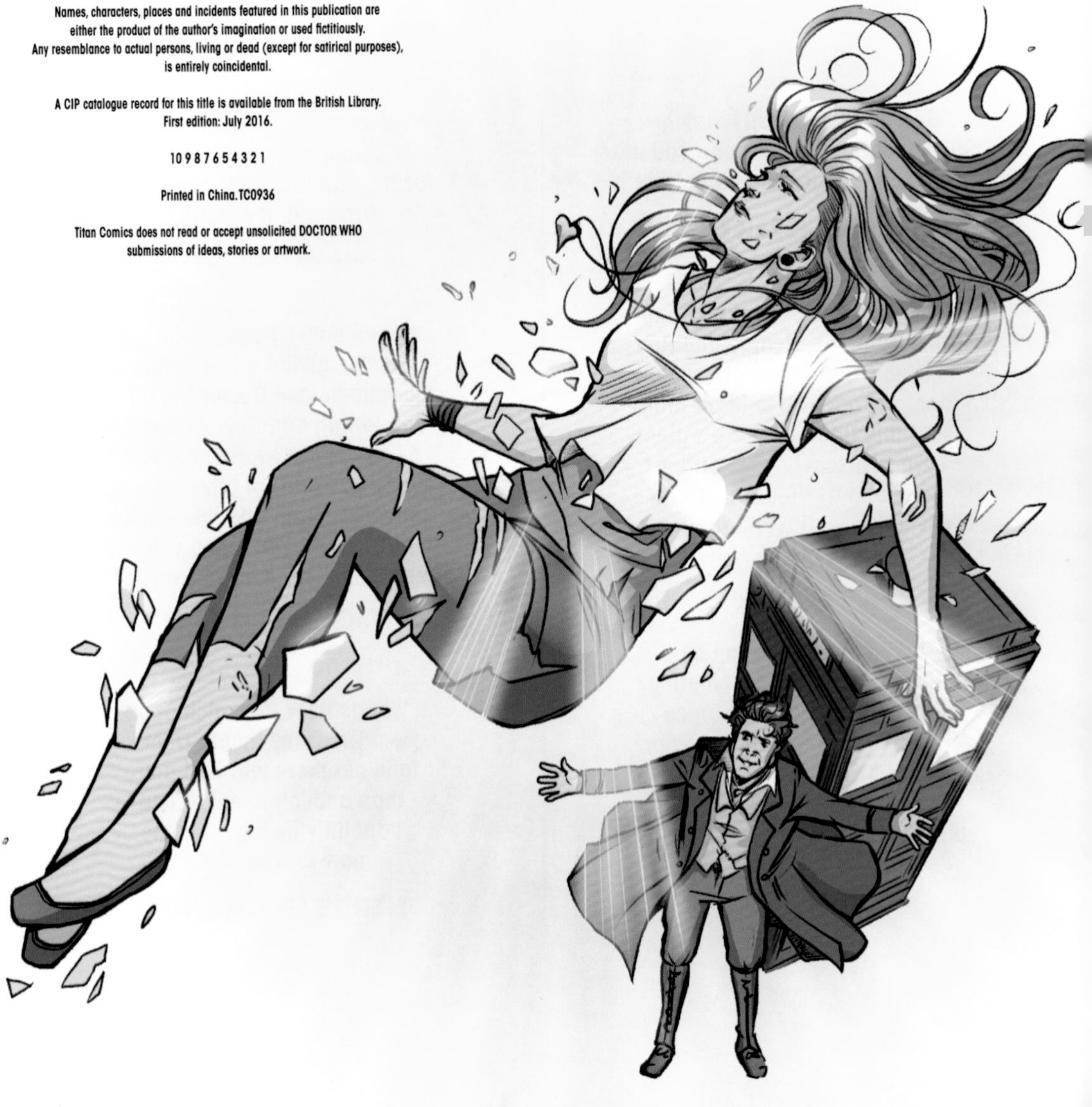

DOCTOR WHO
THE EIGHTH DOCTOR

BBC

VOL 1: A MATTER OF LIFE AND DEATH

WRITER: GEORGE MANN

ARTIST: EMMA VIECELI

COLORIST: HI FI

LETTERS: RICHARD STARKINGS AND COMICRAFT'S JIMMY BETANCOURT

www.titan-comics.com

BBC

DOCTOR WHO

THE EIGHTH DOCTOR

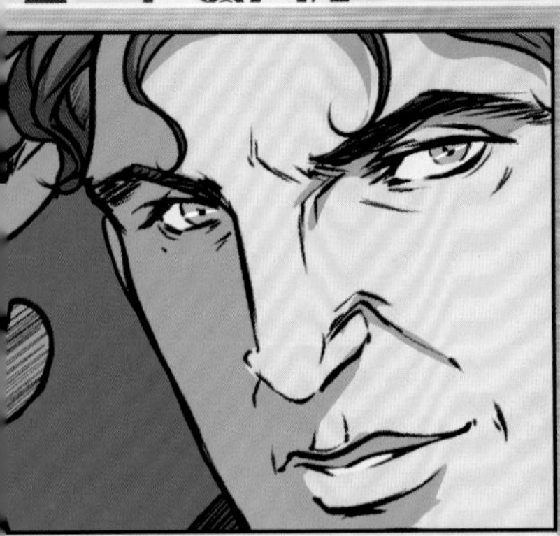

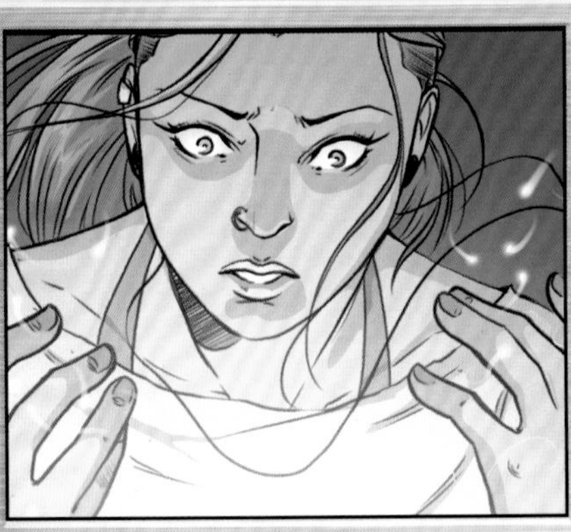

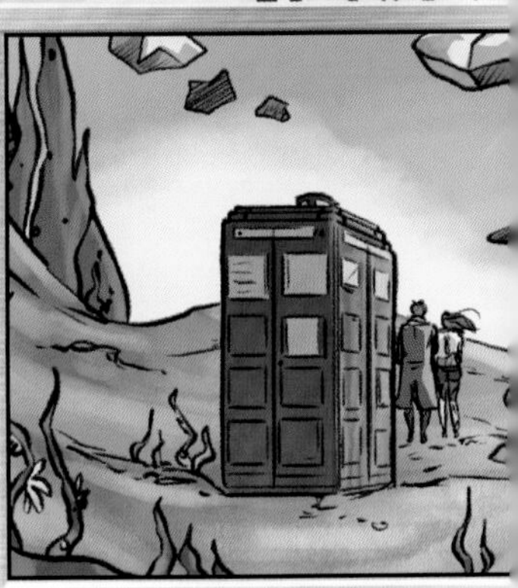

THE DOCTOR

A Time Lord of Gallifrey, the Eighth Doctor is an effortlessly charming, romantic soul wandering the universe in search of culture, companionship and adventure. He is passionate, enthusiastic and eccentric – even in the darkest of days!

JOSEPHINE DAY

Better known as Josie, this cyan-haired artist from Earth is about to capture the Doctor's attention with her mysterious paintings. Don't hang around – turn the page and meet her for the very first time!

THE TARDIS

'Time and Relative Dimension in Space'. Bigger on the inside, this unassuming blue box is your ticket to unforgettable adventure! The Doctor likes to think he's in control, but often the TARDIS takes him where and when he needs to be...

PREVIOUSLY...

The Eighth Doctor has come a long way since he regenerated in the morgue of Grace Holloway's hospital. He has known many friends and fast companions in his life – Charley Pollard, C'rizz, Lucie Miller, Tamsin Drew, Molly O'Sullivan, and many more.

Now traveling alone after an intense period in his long life, the Doctor has returned to his most regular haunt... Earth.

When you've finished reading the collection, please email your thoughts to doctorwhocomic@titanemail.com

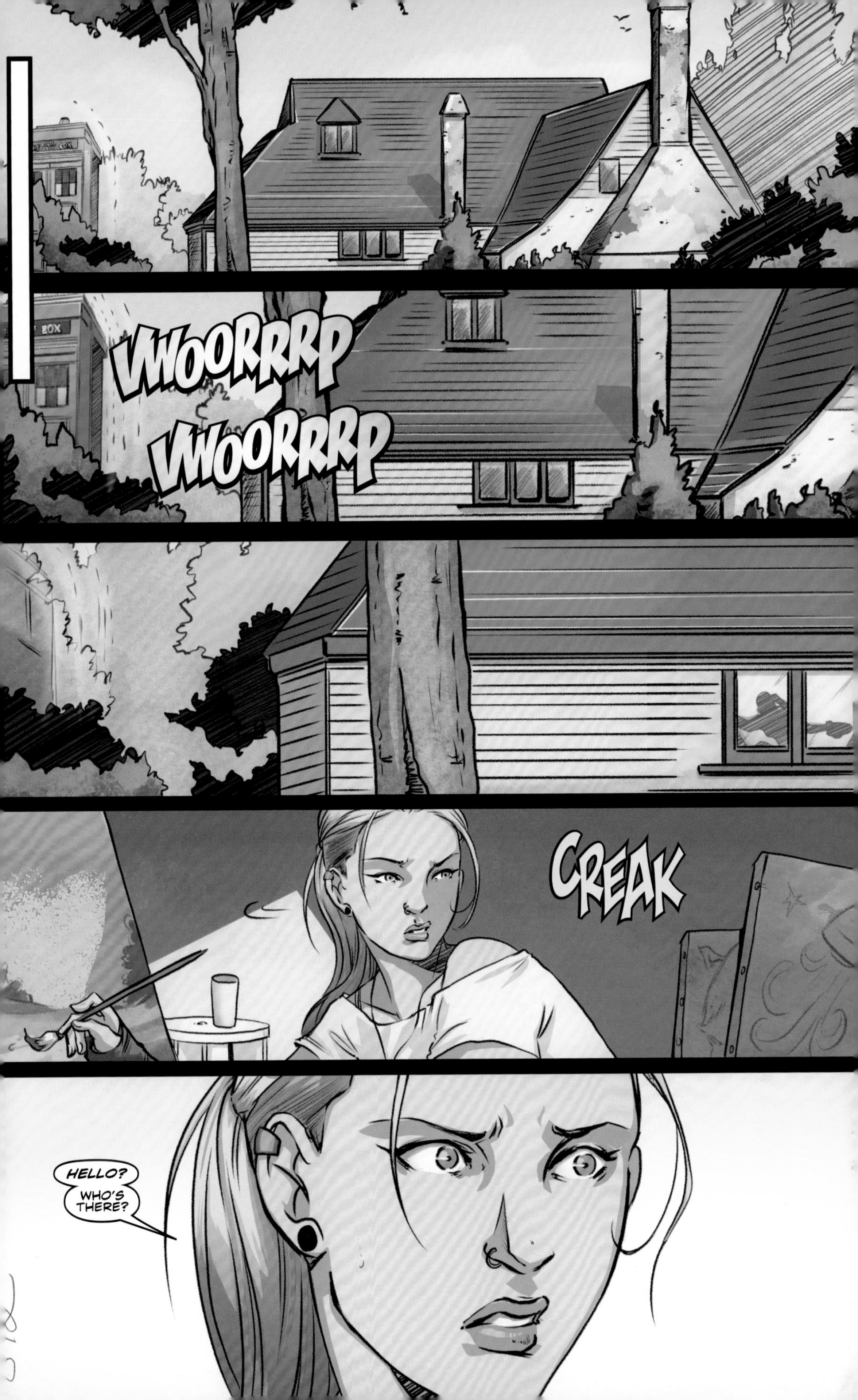
VWOORRRP
VWOORRRP
CREAK
HELLO? WHO'S THERE?

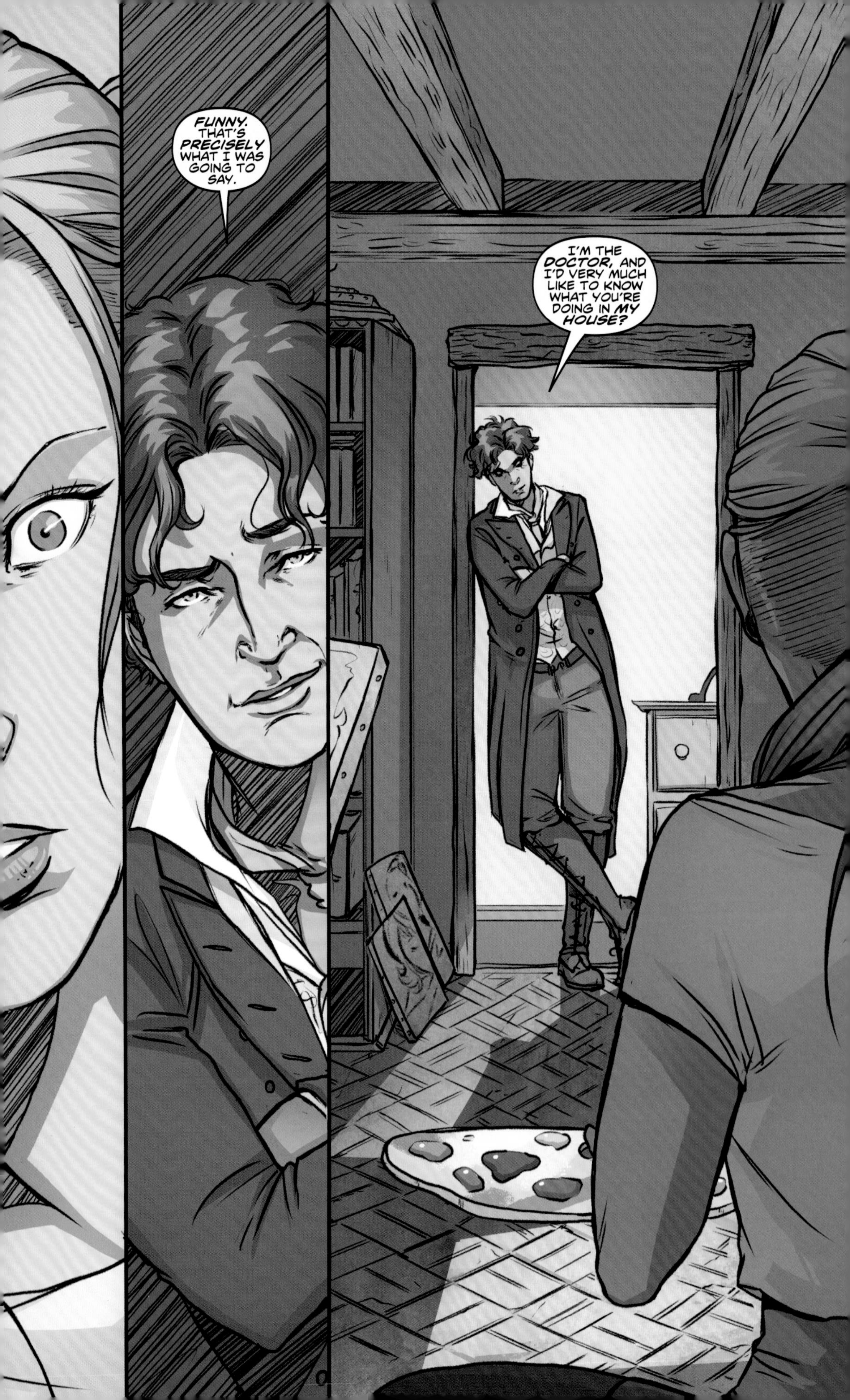
FUNNY. THAT'S PRECISELY WHAT I WAS GOING TO SAY.
I'M THE DOCTOR, AND I'D VERY MUCH LIKE TO KNOW WHAT YOU'RE DOING IN MY HOUSE?

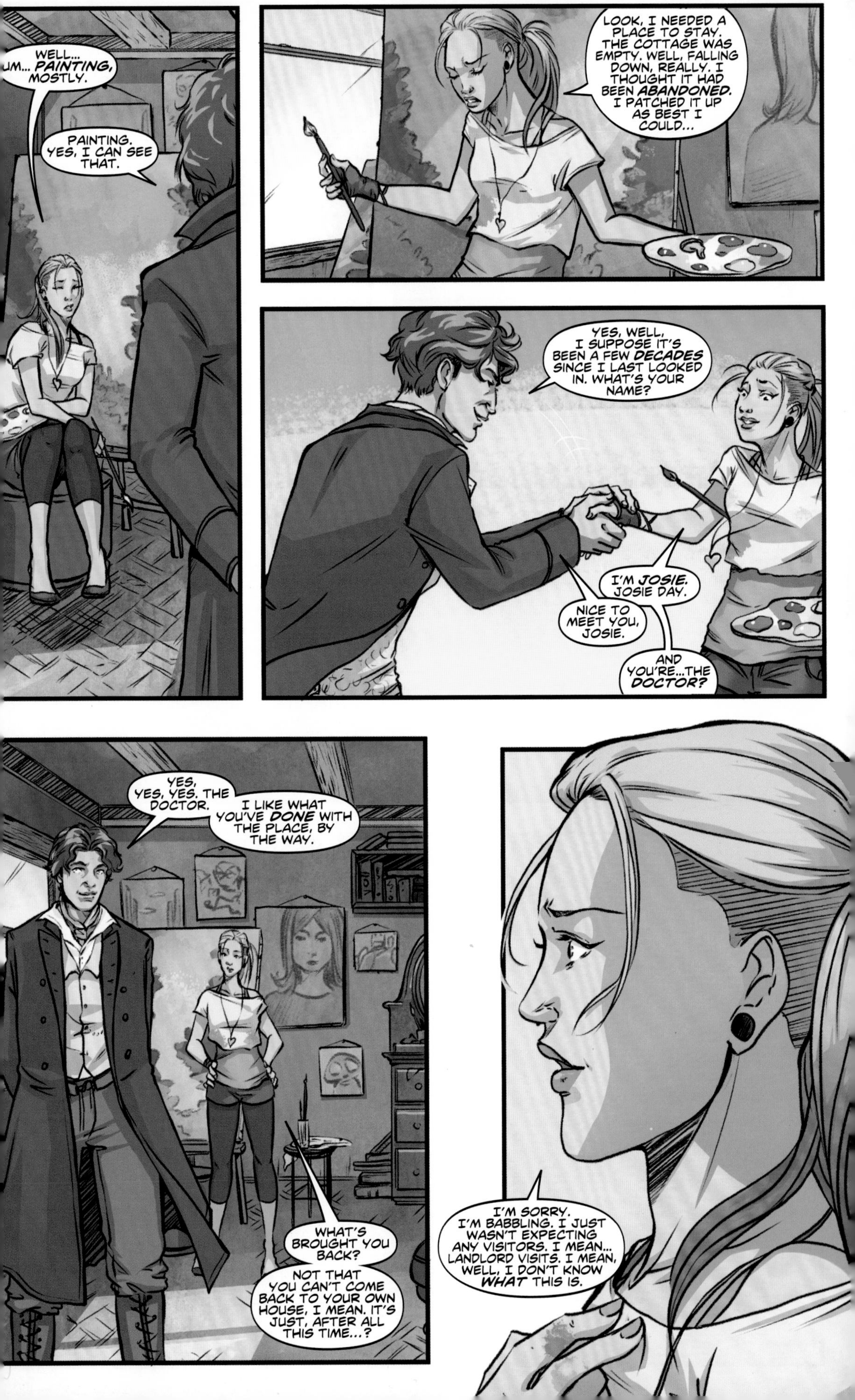
WELL... UM... PAINTING, MOSTLY.
PAINTING. YES, I CAN SEE THAT.
LOOK, I NEEDED A PLACE TO STAY. THE COTTAGE WAS EMPTY. WELL, FALLING DOWN, REALLY. I THOUGHT IT HAD BEEN ABANDONED. I PATCHED IT UP AS BEST I COULD...
YES, WELL, I SUPPOSE IT'S BEEN A FEW DECADES SINCE I LAST LOOKED IN. WHAT'S YOUR NAME?
I'M JOSIE. JOSIE DAY.
NICE TO MEET YOU, JOSIE.
AND YOU'RE...THE DOCTOR?
YES, YES, YES. THE DOCTOR.
I LIKE WHAT YOU'VE DONE WITH THE PLACE, BY THE WAY.
WHAT'S BROUGHT YOU BACK?
NOT THAT YOU CAN'T COME BACK TO YOUR OWN HOUSE, I MEAN. IT'S JUST, AFTER ALL THIS TIME...?
I'M SORRY. I'M BABBLING. I JUST WASN'T EXPECTING ANY VISITORS. I MEAN... LANDLORD VISITS. I MEAN, WELL, I DON'T KNOW WHAT THIS IS.

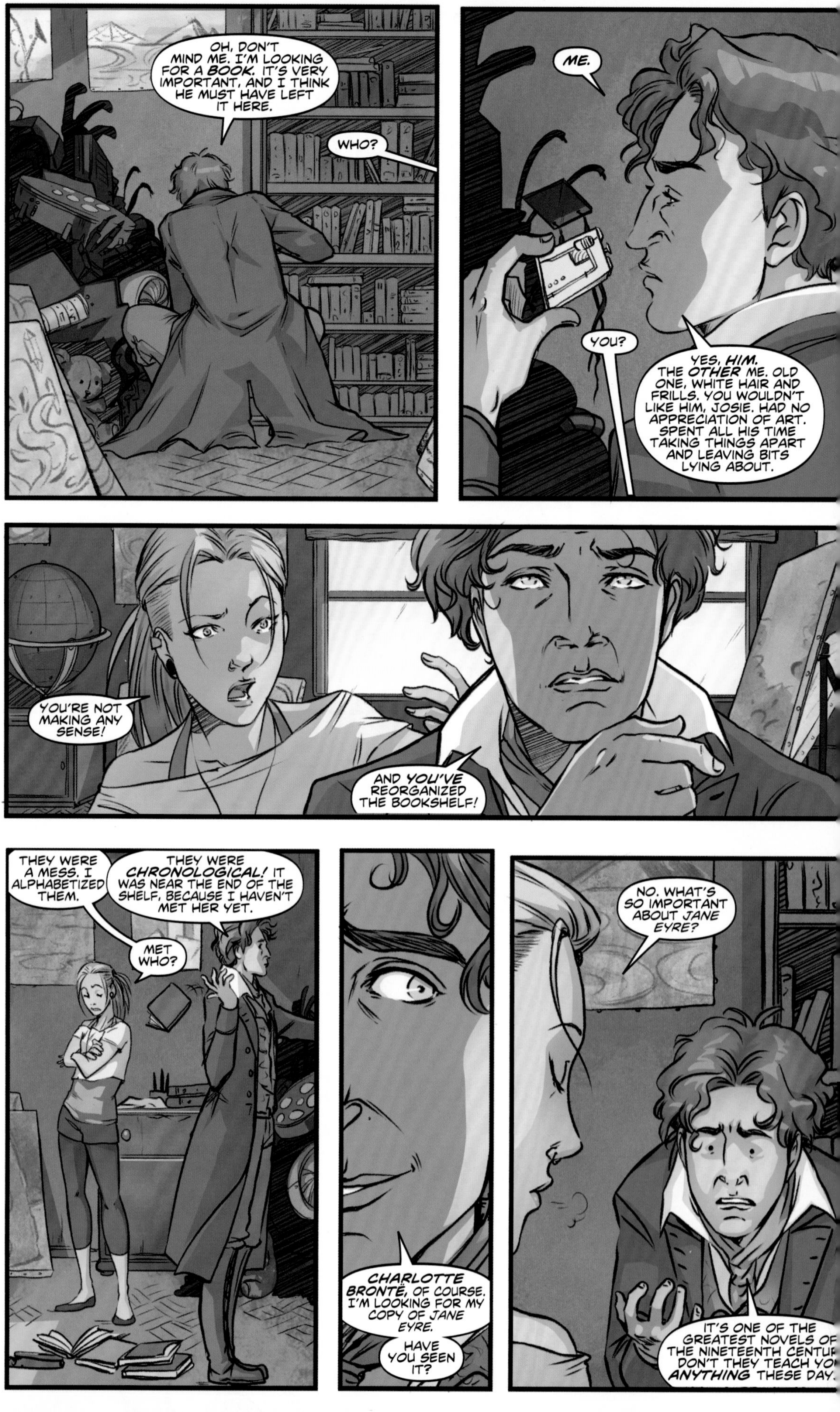
OH, DON'T MIND ME. I'M LOOKING FOR A *BOOK*. IT'S VERY IMPORTANT, AND I THINK HE MUST HAVE LEFT IT HERE.
WHO?
ME.
YOU?
YES, *HIM.* THE *OTHER* ME. OLD ONE, WHITE HAIR AND FRILLS. YOU WOULDN'T LIKE HIM, JOSIE. HAD NO APPRECIATION OF ART. SPENT ALL HIS TIME TAKING THINGS APART AND LEAVING BITS LYING ABOUT.
YOU'RE NOT MAKING ANY SENSE!
AND *YOU'VE* REORGANIZED THE BOOKSHELF!
THEY WERE A MESS. I ALPHABETIZED THEM.
THEY WERE *CHRONOLOGICAL!* IT WAS NEAR THE END OF THE SHELF, BECAUSE I HAVEN'T MET HER YET.
MET WHO?
CHARLOTTE BRONTË, OF COURSE. I'M LOOKING FOR MY COPY OF *JANE EYRE*.
HAVE YOU SEEN IT?
NO. WHAT'S SO IMPORTANT ABOUT *JANE EYRE*?
IT'S ONE OF THE GREATEST NOVELS OF THE NINETEENTH CENTUR DON'T THEY TEACH YO *ANYTHING* THESE DAY

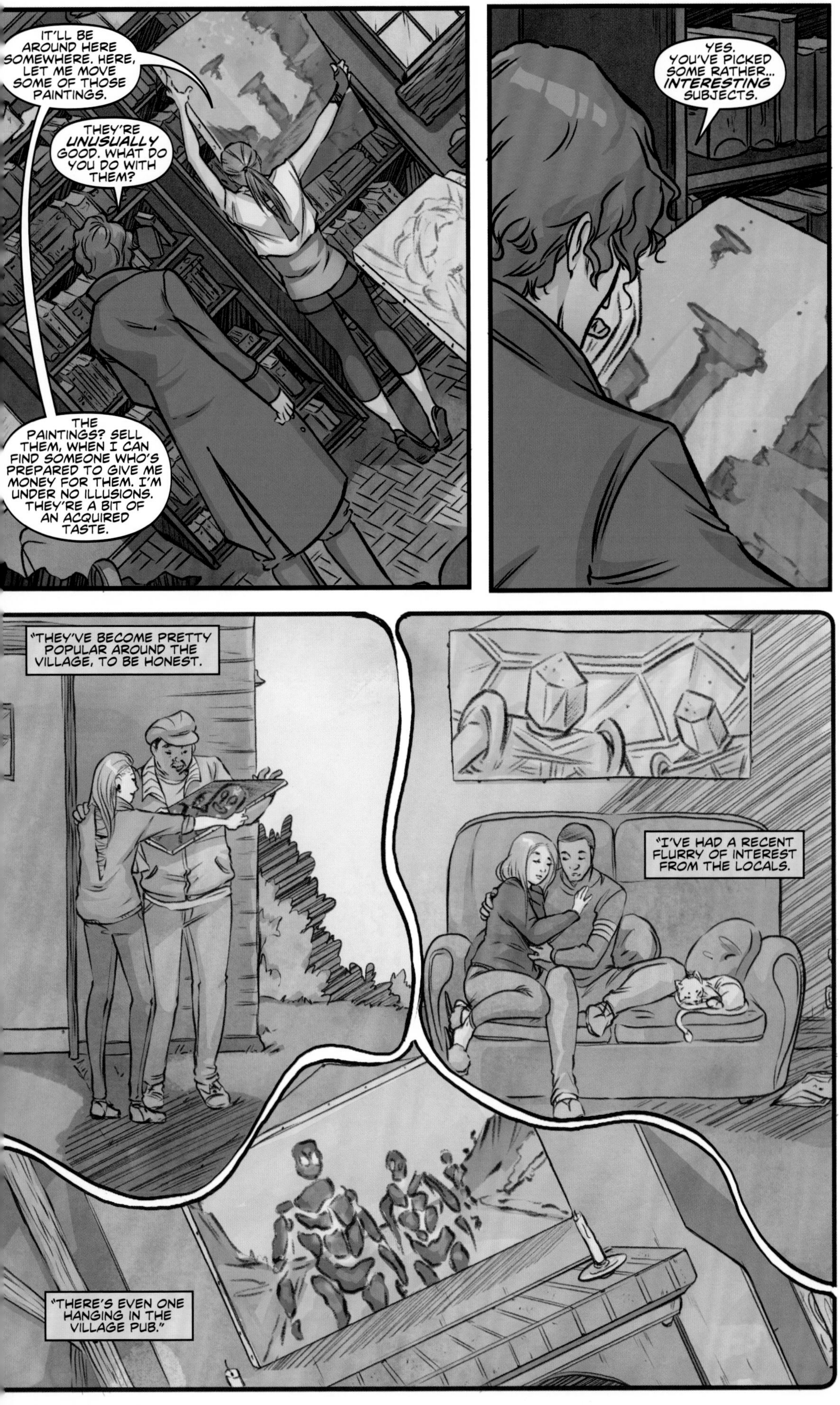
IT'LL BE AROUND HERE SOMEWHERE. HERE, LET ME MOVE SOME OF THOSE PAINTINGS.
THEY'RE *UNUSUALLY* GOOD. WHAT DO YOU DO WITH THEM?
THE PAINTINGS? SELL THEM, WHEN I CAN FIND SOMEONE WHO'S PREPARED TO GIVE ME MONEY FOR THEM. I'M UNDER NO ILLUSIONS. THEY'RE A BIT OF AN ACQUIRED TASTE.
YES. YOU'VE PICKED SOME RATHER... *INTERESTING* SUBJECTS.
"THEY'VE BECOME PRETTY POPULAR AROUND THE VILLAGE, TO BE HONEST.
"I'VE HAD A RECENT FLURRY OF INTEREST FROM THE LOCALS.
"THERE'S EVEN ONE HANGING IN THE VILLAGE PUB."

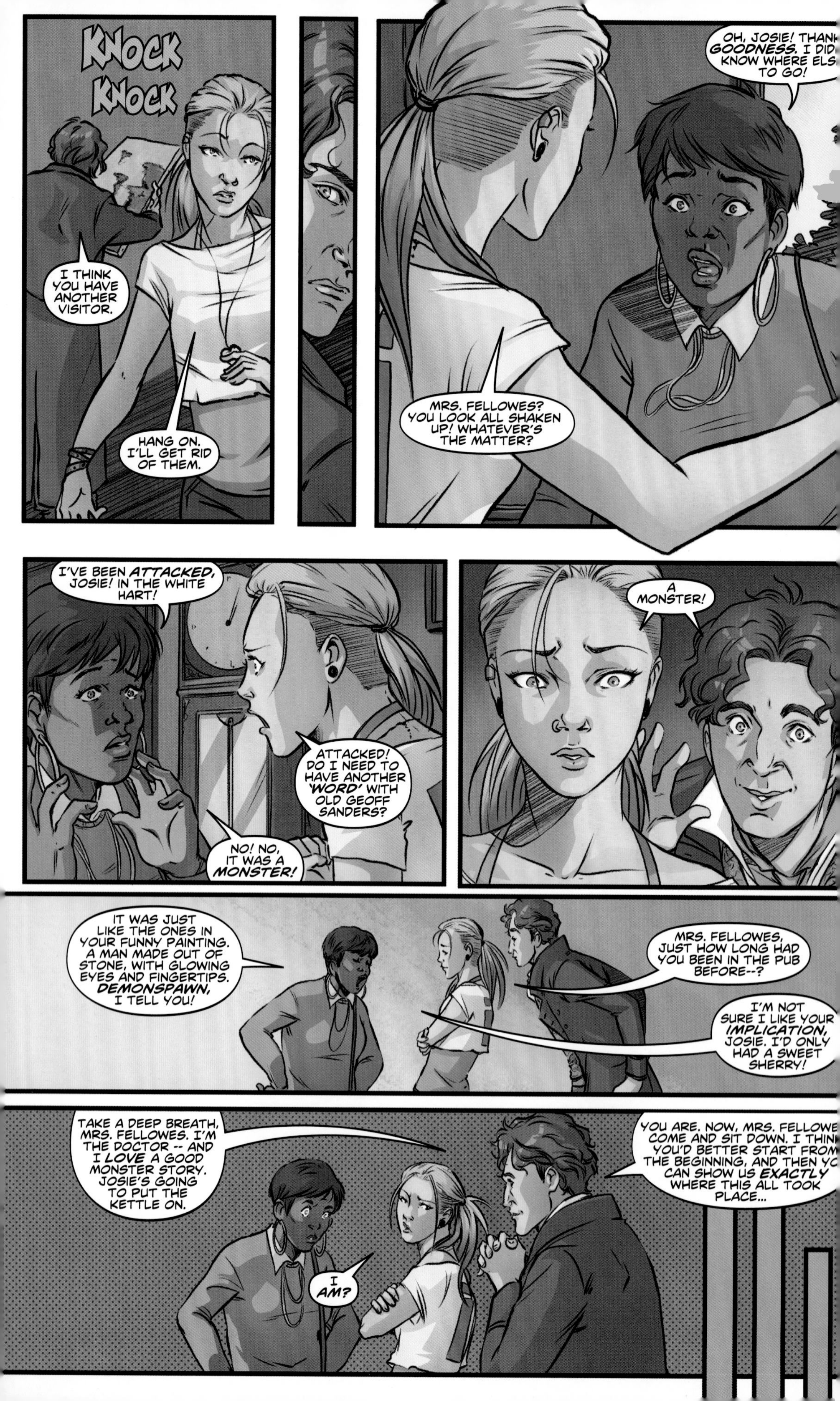
KNOCK KNOCK
I THINK YOU HAVE ANOTHER VISITOR.
HANG ON. I'LL GET RID OF THEM.
OH, JOSIE! THANK GOODNESS. I DIDN'T KNOW WHERE ELSE TO GO!
MRS. FELLOWES? YOU LOOK ALL SHAKEN UP! WHATEVER'S THE MATTER?
I'VE BEEN ATTACKED, JOSIE! IN THE WHITE HART!
ATTACKED! DO I NEED TO HAVE ANOTHER 'WORD' WITH OLD GEOFF SANDERS?
NO! NO, IT WAS A MONSTER!
A MONSTER!
IT WAS JUST LIKE THE ONES IN YOUR FUNNY PAINTING. A MAN MADE OUT OF STONE, WITH GLOWING EYES AND FINGERTIPS. DEMONSPAWN, I TELL YOU!
MRS. FELLOWES, JUST HOW LONG HAD YOU BEEN IN THE PUB BEFORE--?
I'M NOT SURE I LIKE YOUR IMPLICATION, JOSIE. I'D ONLY HAD A SWEET SHERRY!
TAKE A DEEP BREATH, MRS. FELLOWES. I'M THE DOCTOR -- AND I LOVE A GOOD MONSTER STORY. JOSIE'S GOING TO PUT THE KETTLE ON.
I AM?
YOU ARE. NOW, MRS. FELLOWES, COME AND SIT DOWN. I THINK YOU'D BETTER START FROM THE BEGINNING, AND THEN YOU CAN SHOW US EXACTLY WHERE THIS ALL TOOK PLACE...

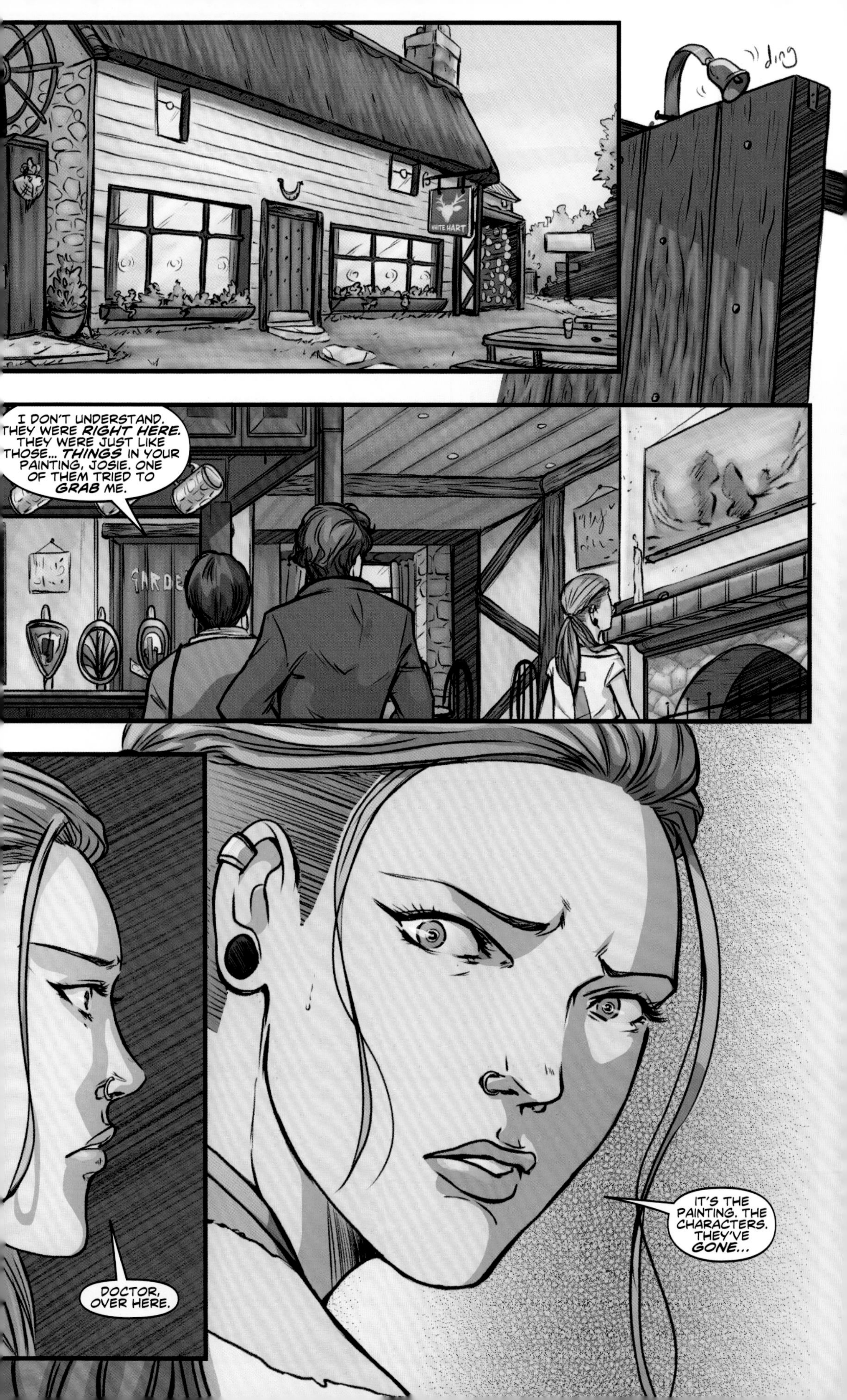
ding
WHITE HART
I DON'T UNDERSTAND. THEY WERE RIGHT HERE. THEY WERE JUST LIKE THOSE... THINGS IN YOUR PAINTING, JOSIE. ONE OF THEM TRIED TO GRAB ME.
IT'S THE PAINTING. THE CHARACTERS. THEY'VE GONE...
DOCTOR, OVER HERE.

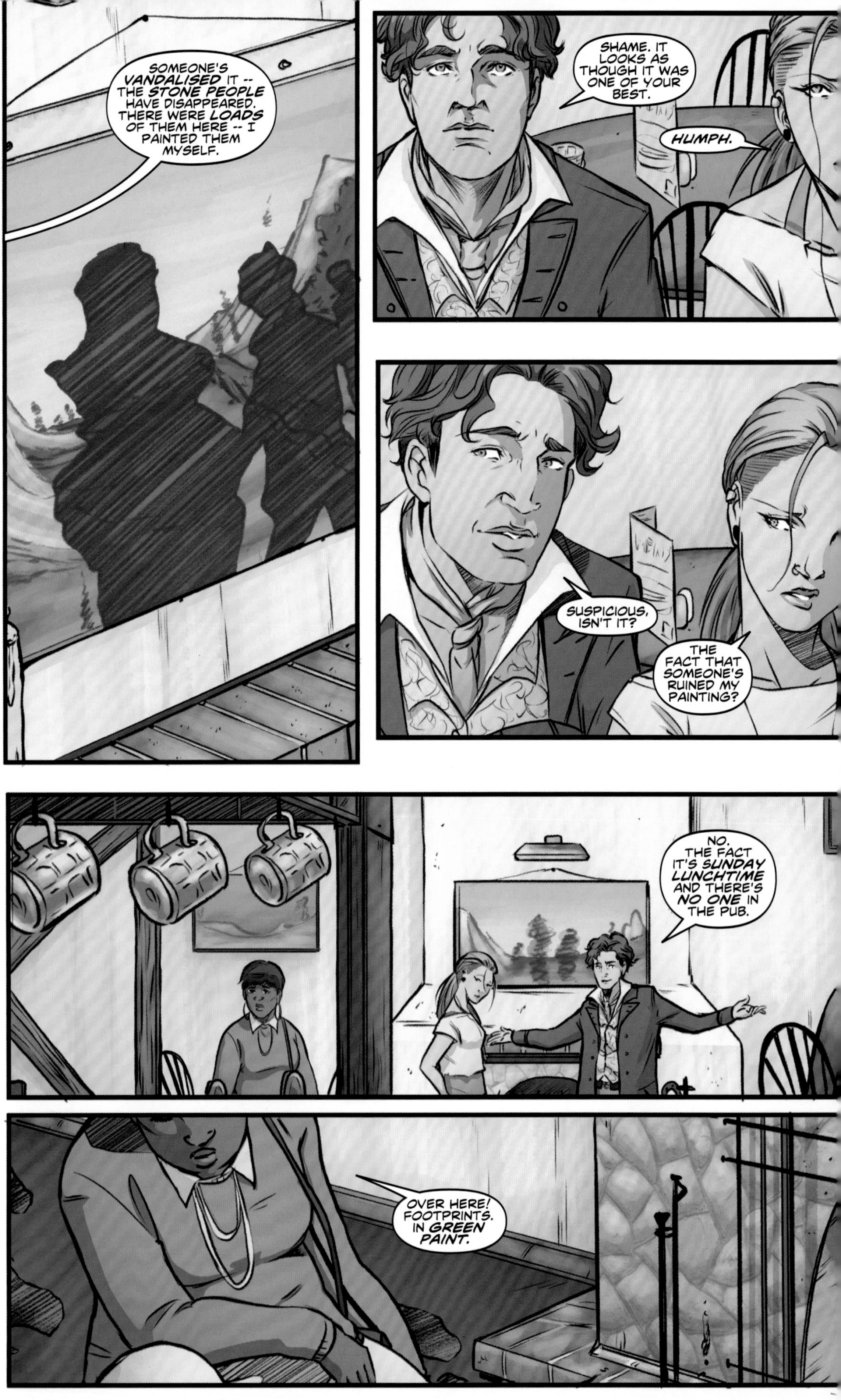
SOMEONE'S VANDALISED IT -- THE STONE PEOPLE HAVE DISAPPEARED. THERE WERE LOADS OF THEM HERE -- I PAINTED THEM MYSELF.
SHAME. IT LOOKS AS THOUGH IT WAS ONE OF YOUR BEST.
HUMPH.
SUSPICIOUS, ISN'T IT?
THE FACT THAT SOMEONE'S RUINED MY PAINTING?
NO. THE FACT IT'S SUNDAY LUNCHTIME AND THERE'S NO ONE IN THE PUB.
OVER HERE! FOOTPRINTS. IN GREEN PAINT.

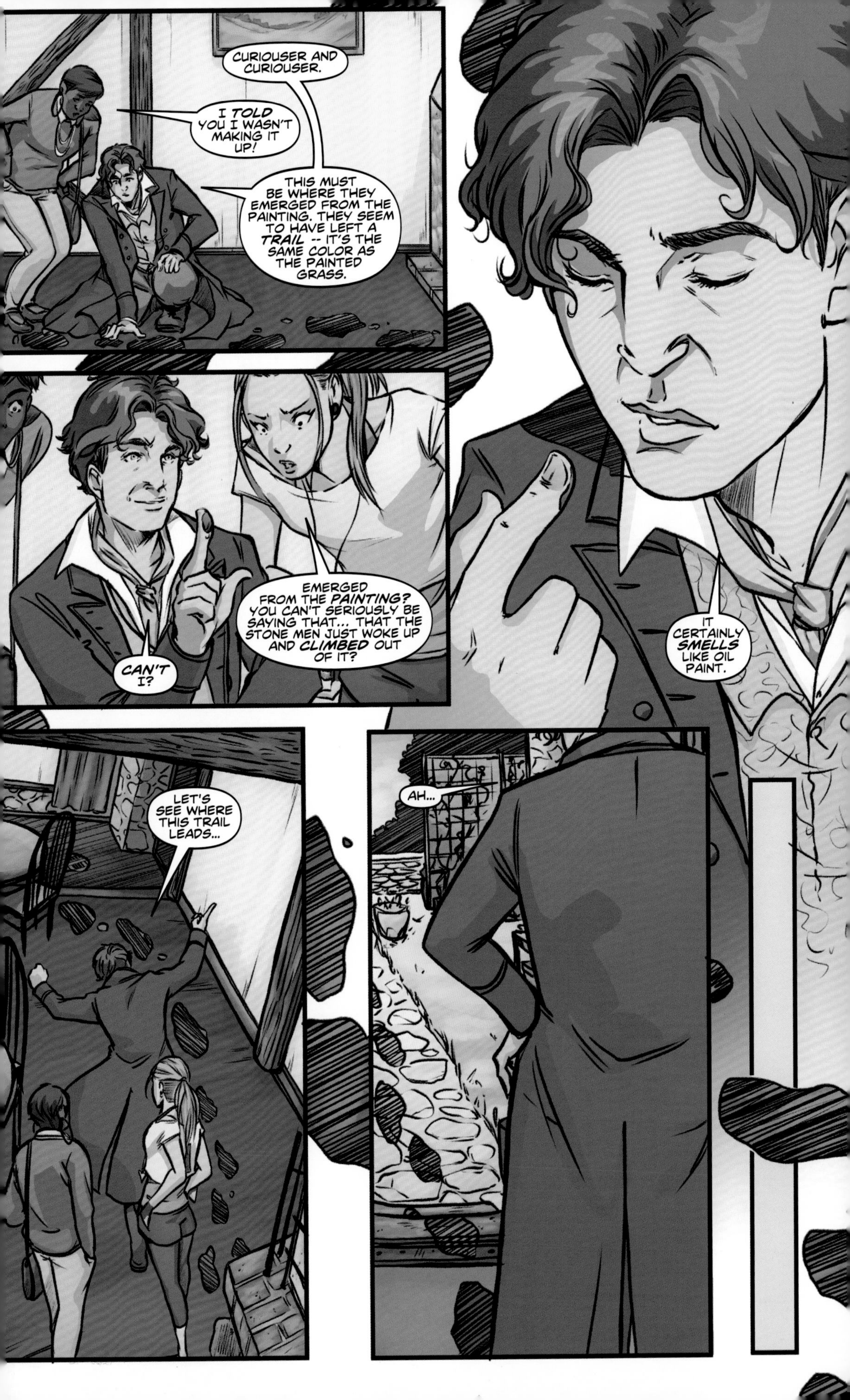
CURIOUSER AND CURIOUSER.
I TOLD YOU I WASN'T MAKING IT UP!
THIS MUST BE WHERE THEY EMERGED FROM THE PAINTING. THEY SEEM TO HAVE LEFT A TRAIL -- IT'S THE SAME COLOR AS THE PAINTED GRASS.
IT CERTAINLY SMELLS LIKE OIL PAINT.
EMERGED FROM THE PAINTING? YOU CAN'T SERIOUSLY BE SAYING THAT... THAT THE STONE MEN JUST WOKE UP AND CLIMBED OUT OF IT?
CAN'T I?
LET'S SEE WHERE THIS TRAIL LEADS...
AH...

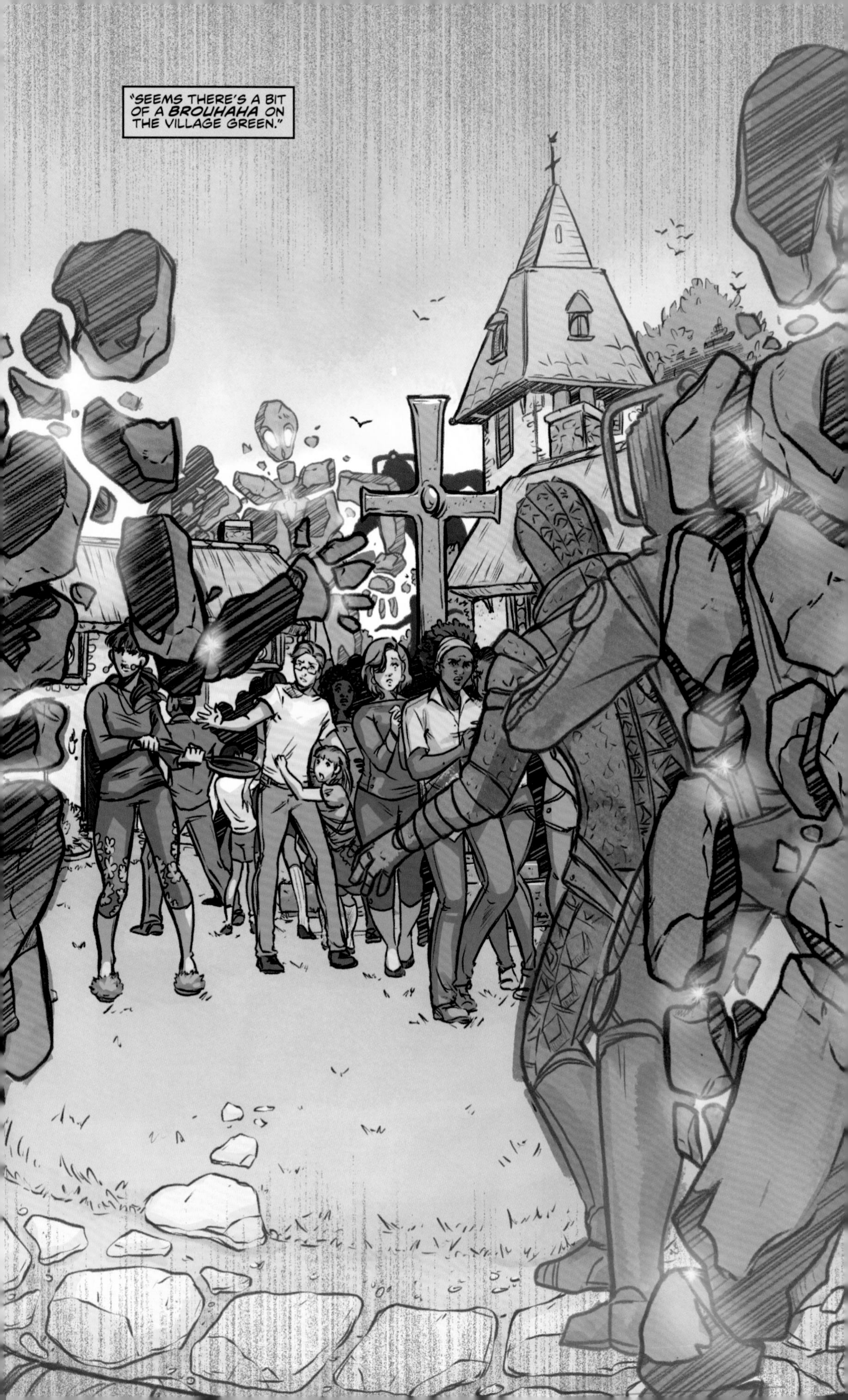
"SEEMS THERE'S A BIT
OF A BROUHAHA ON
THE VILLAGE GREEN."

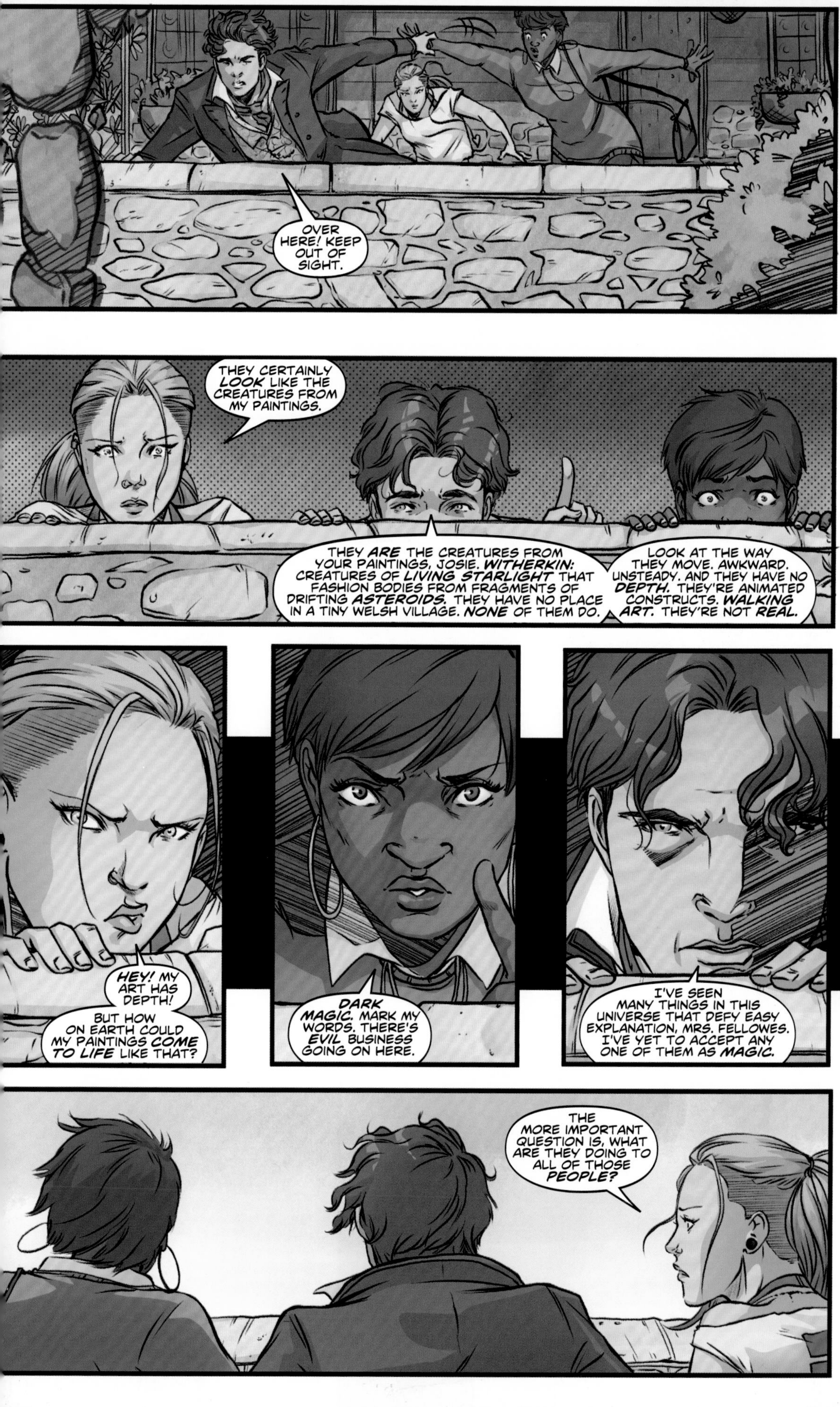
OVER HERE! KEEP OUT OF SIGHT.
THEY CERTAINLY LOOK LIKE THE CREATURES FROM MY PAINTINGS.
THEY ARE THE CREATURES FROM YOUR PAINTINGS, JOSIE. WITHERKIN: CREATURES OF LIVING STARLIGHT THAT FASHION BODIES FROM FRAGMENTS OF DRIFTING ASTEROIDS. THEY HAVE NO PLACE IN A TINY WELSH VILLAGE. NONE OF THEM DO.
LOOK AT THE WAY THEY MOVE. AWKWARD. UNSTEADY. AND THEY HAVE NO DEPTH. THEY'RE ANIMATED CONSTRUCTS. WALKING ART. THEY'RE NOT REAL.
HEY! MY ART HAS DEPTH!
BUT HOW ON EARTH COULD MY PAINTINGS COME TO LIFE LIKE THAT?
DARK MAGIC. MARK MY WORDS. THERE'S EVIL BUSINESS GOING ON HERE.
I'VE SEEN MANY THINGS IN THIS UNIVERSE THAT DEFY EASY EXPLANATION, MRS. FELLOWES. I'VE YET TO ACCEPT ANY ONE OF THEM AS MAGIC.
THE MORE IMPORTANT QUESTION IS, WHAT ARE THEY DOING TO ALL OF THOSE PEOPLE?

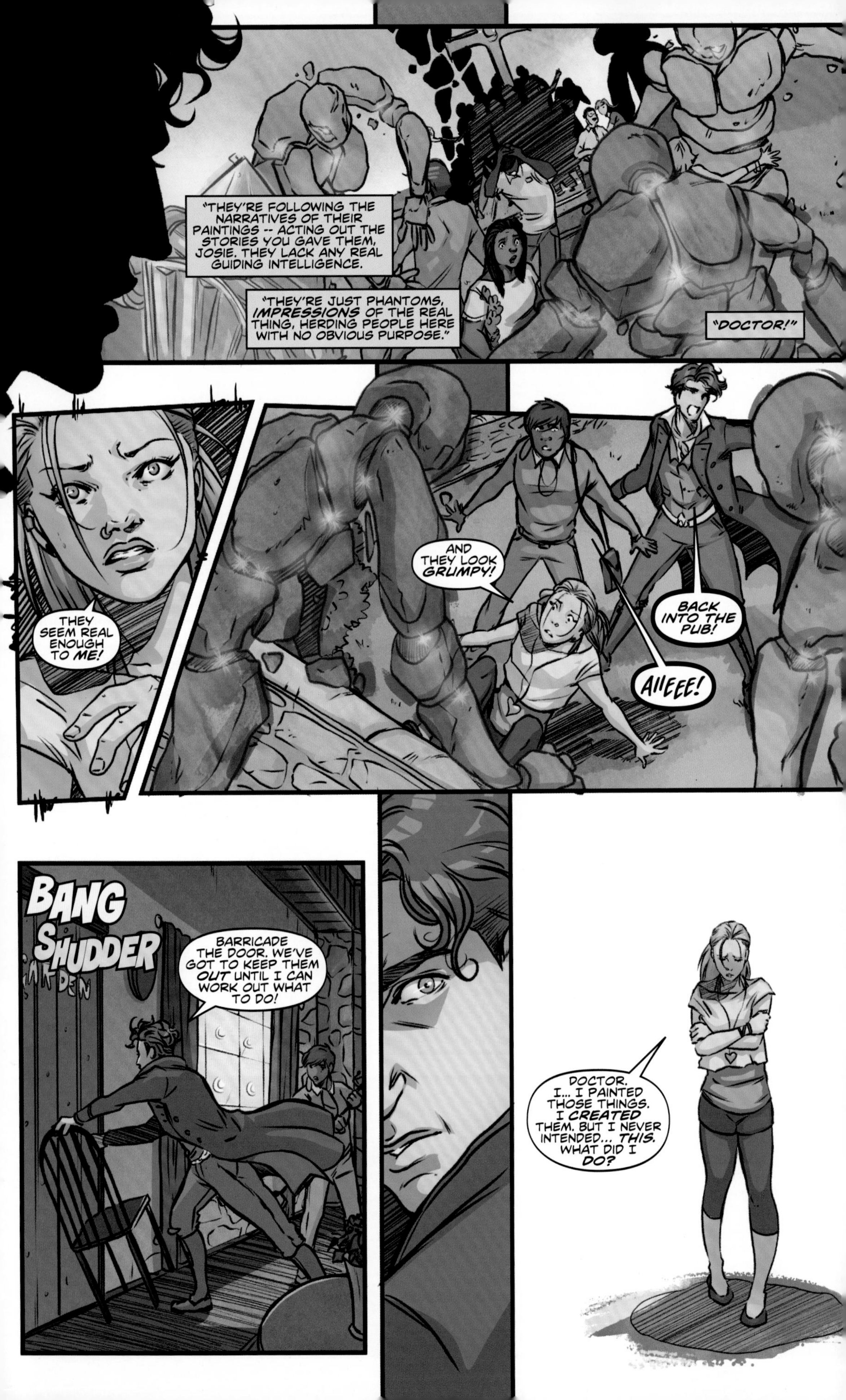
"THEY'RE FOLLOWING THE NARRATIVES OF THEIR PAINTINGS -- ACTING OUT THE STORIES YOU GAVE THEM, JOSIE. THEY LACK ANY REAL GUIDING INTELLIGENCE.
"THEY'RE JUST PHANTOMS, IMPRESSIONS OF THE REAL THING, HERDING PEOPLE HERE WITH NO OBVIOUS PURPOSE."
"DOCTOR!"
THEY SEEM REAL ENOUGH TO ME!
AND THEY LOOK GRUMPY!
BACK INTO THE PUB!
AIIEEE!
BANG
SHUDDER
BARRICADE THE DOOR. WE'VE GOT TO KEEP THEM OUT UNTIL I CAN WORK OUT WHAT TO DO!
DOCTOR. I... I PAINTED THOSE THINGS. I CREATED THEM. BUT I NEVER INTENDED... THIS. WHAT DID I DO?

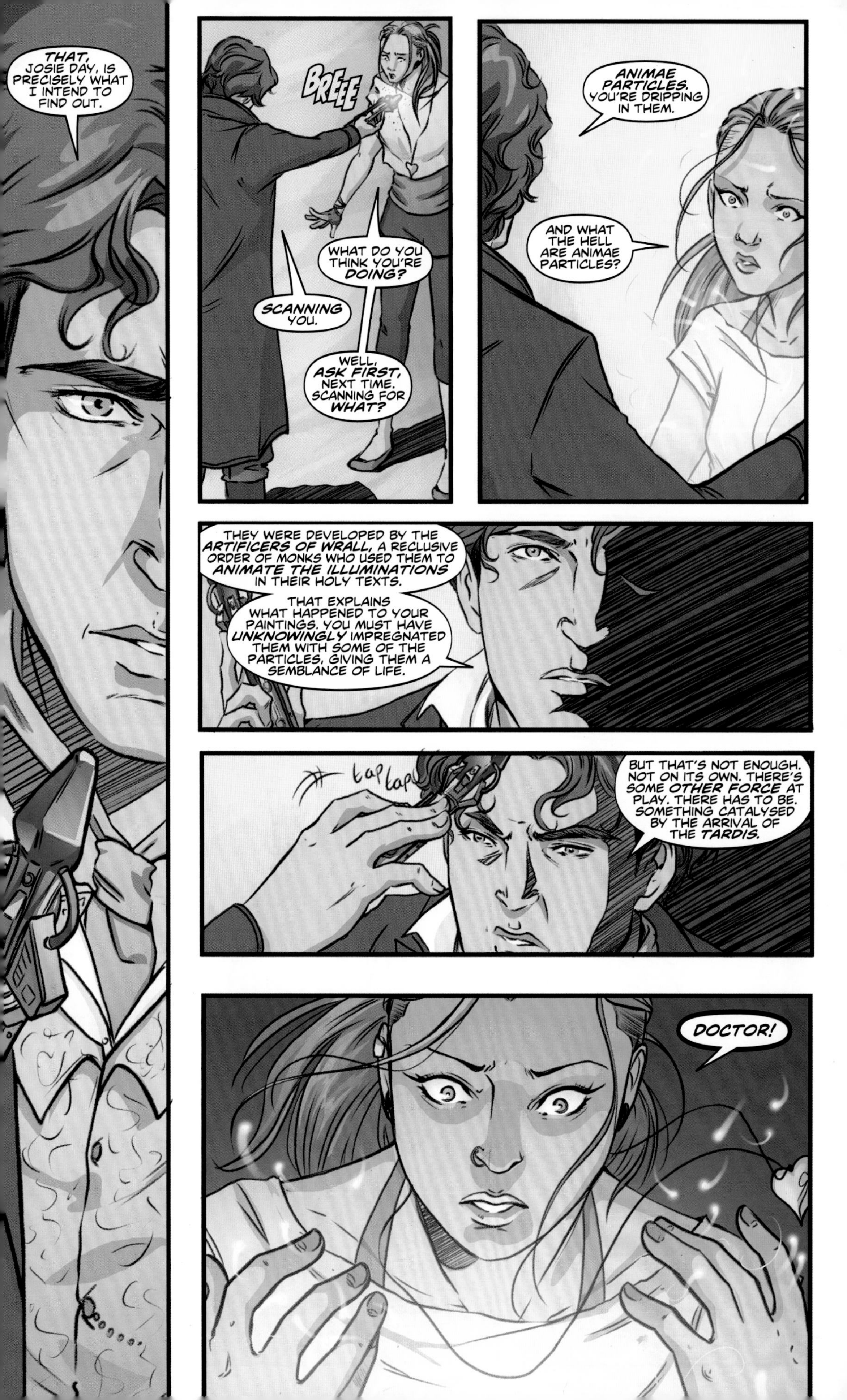
THAT, JOSIE DAY, IS PRECISELY WHAT I INTEND TO FIND OUT.
BREEE
WHAT DO YOU THINK YOU'RE DOING?
SCANNING YOU.
WELL, ASK FIRST, NEXT TIME. SCANNING FOR WHAT?
ANIMAE PARTICLES. YOU'RE DRIPPING IN THEM.
AND WHAT THE HELL ARE ANIMAE PARTICLES?
THEY WERE DEVELOPED BY THE ARTIFICERS OF WRALL, A RECLUSIVE ORDER OF MONKS WHO USED THEM TO ANIMATE THE ILLUMINATIONS IN THEIR HOLY TEXTS.
THAT EXPLAINS WHAT HAPPENED TO YOUR PAINTINGS. YOU MUST HAVE UNKNOWINGLY IMPREGNATED THEM WITH SOME OF THE PARTICLES, GIVING THEM A SEMBLANCE OF LIFE.
tap tap
BUT THAT'S NOT ENOUGH. NOT ON ITS OWN. THERE'S SOME OTHER FORCE AT PLAY. THERE HAS TO BE. SOMETHING CATALYSED BY THE ARRIVAL OF THE TARDIS.
DOCTOR!

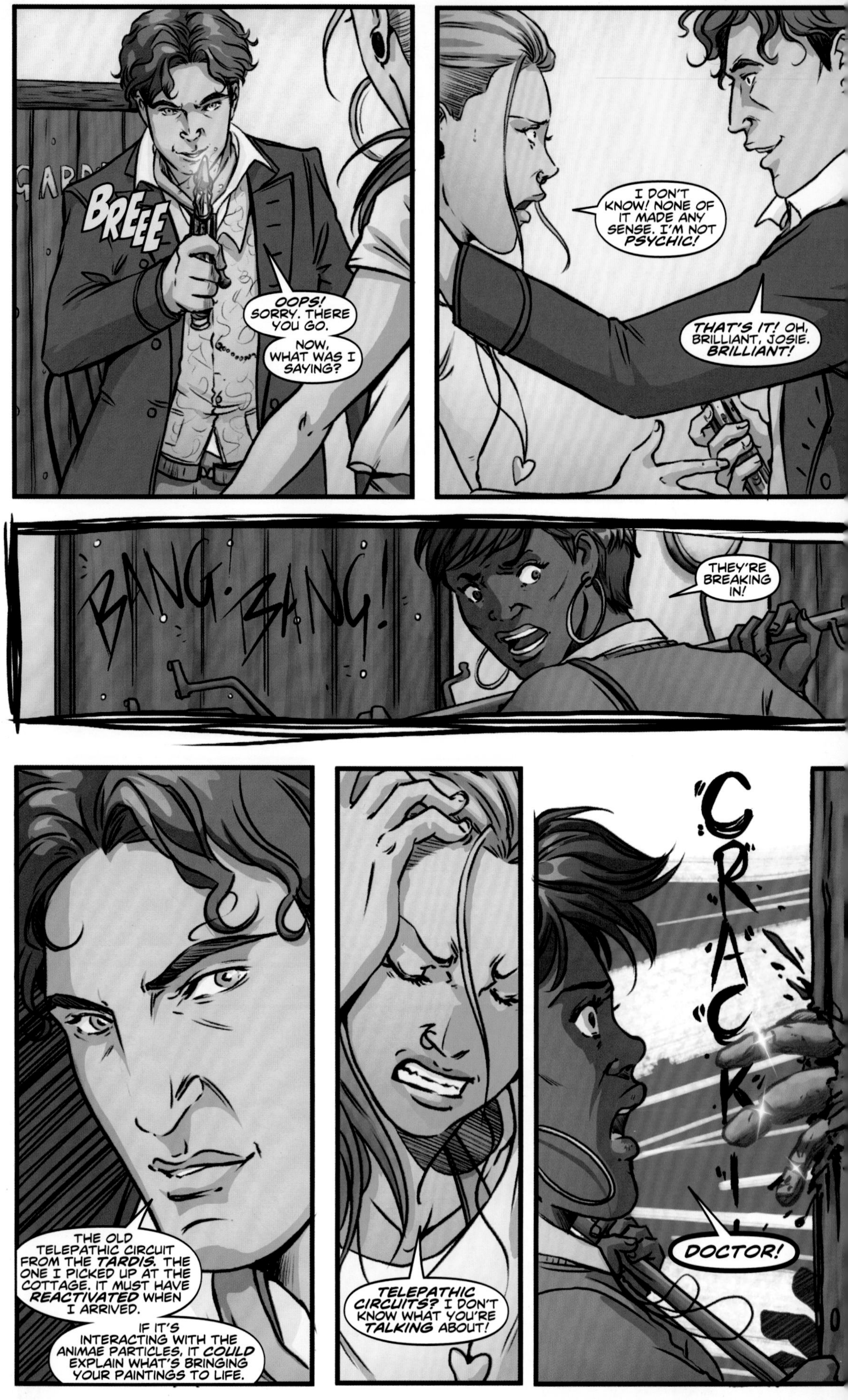
GARD
BREEE
OOPS! SORRY. THERE YOU GO.
NOW, WHAT WAS I SAYING?
I DON'T KNOW! NONE OF IT MADE ANY SENSE. I'M NOT PSYCHIC!
THAT'S IT! OH, BRILLIANT, JOSIE. BRILLIANT!
BANG! BANG!
THEY'RE BREAKING IN!
THE OLD TELEPATHIC CIRCUIT FROM THE TARDIS. THE ONE I PICKED UP AT THE COTTAGE. IT MUST HAVE REACTIVATED WHEN I ARRIVED.
IF IT'S INTERACTING WITH THE ANIMAE PARTICLES, IT COULD EXPLAIN WHAT'S BRINGING YOUR PAINTINGS TO LIFE.
TELEPATHIC CIRCUITS? I DON'T KNOW WHAT YOU'RE TALKING ABOUT!
CRACK!
DOCTOR!

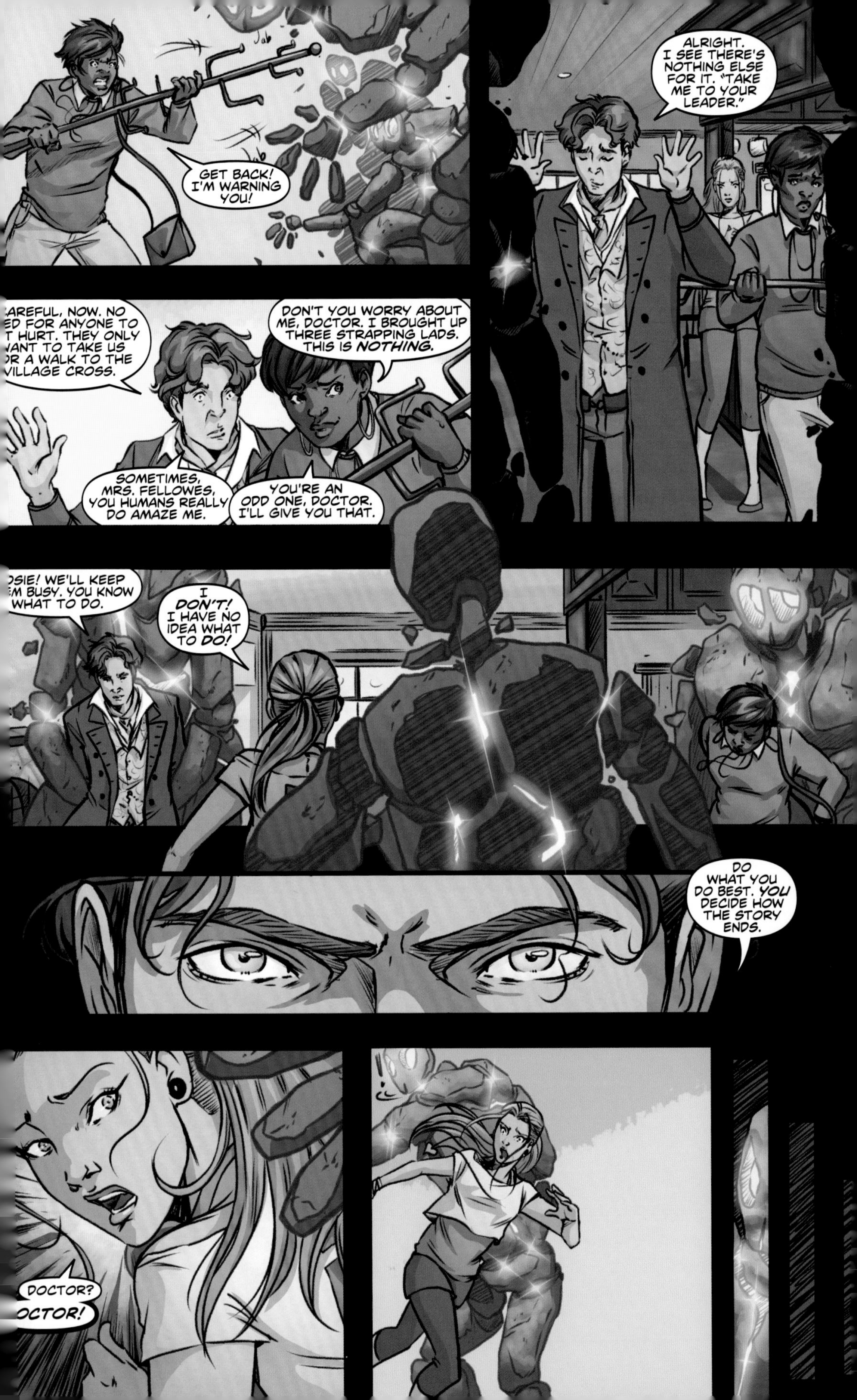
Jab
Jab
GET BACK! I'M WARNING YOU!
ALRIGHT. I SEE THERE'S NOTHING ELSE FOR IT. "TAKE ME TO YOUR LEADER."
AREFUL, NOW. NO ED FOR ANYONE TO T HURT. THEY ONLY VANT TO TAKE US OR A WALK TO THE VILLAGE CROSS.
DON'T YOU WORRY ABOUT ME, DOCTOR. I BROUGHT UP THREE STRAPPING LADS. THIS IS NOTHING.
SOMETIMES, MRS. FELLOWES, YOU HUMANS REALLY DO AMAZE ME.
YOU'RE AN ODD ONE, DOCTOR. I'LL GIVE YOU THAT.
OSIE! WE'LL KEEP EM BUSY. YOU KNOW WHAT TO DO.
I DON'T! I HAVE NO IDEA WHAT TO DO!
DO WHAT YOU DO BEST. YOU DECIDE HOW THE STORY ENDS.
DOCTOR?
OCTOR!

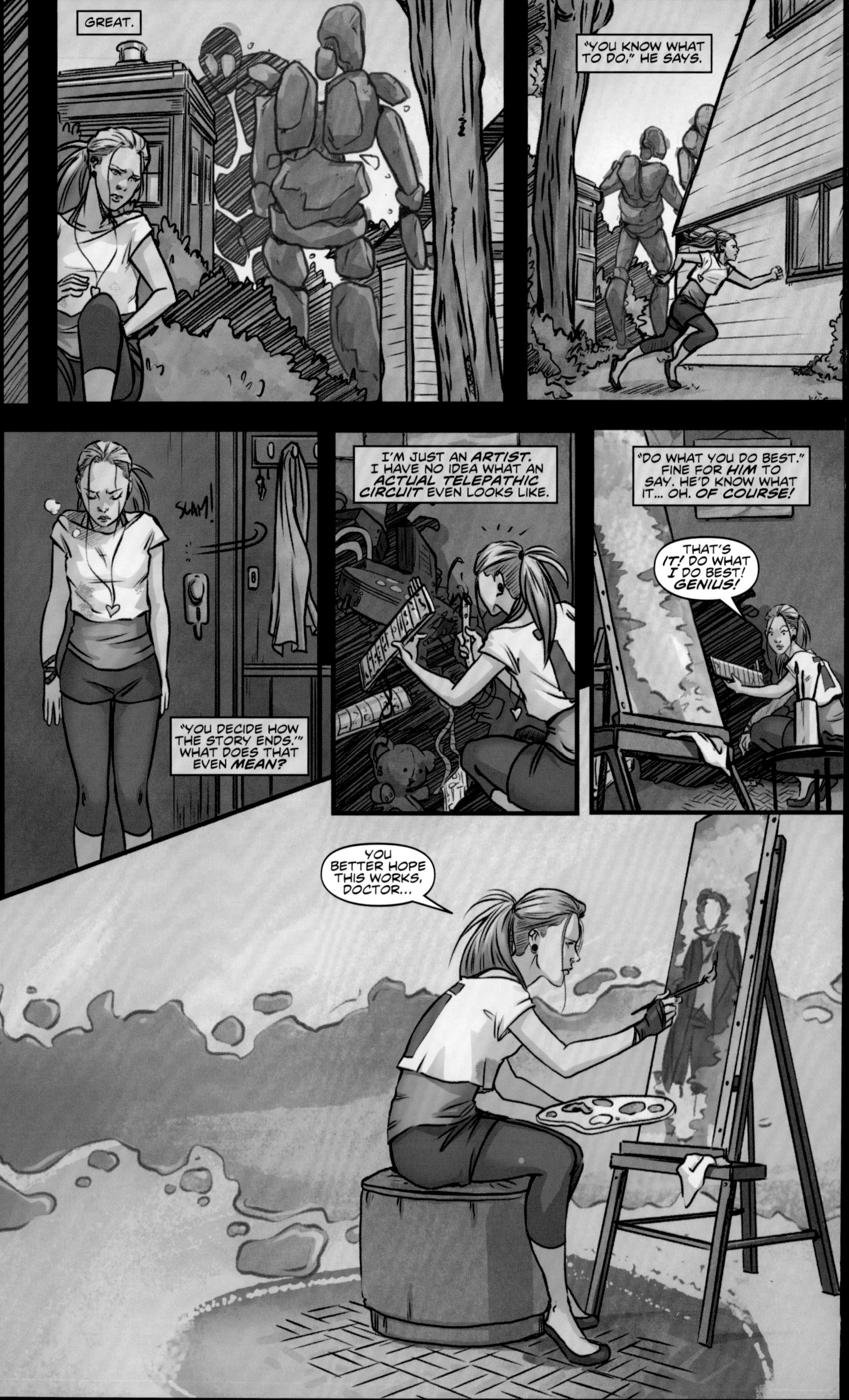

GREAT.
"YOU KNOW WHAT TO DO," HE SAYS.
SLAM!
"YOU DECIDE HOW THE STORY ENDS." WHAT DOES THAT EVEN MEAN?
I'M JUST AN ARTIST. I HAVE NO IDEA WHAT AN ACTUAL TELEPATHIC CIRCUIT EVEN LOOKS LIKE.
"DO WHAT YOU DO BEST." FINE FOR HIM TO SAY. HE'D KNOW WHAT IT... OH. OF COURSE!
THAT'S IT! DO WHAT I DO BEST! GENIUS!
YOU BETTER HOPE THIS WORKS, DOCTOR...

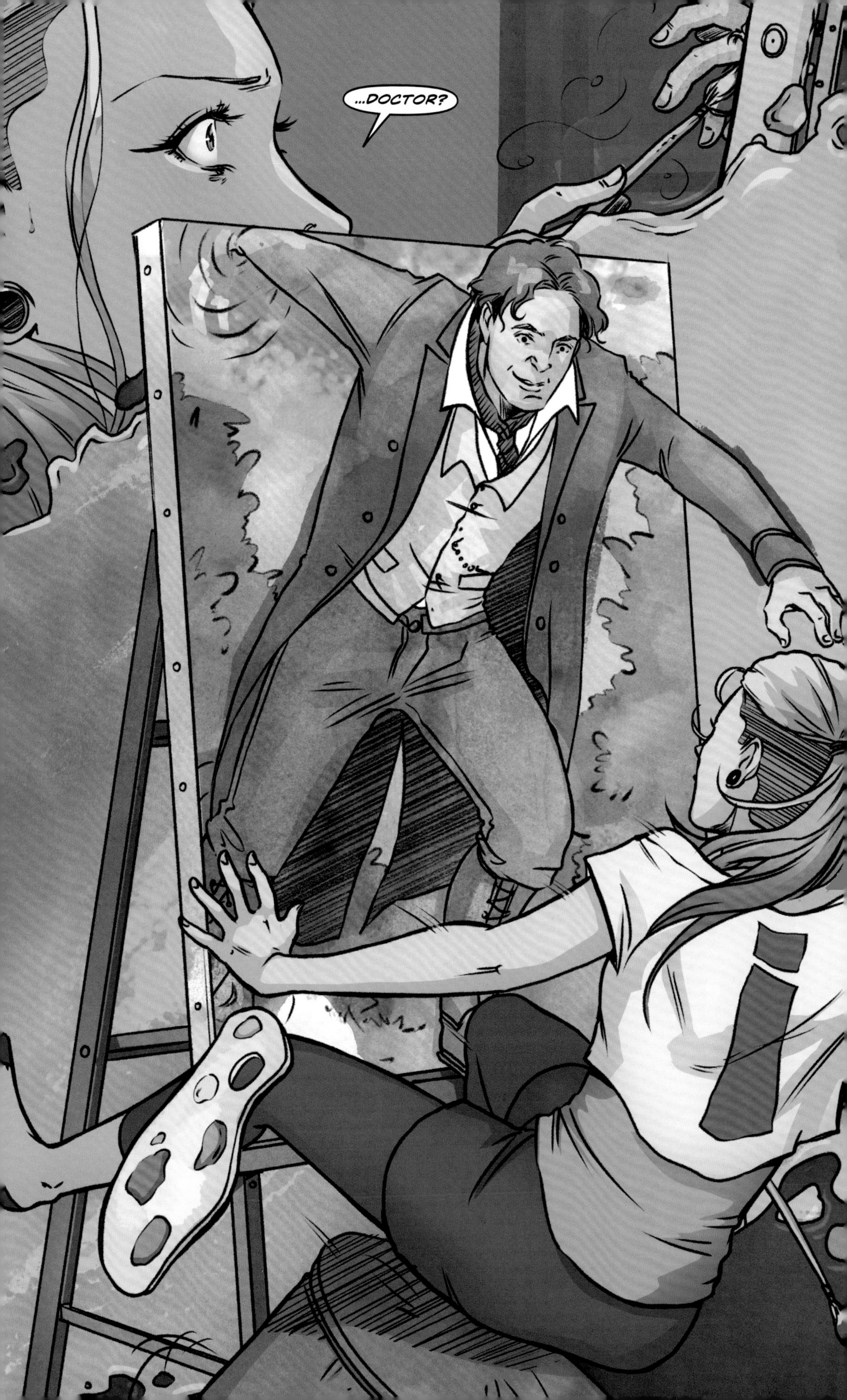
...DOCTOR?

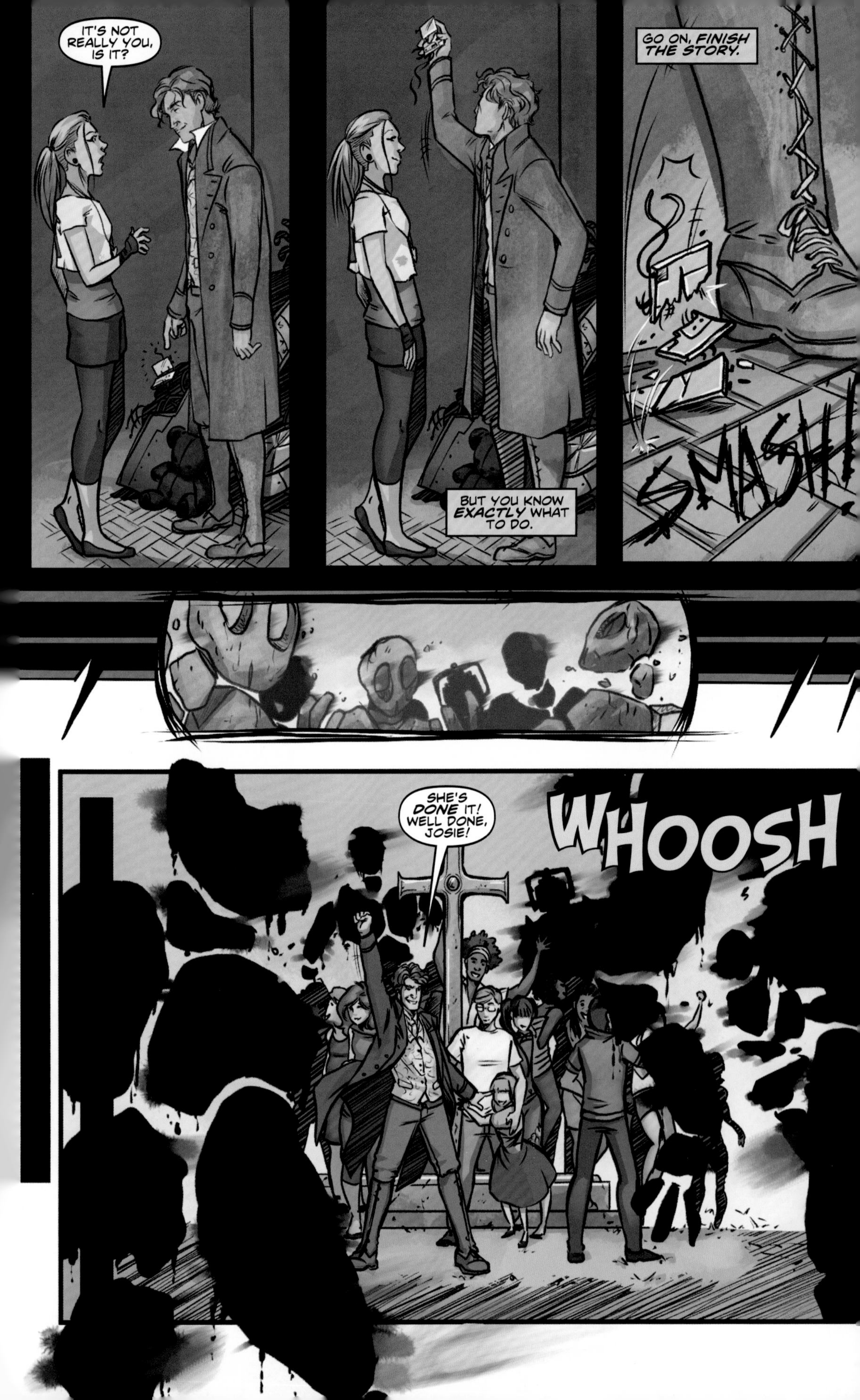
IT'S NOT REALLY YOU, IS IT?
BUT YOU KNOW EXACTLY WHAT TO DO.
GO ON, FINISH THE STORY.
SMASH!
SHE'S DONE IT! WELL DONE, JOSIE!
WHOOSH

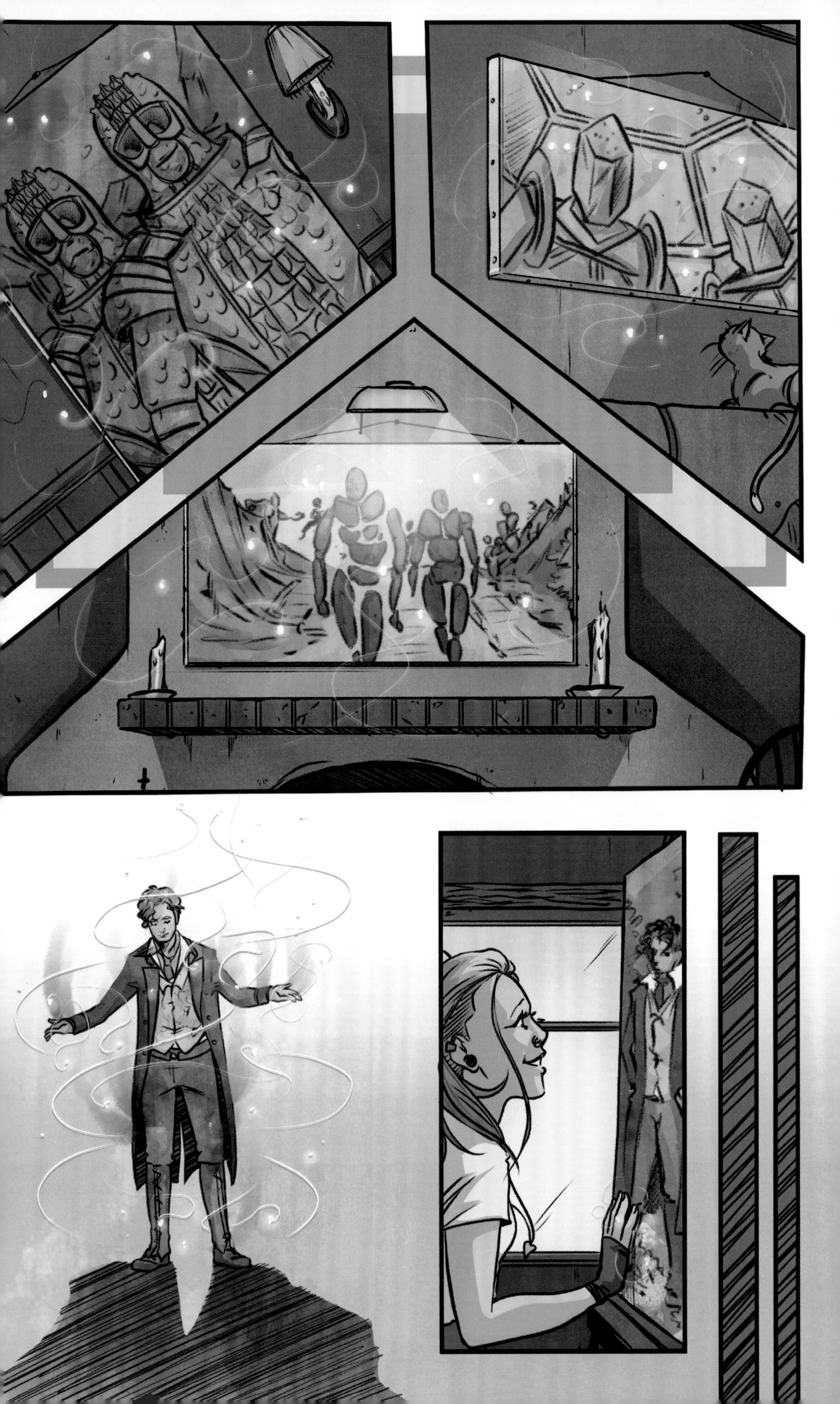

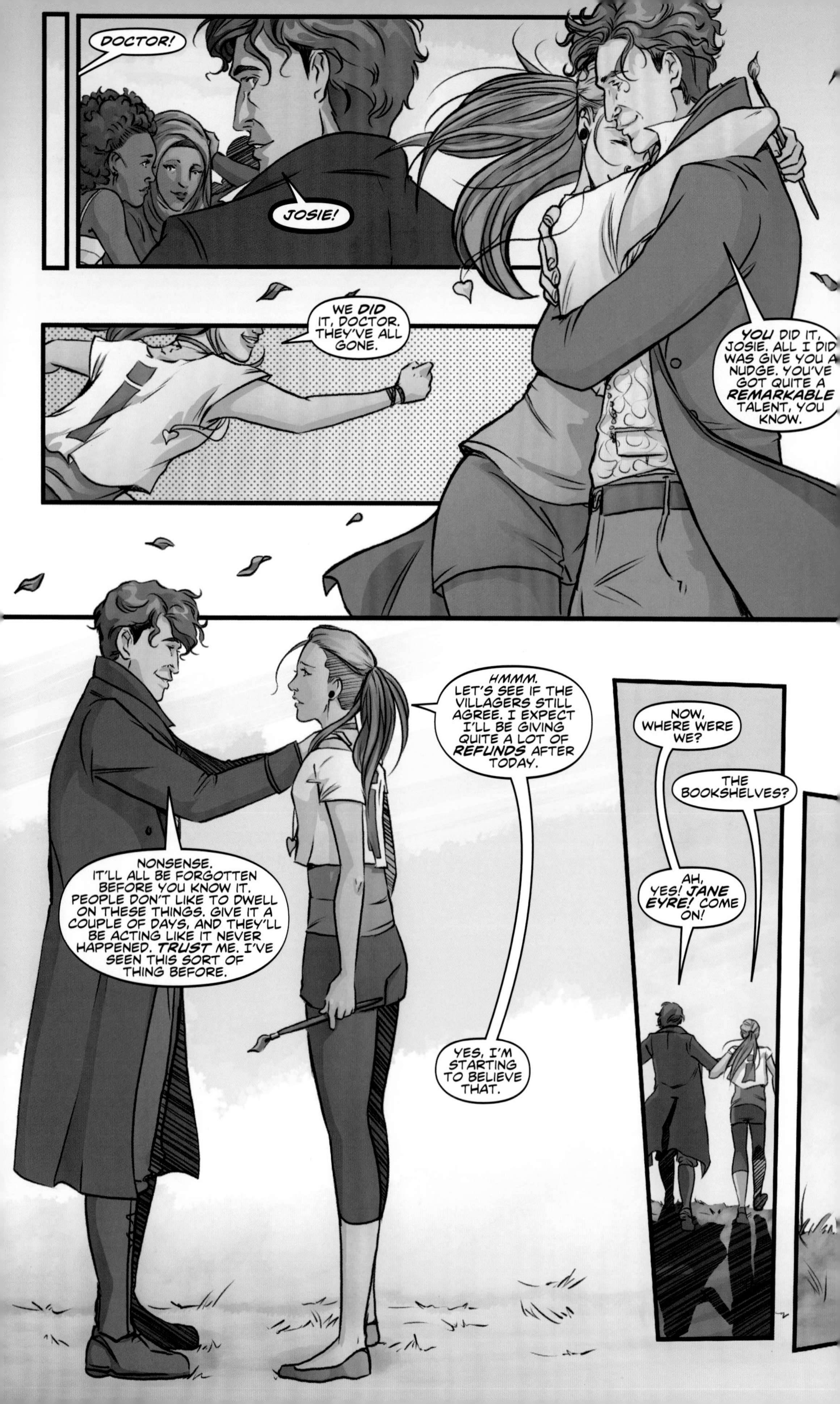
DOCTOR!
JOSIE!
WE DID IT, DOCTOR. THEY'VE ALL GONE.
YOU DID IT, JOSIE. ALL I DID WAS GIVE YOU A NUDGE. YOU'VE GOT QUITE A REMARKABLE TALENT, YOU KNOW.
HMMM. LET'S SEE IF THE VILLAGERS STILL AGREE. I EXPECT I'LL BE GIVING QUITE A LOT OF REFUNDS AFTER TODAY.
NONSENSE. IT'LL ALL BE FORGOTTEN BEFORE YOU KNOW IT. PEOPLE DON'T LIKE TO DWELL ON THESE THINGS. GIVE IT A COUPLE OF DAYS, AND THEY'LL BE ACTING LIKE IT NEVER HAPPENED. TRUST ME. I'VE SEEN THIS SORT OF THING BEFORE.
YES, I'M STARTING TO BELIEVE THAT.
NOW, WHERE WERE WE?
THE BOOKSHELVES?
AH, YES! JANE EYRE! COME ON!

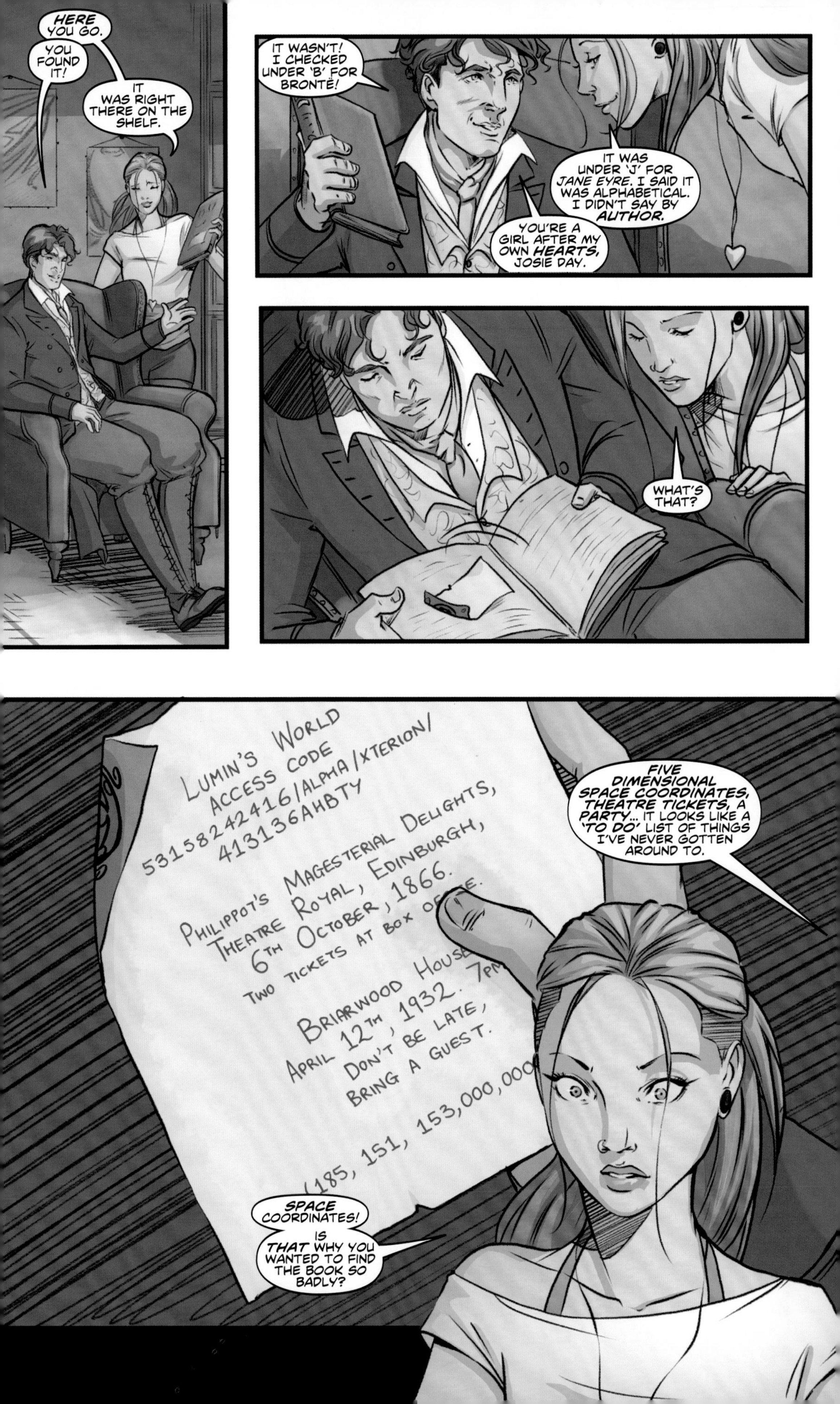
HERE YOU GO.
YOU FOUND IT!
IT WAS RIGHT THERE ON THE SHELF.
IT WASN'T! I CHECKED UNDER 'B' FOR BRONTË!
IT WAS UNDER 'J' FOR JANE EYRE. I SAID IT WAS ALPHABETICAL. I DIDN'T SAY BY AUTHOR.
YOU'RE A GIRL AFTER MY OWN HEARTS, JOSIE DAY.
WHAT'S THAT?
LUMIN'S WORLD
ACCESS CODE
53158242416/ALPHA/XTERION/
413136AHBTY
PHILIPPOT'S MAGESTERIAL DELIGHTS,
THEATRE ROYAL, EDINBURGH,
6TH OCTOBER, 1866.
TWO TICKETS AT BOX OF
BRIARWOOD HOUSE
APRIL 12TH, 1932. 7PM
DON'T BE LATE,
BRING A GUEST.
(185, 151, 153,000,000
FIVE DIMENSIONAL SPACE COORDINATES, THEATRE TICKETS, A PARTY... IT LOOKS LIKE A 'TO DO' LIST OF THINGS I'VE NEVER GOTTEN AROUND TO.
SPACE COORDINATES!
IS THAT WHY YOU WANTED TO FIND THE BOOK SO BADLY?

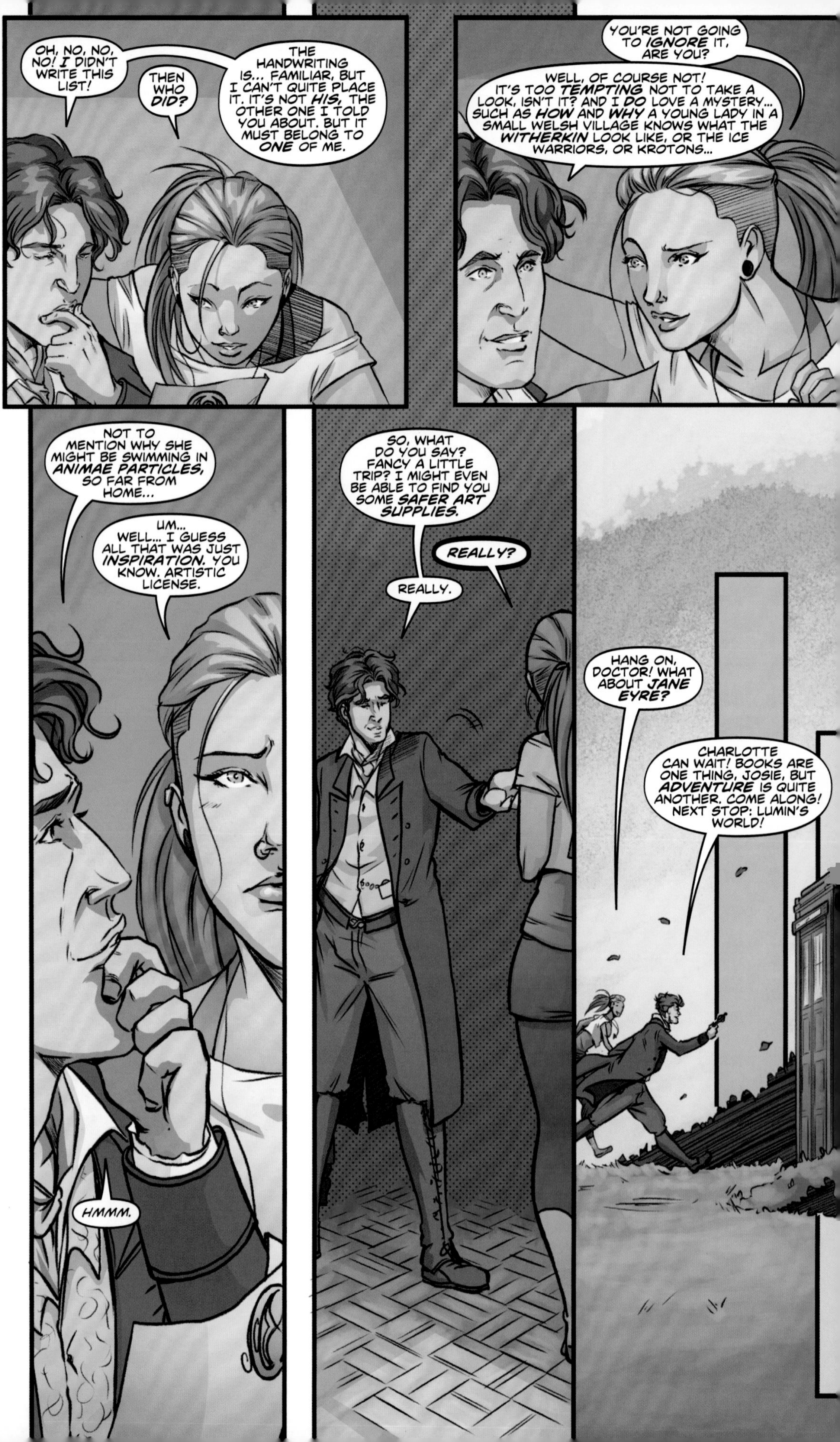

OH, NO, NO, NO! I DIDN'T WRITE THIS LIST!
THEN WHO DID?
THE HANDWRITING IS... FAMILIAR, BUT I CAN'T QUITE PLACE IT. IT'S NOT HIS, THE OTHER ONE I TOLD YOU ABOUT. BUT IT MUST BELONG TO ONE OF ME.
YOU'RE NOT GOING TO IGNORE IT, ARE YOU?
WELL, OF COURSE NOT! IT'S TOO TEMPTING NOT TO TAKE A LOOK, ISN'T IT? AND I DO LOVE A MYSTERY... SUCH AS HOW AND WHY A YOUNG LADY IN A SMALL WELSH VILLAGE KNOWS WHAT THE WITHERKIN LOOK LIKE, OR THE ICE WARRIORS, OR KROTONS...
NOT TO MENTION WHY SHE MIGHT BE SWIMMING IN ANIMAE PARTICLES, SO FAR FROM HOME...
UM... WELL... I GUESS ALL THAT WAS JUST INSPIRATION. YOU KNOW. ARTISTIC LICENSE.
HMMM.
SO, WHAT DO YOU SAY? FANCY A LITTLE TRIP? I MIGHT EVEN BE ABLE TO FIND YOU SOME SAFER ART SUPPLIES.
REALLY?
REALLY.
HANG ON, DOCTOR! WHAT ABOUT JANE EYRE?
CHARLOTTE CAN WAIT! BOOKS ARE ONE THING, JOSIE, BUT ADVENTURE IS QUITE ANOTHER. COME ALONG! NEXT STOP: LUMIN'S WORLD!

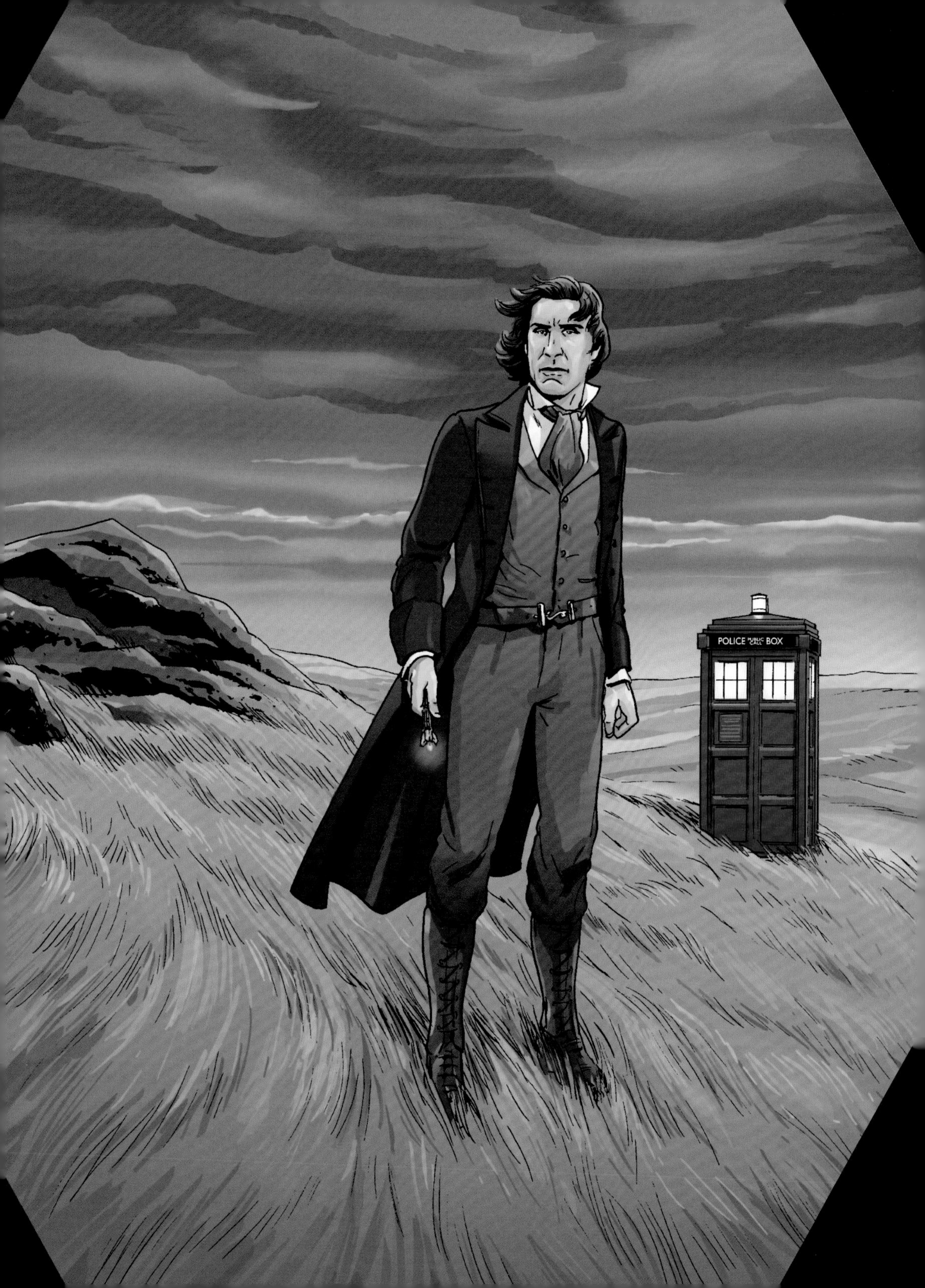
POLICE PUBLIC CALL BOX

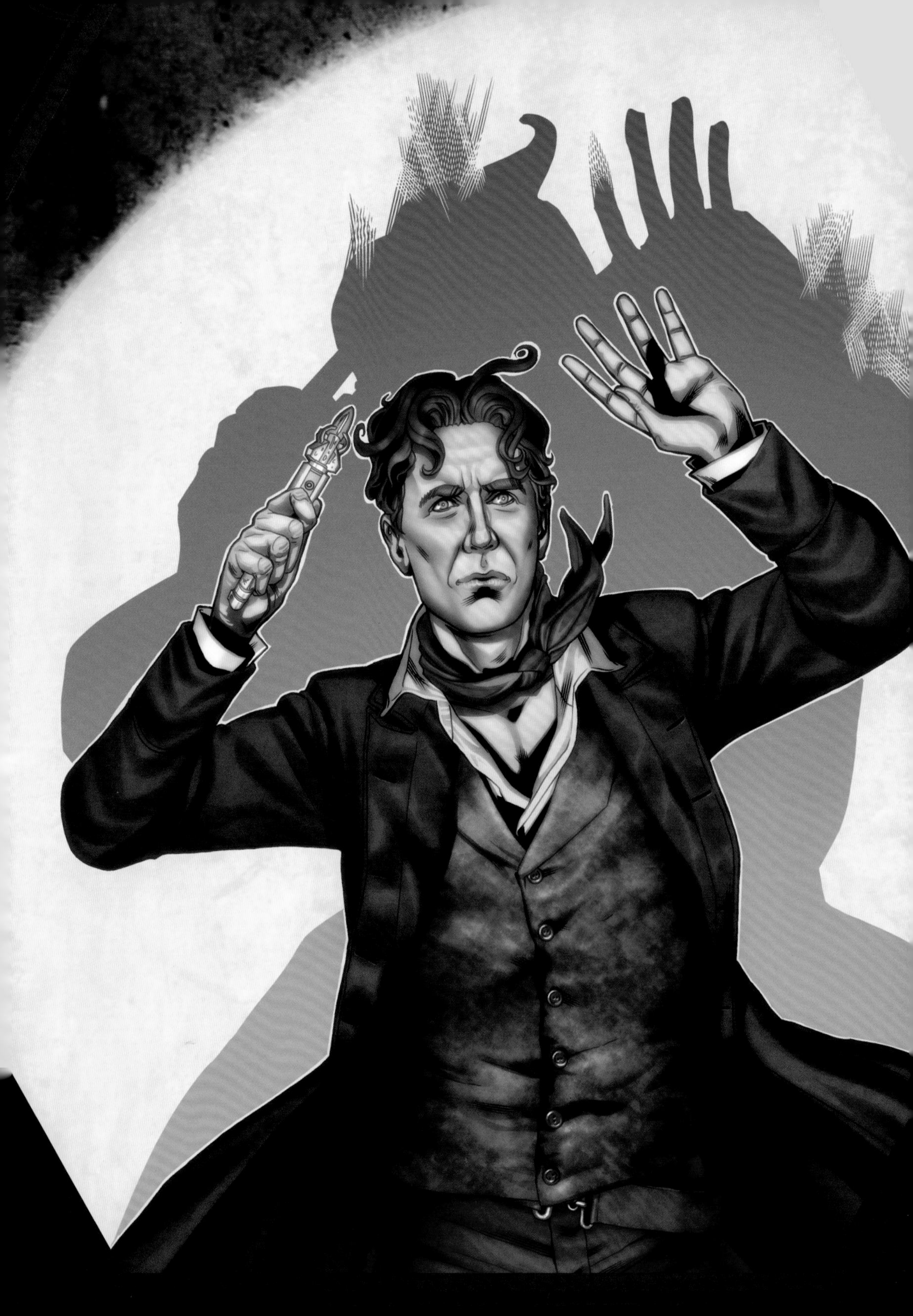

8D #2 Cover A: RACHAEL STOTT & LUIS GUERRERO

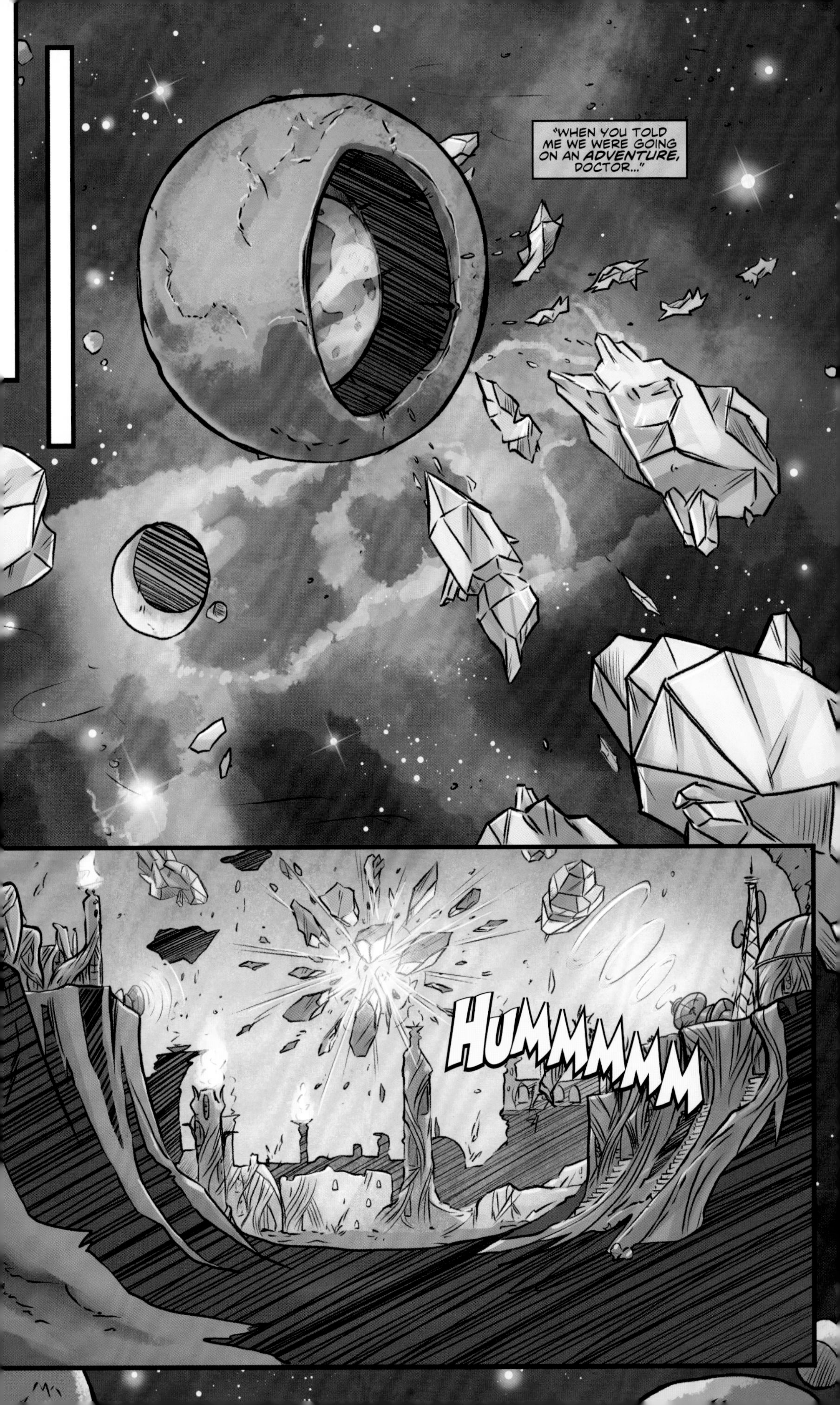
"WHEN YOU TOLD ME WE WERE GOING ON AN *ADVENTURE*, DOCTOR..."
HUMMMMMM

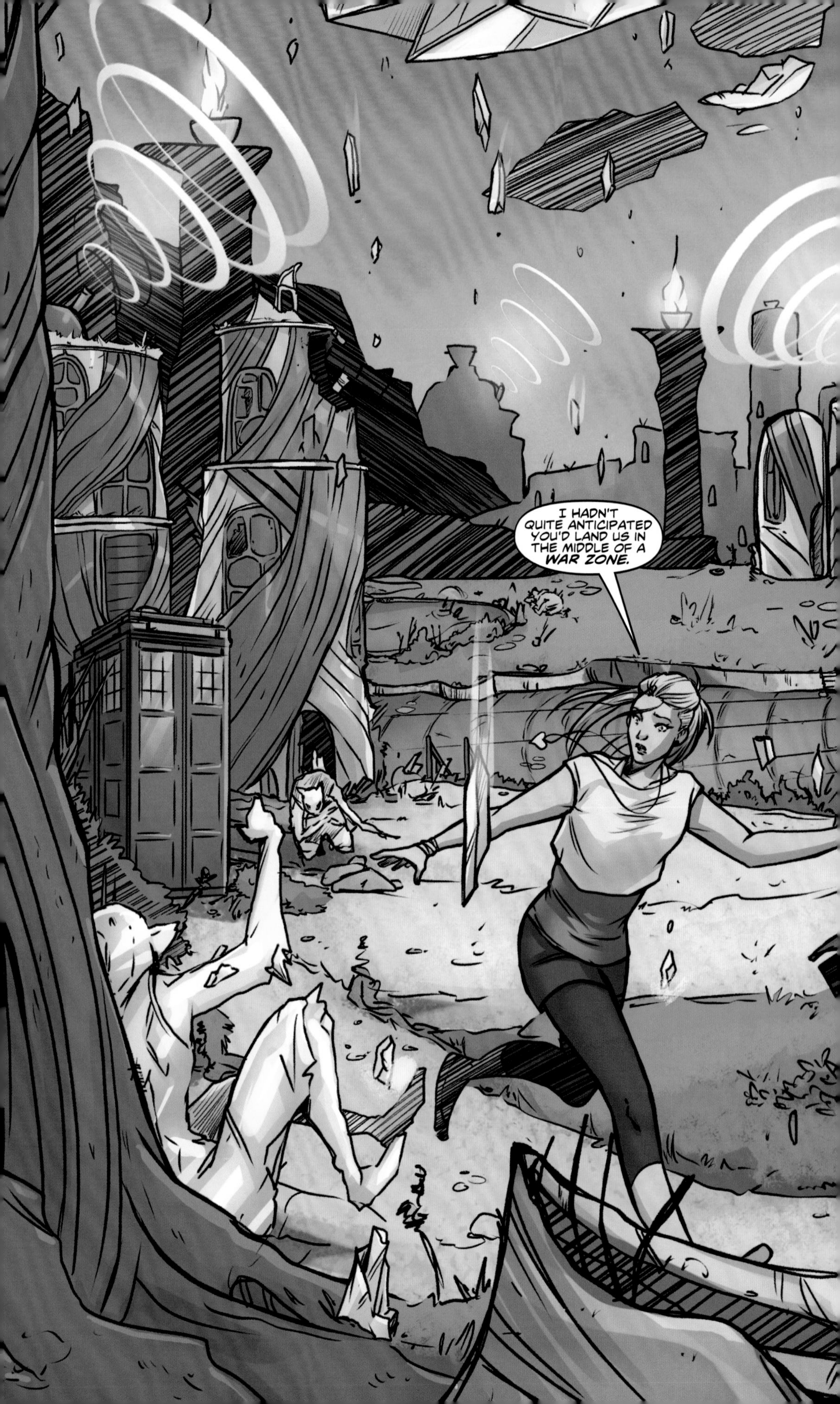
I HADN'T QUITE ANTICIPATED YOU'D LAND US IN THE MIDDLE OF A WAR ZONE.

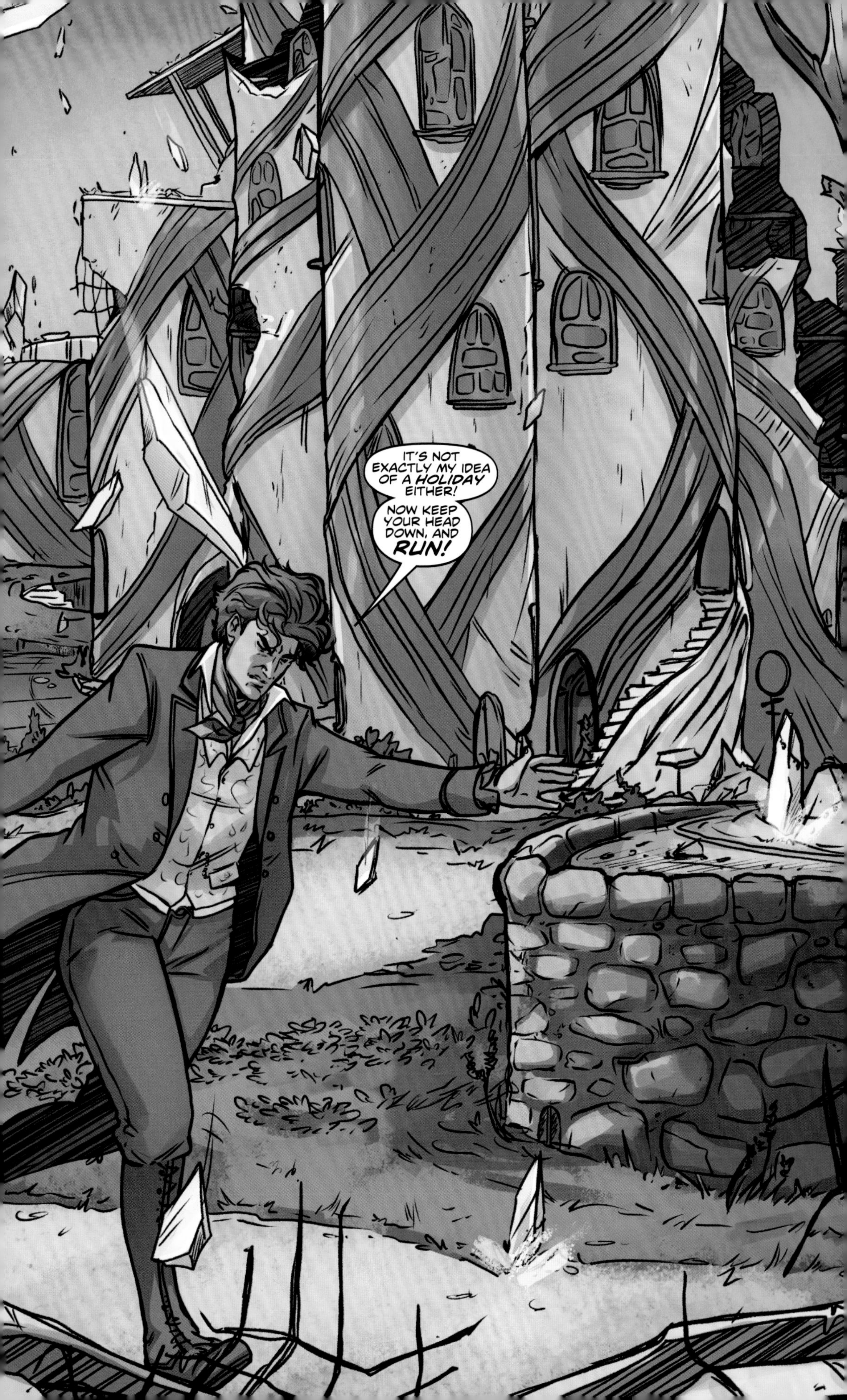
IT'S NOT EXACTLY MY IDEA OF A *HOLIDAY* EITHER!
NOW KEEP YOUR HEAD DOWN, AND ***RUN!***

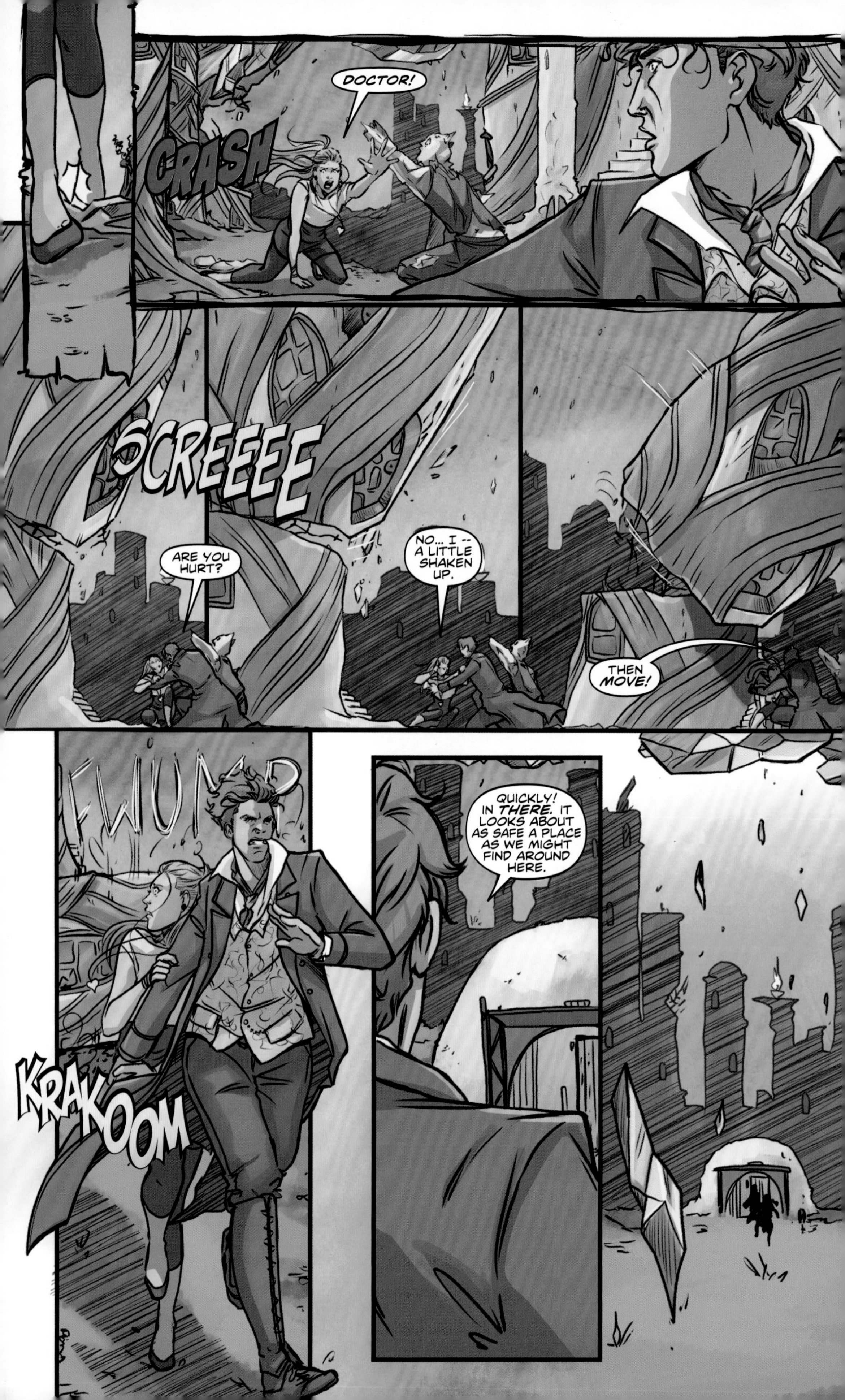
DOCTOR!
CRASH
SCREEEE
ARE YOU HURT?
NO... I -- A LITTLE SHAKEN UP.
THEN *MOVE!*
FWUMP
KRAKOOM
QUICKLY! IN *THERE.* IT LOOKS ABOUT AS SAFE A PLACE AS WE MIGHT FIND AROUND HERE.

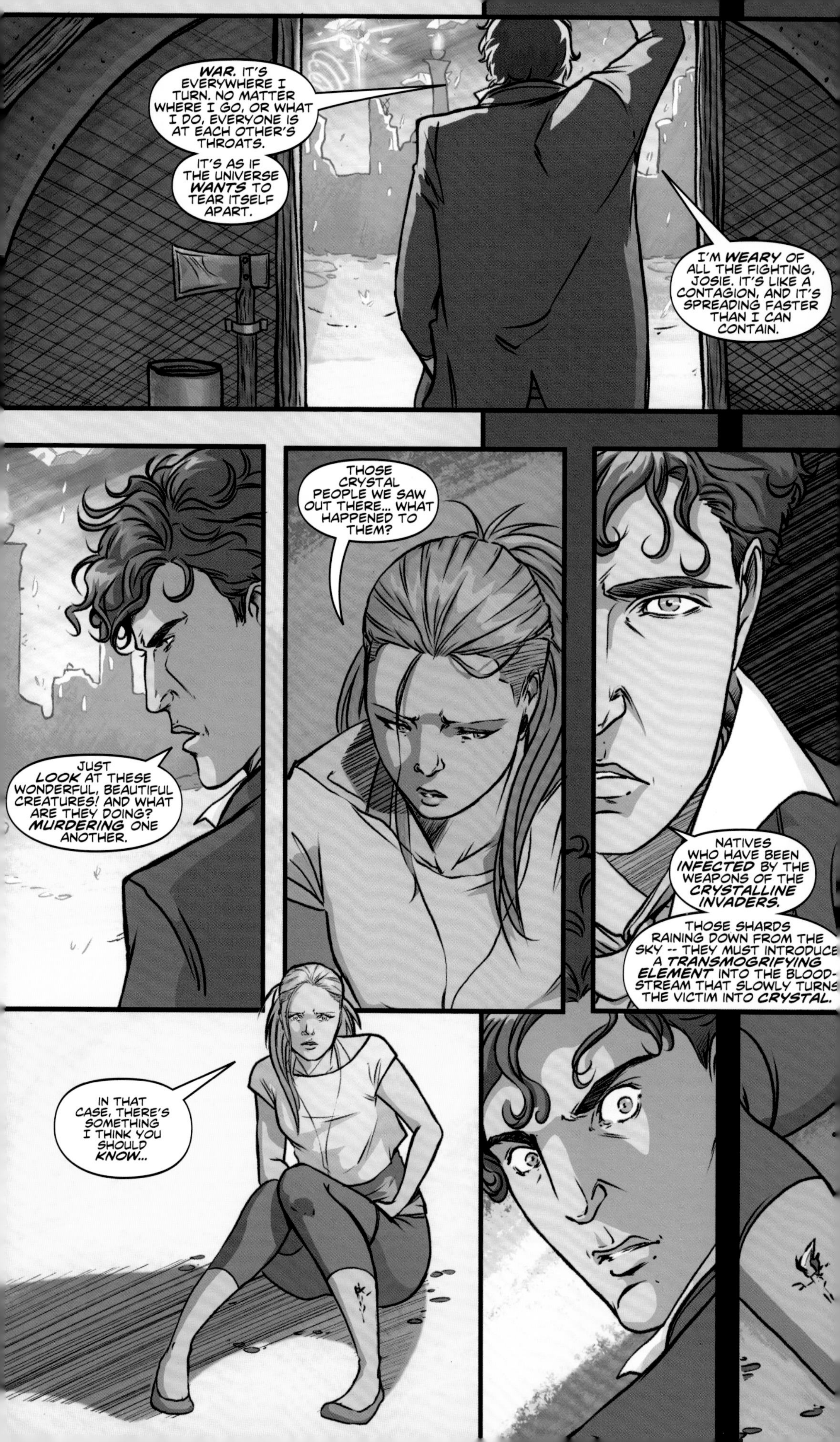
WAR. IT'S EVERYWHERE I TURN. NO MATTER WHERE I GO, OR WHAT I DO, EVERYONE IS AT EACH OTHER'S THROATS.
IT'S AS IF THE UNIVERSE WANTS TO TEAR ITSELF APART.
I'M WEARY OF ALL THE FIGHTING, JOSIE. IT'S LIKE A CONTAGION, AND IT'S SPREADING FASTER THAN I CAN CONTAIN.
JUST LOOK AT THESE WONDERFUL, BEAUTIFUL CREATURES! AND WHAT ARE THEY DOING? MURDERING ONE ANOTHER.
THOSE CRYSTAL PEOPLE WE SAW OUT THERE... WHAT HAPPENED TO THEM?
NATIVES WHO HAVE BEEN INFECTED BY THE WEAPONS OF THE CRYSTALLINE INVADERS.
THOSE SHARDS RAINING DOWN FROM THE SKY -- THEY MUST INTRODUCE A TRANSMOGRIFYING ELEMENT INTO THE BLOOD-STREAM THAT SLOWLY TURNS THE VICTIM INTO CRYSTAL.
IN THAT CASE, THERE'S SOMETHING I THINK YOU SHOULD KNOW...

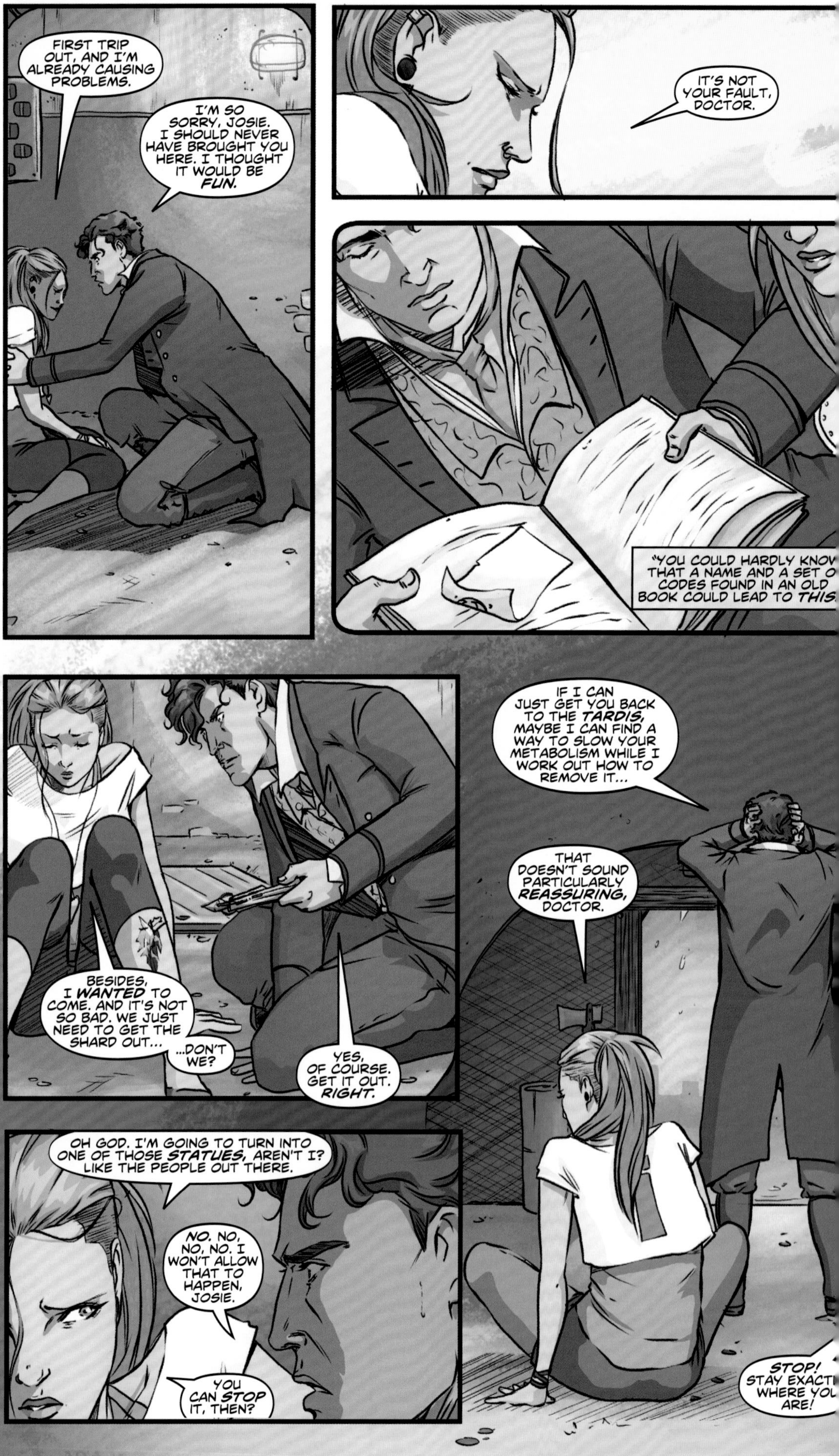
FIRST TRIP OUT, AND I'M ALREADY CAUSING PROBLEMS.
I'M SO SORRY, JOSIE. I SHOULD NEVER HAVE BROUGHT YOU HERE. I THOUGHT IT WOULD BE FUN.
IT'S NOT YOUR FAULT, DOCTOR.
"YOU COULD HARDLY KNOW THAT A NAME AND A SET OF CODES FOUND IN AN OLD BOOK COULD LEAD TO THIS.
BESIDES, I WANTED TO COME. AND IT'S NOT SO BAD. WE JUST NEED TO GET THE SHARD OUT...
...DON'T WE?
YES, OF COURSE. GET IT OUT. RIGHT.
IF I CAN JUST GET YOU BACK TO THE TARDIS, MAYBE I CAN FIND A WAY TO SLOW YOUR METABOLISM WHILE I WORK OUT HOW TO REMOVE IT...
THAT DOESN'T SOUND PARTICULARLY REASSURING, DOCTOR.
OH GOD. I'M GOING TO TURN INTO ONE OF THOSE STATUES, AREN'T I? LIKE THE PEOPLE OUT THERE.
NO. NO, NO, NO. I WON'T ALLOW THAT TO HAPPEN, JOSIE.
YOU CAN STOP IT, THEN?
STOP! STAY EXACT WHERE YOU ARE!

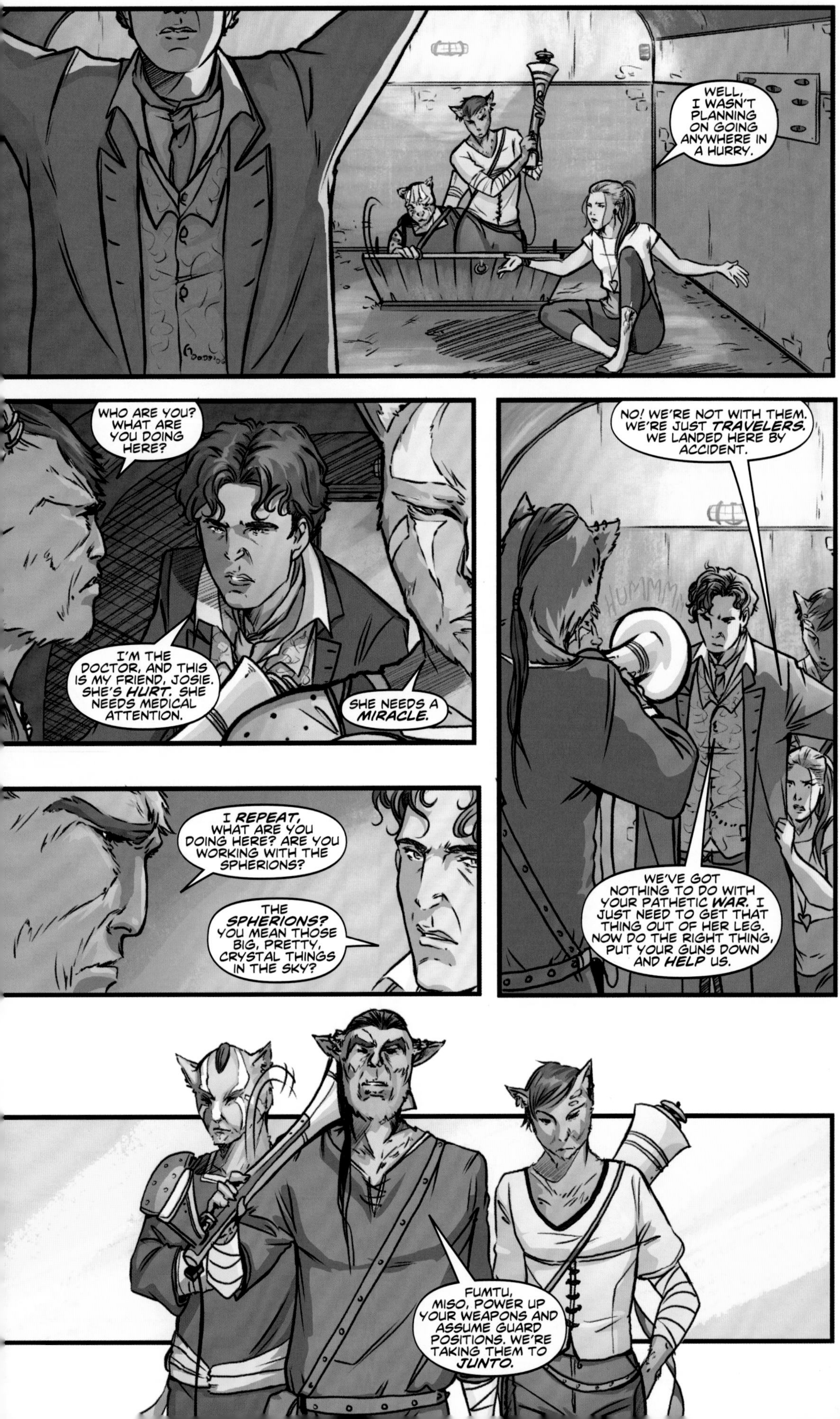
WELL, I WASN'T PLANNING ON GOING ANYWHERE IN A HURRY.
WHO ARE YOU? WHAT ARE YOU DOING HERE?
I'M THE DOCTOR, AND THIS IS MY FRIEND, JOSIE. SHE'S HURT. SHE NEEDS MEDICAL ATTENTION.
SHE NEEDS A MIRACLE.
I REPEAT, WHAT ARE YOU DOING HERE? ARE YOU WORKING WITH THE SPHERIONS?
THE SPHERIONS? YOU MEAN THOSE BIG, PRETTY, CRYSTAL THINGS IN THE SKY?
NO! WE'RE NOT WITH THEM. WE'RE JUST TRAVELERS. WE LANDED HERE BY ACCIDENT.
HUMMMM
WE'VE GOT NOTHING TO DO WITH YOUR PATHETIC WAR. I JUST NEED TO GET THAT THING OUT OF HER LEG. NOW DO THE RIGHT THING, PUT YOUR GUNS DOWN AND HELP US.
FUMTU, MISO, POWER UP YOUR WEAPONS AND ASSUME GUARD POSITIONS. WE'RE TAKING THEM TO JUNTO.

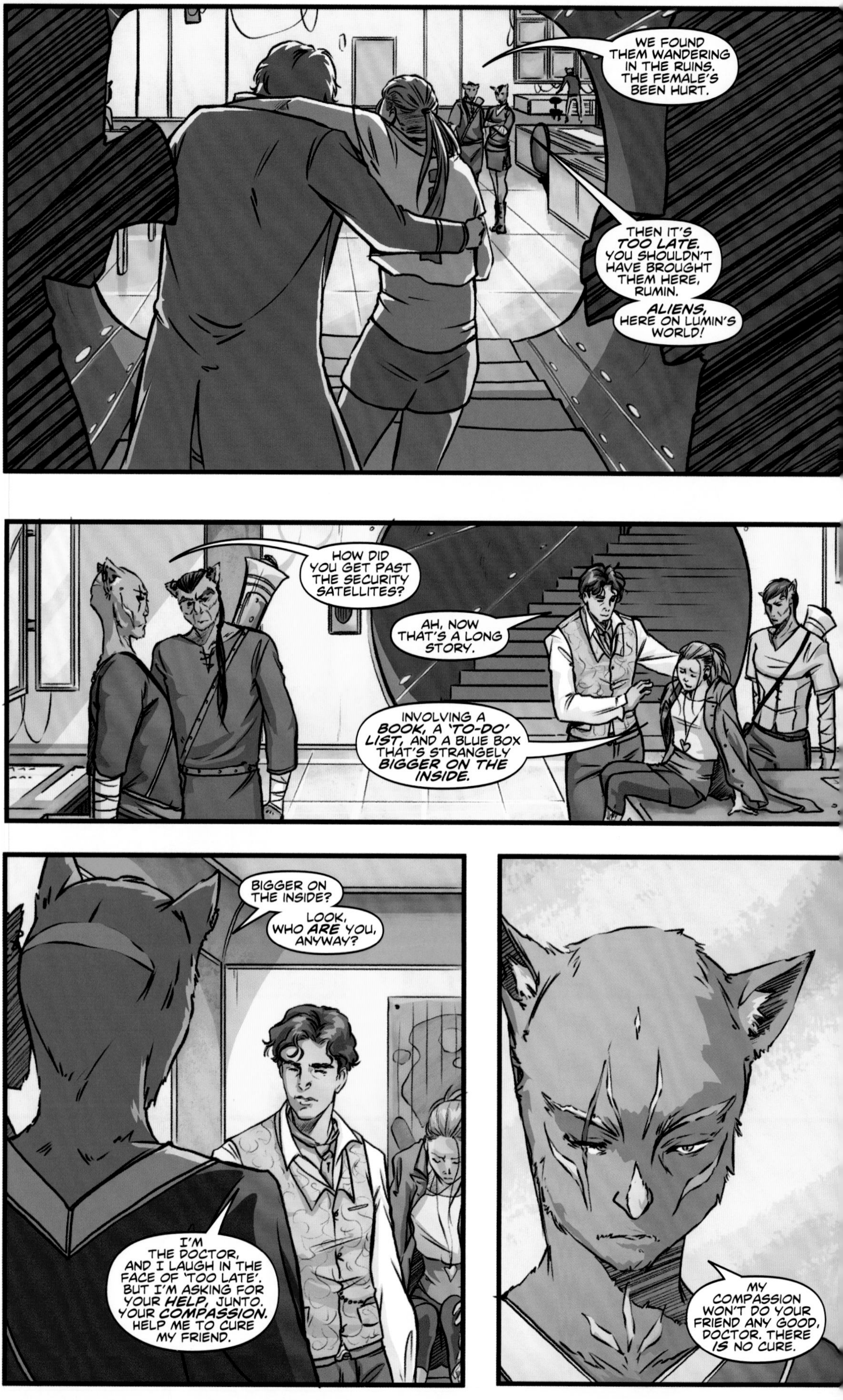
WE FOUND THEM WANDERING IN THE RUINS. THE FEMALE'S BEEN HURT.
THEN IT'S *TOO LATE*. YOU SHOULDN'T HAVE BROUGHT THEM HERE, RUMIN.
ALIENS, HERE ON LUMIN'S WORLD!
HOW DID YOU GET PAST THE SECURITY SATELLITES?
AH, NOW THAT'S A LONG STORY.
INVOLVING A ***BOOK***, A ***'TO-DO' LIST***, AND A BLUE BOX THAT'S STRANGELY ***BIGGER ON THE INSIDE.***
BIGGER ON THE INSIDE?
LOOK, WHO ***ARE*** YOU, ANYWAY?
I'M THE DOCTOR, AND I LAUGH IN THE FACE OF 'TOO LATE'. BUT I'M ASKING FOR YOUR ***HELP***, JUNTO. YOUR ***COMPASSION.*** HELP ME TO CURE MY FRIEND.
MY COMPASSION WON'T DO YOUR FRIEND ANY GOOD, DOCTOR. THERE ***IS*** NO CURE.

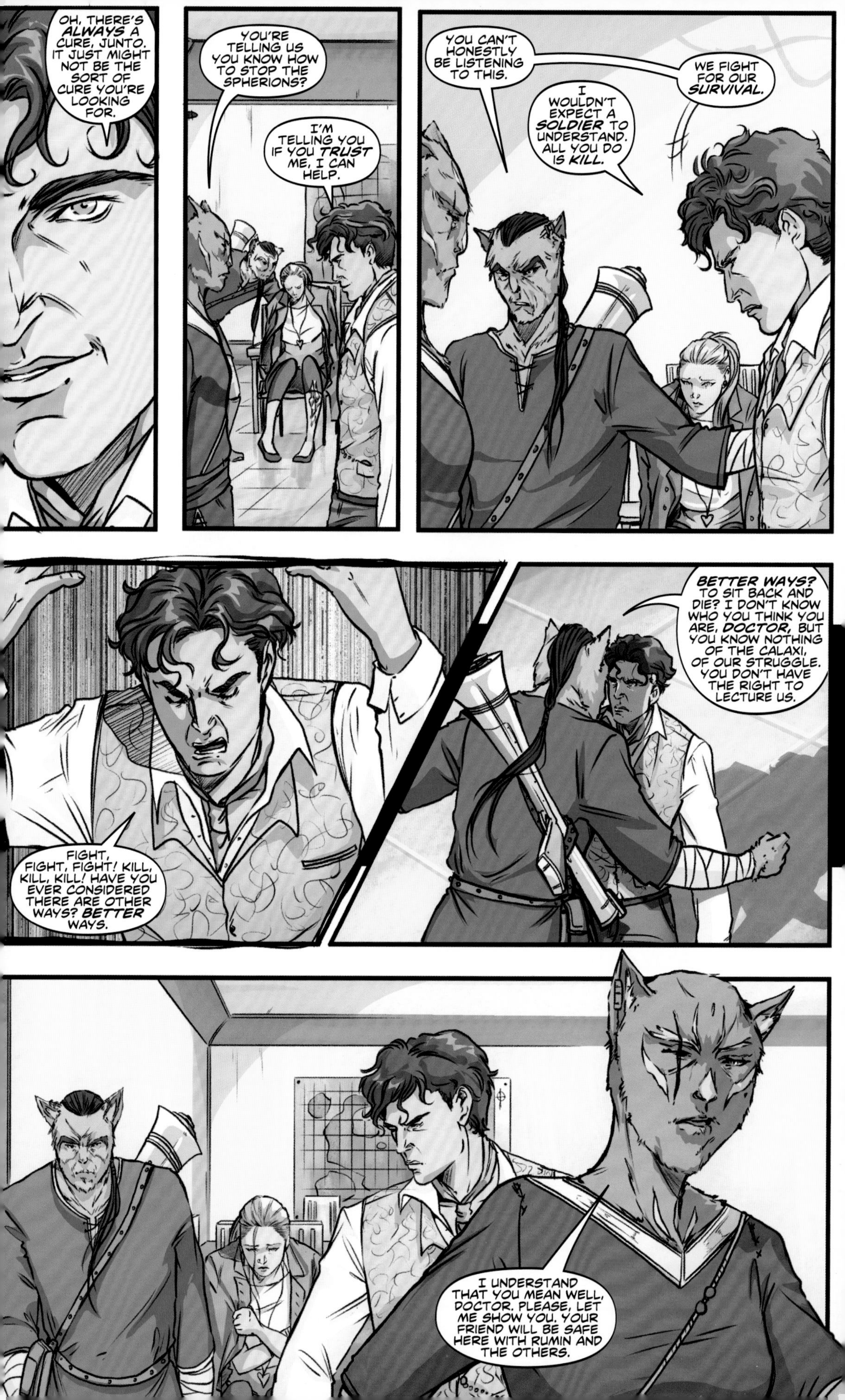
OH, THERE'S ALWAYS A CURE, JUNTO. IT JUST MIGHT NOT BE THE SORT OF CURE YOU'RE LOOKING FOR.
YOU'RE TELLING US YOU KNOW HOW TO STOP THE SPHERIONS?
I'M TELLING YOU IF YOU TRUST ME, I CAN HELP.
YOU CAN'T HONESTLY BE LISTENING TO THIS.
WE FIGHT FOR OUR SURVIVAL.
I WOULDN'T EXPECT A SOLDIER TO UNDERSTAND. ALL YOU DO IS KILL.
FIGHT, FIGHT, FIGHT! KILL, KILL, KILL! HAVE YOU EVER CONSIDERED THERE ARE OTHER WAYS? BETTER WAYS.
BETTER WAYS? TO SIT BACK AND DIE? I DON'T KNOW WHO YOU THINK YOU ARE, DOCTOR, BUT YOU KNOW NOTHING OF THE CALAXI, OF OUR STRUGGLE. YOU DON'T HAVE THE RIGHT TO LECTURE US.
I UNDERSTAND THAT YOU MEAN WELL, DOCTOR. PLEASE, LET ME SHOW YOU. YOUR FRIEND WILL BE SAFE HERE WITH RUMIN AND THE OTHERS.

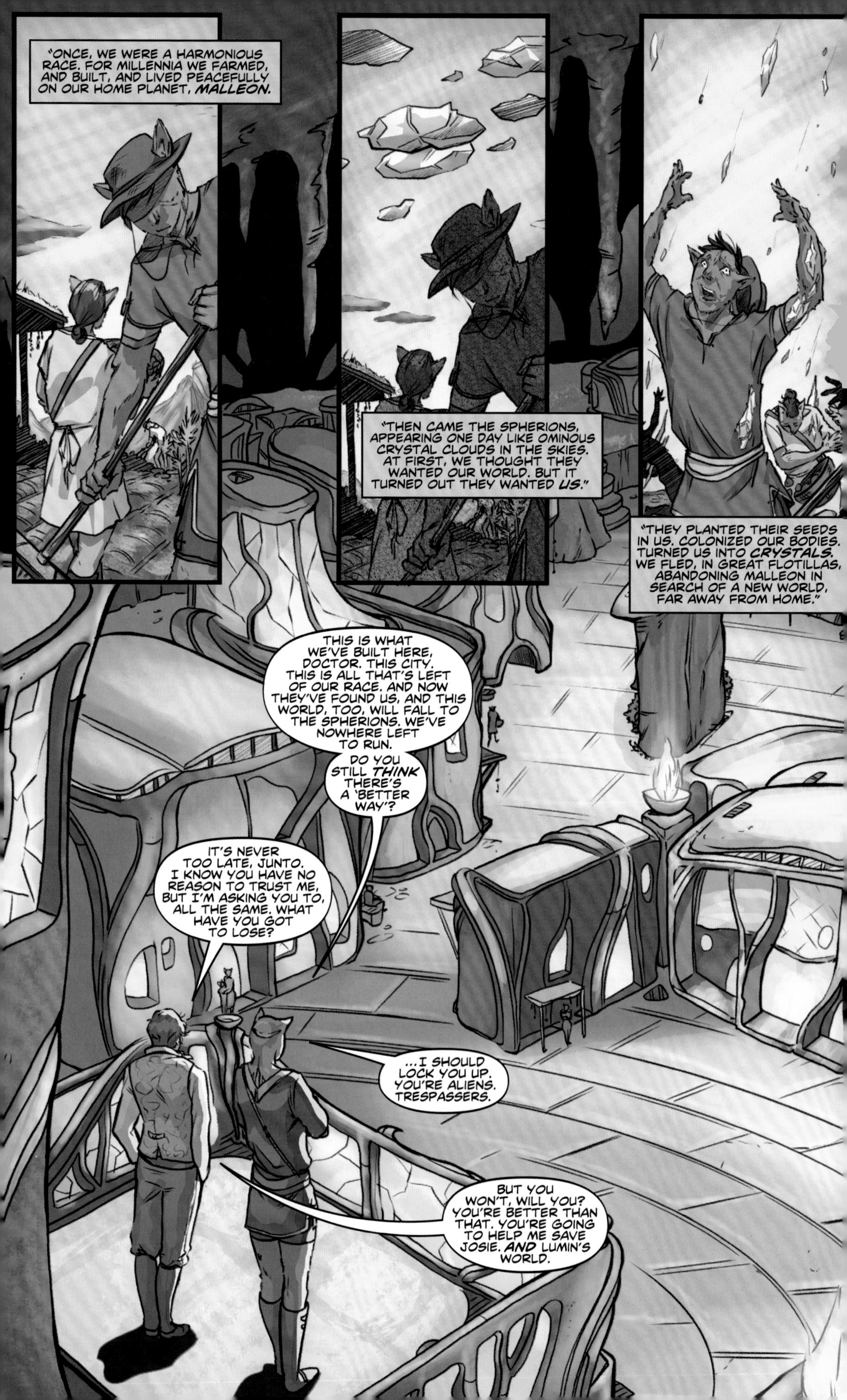
"ONCE, WE WERE A HARMONIOUS RACE. FOR MILLENNIA WE FARMED, AND BUILT, AND LIVED PEACEFULLY ON OUR HOME PLANET, MALLEON.
"THEN CAME THE SPHERIONS, APPEARING ONE DAY LIKE OMINOUS CRYSTAL CLOUDS IN THE SKIES. AT FIRST, WE THOUGHT THEY WANTED OUR WORLD. BUT IT TURNED OUT THEY WANTED US."
"THEY PLANTED THEIR SEEDS IN US. COLONIZED OUR BODIES. TURNED US INTO CRYSTALS. WE FLED, IN GREAT FLOTILLAS, ABANDONING MALLEON IN SEARCH OF A NEW WORLD, FAR AWAY FROM HOME."
THIS IS WHAT WE'VE BUILT HERE, DOCTOR. THIS CITY. THIS IS ALL THAT'S LEFT OF OUR RACE. AND NOW THEY'VE FOUND US, AND THIS WORLD, TOO, WILL FALL TO THE SPHERIONS. WE'VE NOWHERE LEFT TO RUN.
DO YOU STILL THINK THERE'S A 'BETTER WAY'?
IT'S NEVER TOO LATE, JUNTO. I KNOW YOU HAVE NO REASON TO TRUST ME, BUT I'M ASKING YOU TO, ALL THE SAME. WHAT HAVE YOU GOT TO LOSE?
...I SHOULD LOCK YOU UP. YOU'RE ALIENS. TRESPASSERS.
BUT YOU WON'T, WILL YOU? YOU'RE BETTER THAN THAT. YOU'RE GOING TO HELP ME SAVE JOSIE. AND LUMIN'S WORLD.

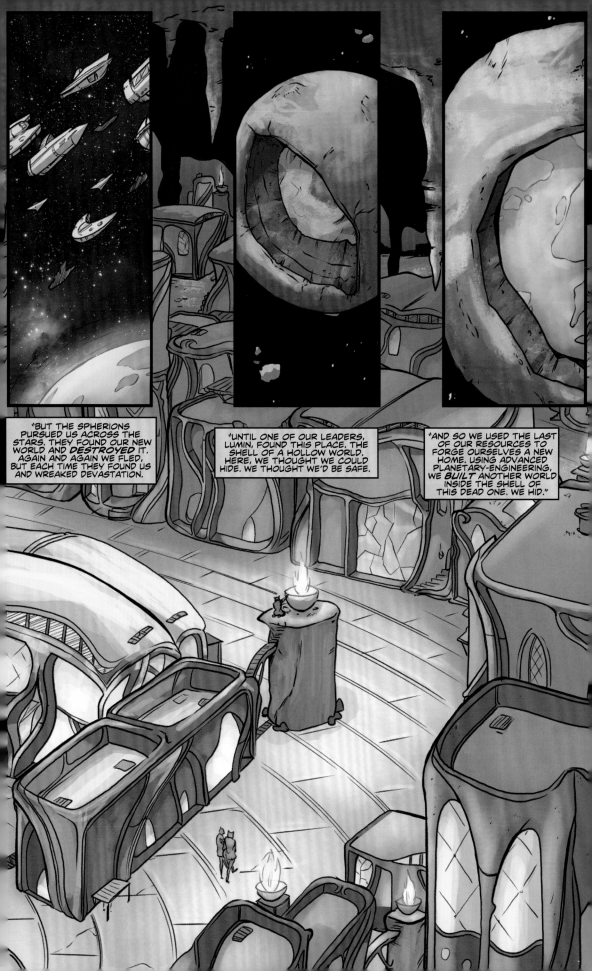

"BUT THE SPHERIONS PURSUED US ACROSS THE STARS. THEY FOUND OUR NEW WORLD AND *DESTROYED* IT. AGAIN AND AGAIN WE FLED, BUT EACH TIME THEY FOUND US AND WREAKED DEVASTATION.

"UNTIL ONE OF OUR LEADERS, LUMIN, FOUND THIS PLACE. THE SHELL OF A HOLLOW WORLD. HERE, WE THOUGHT WE COULD HIDE. WE THOUGHT WE'D BE SAFE.

"AND SO WE USED THE LAST OF OUR RESOURCES TO FORGE OURSELVES A NEW HOME. USING ADVANCED PLANETARY-ENGINEERING, WE *BUILT* ANOTHER WORLD INSIDE THE SHELL OF THIS DEAD ONE. WE HID."

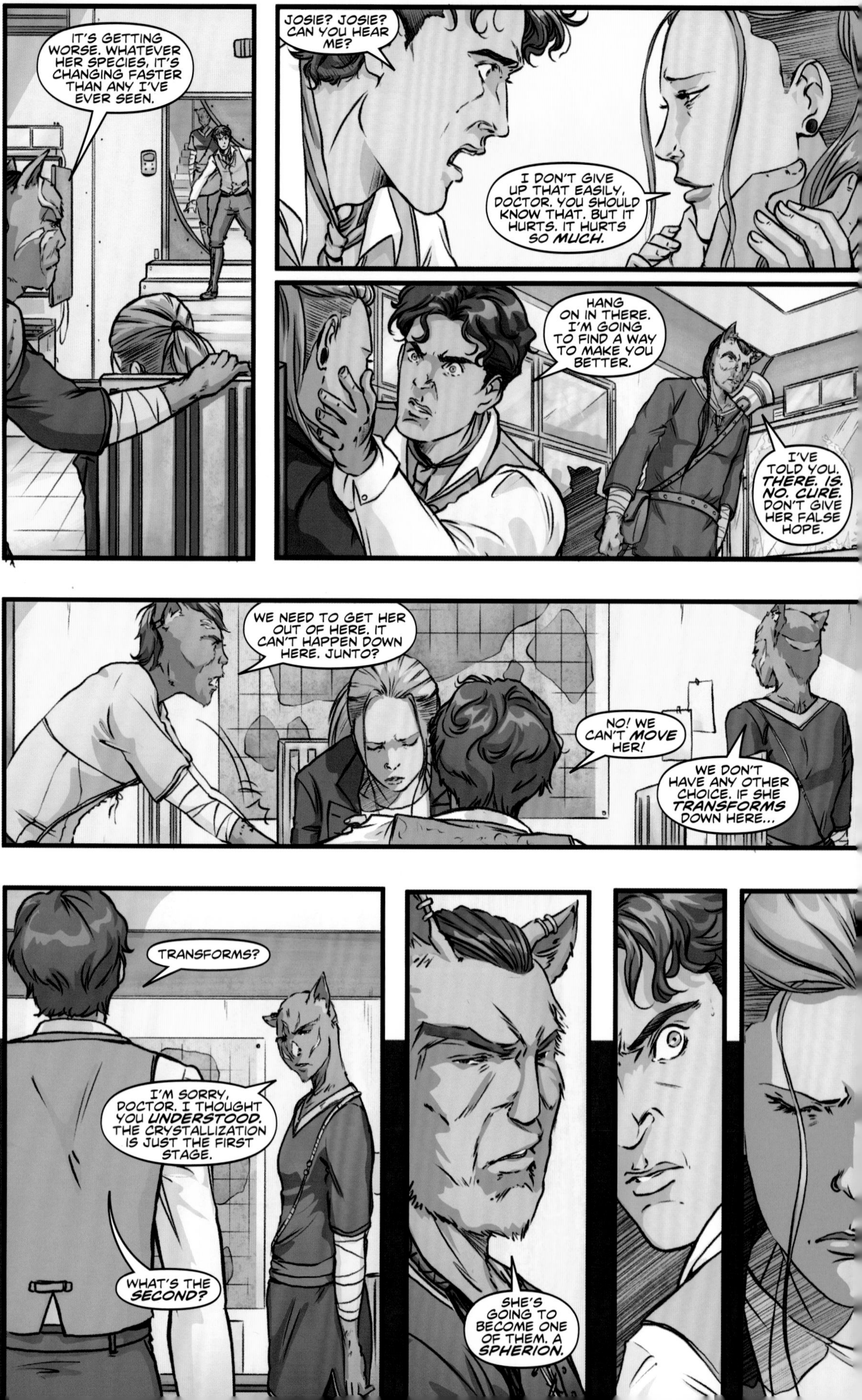
IT'S GETTING WORSE. WHATEVER HER SPECIES, IT'S CHANGING FASTER THAN ANY I'VE EVER SEEN.
JOSIE? JOSIE? CAN YOU HEAR ME?
I DON'T GIVE UP THAT EASILY, DOCTOR. YOU SHOULD KNOW THAT. BUT IT HURTS. IT HURTS SO *MUCH.*
HANG ON IN THERE. I'M GOING TO FIND A WAY TO MAKE YOU BETTER.
I'VE TOLD YOU. ***THERE. IS. NO. CURE.*** DON'T GIVE HER FALSE HOPE.
WE NEED TO GET HER OUT OF HERE. IT CAN'T HAPPEN DOWN HERE. JUNTO?
NO! WE CAN'T *MOVE* HER!
WE DON'T HAVE ANY OTHER CHOICE. IF SHE *TRANSFORMS* DOWN HERE...
TRANSFORMS?
I'M SORRY, DOCTOR. I THOUGHT YOU *UNDERSTOOD.* THE CRYSTALLIZATION IS JUST THE FIRST STAGE.
WHAT'S THE *SECOND?*
SHE'S GOING TO BECOME ONE OF THEM. A *SPHERION.*

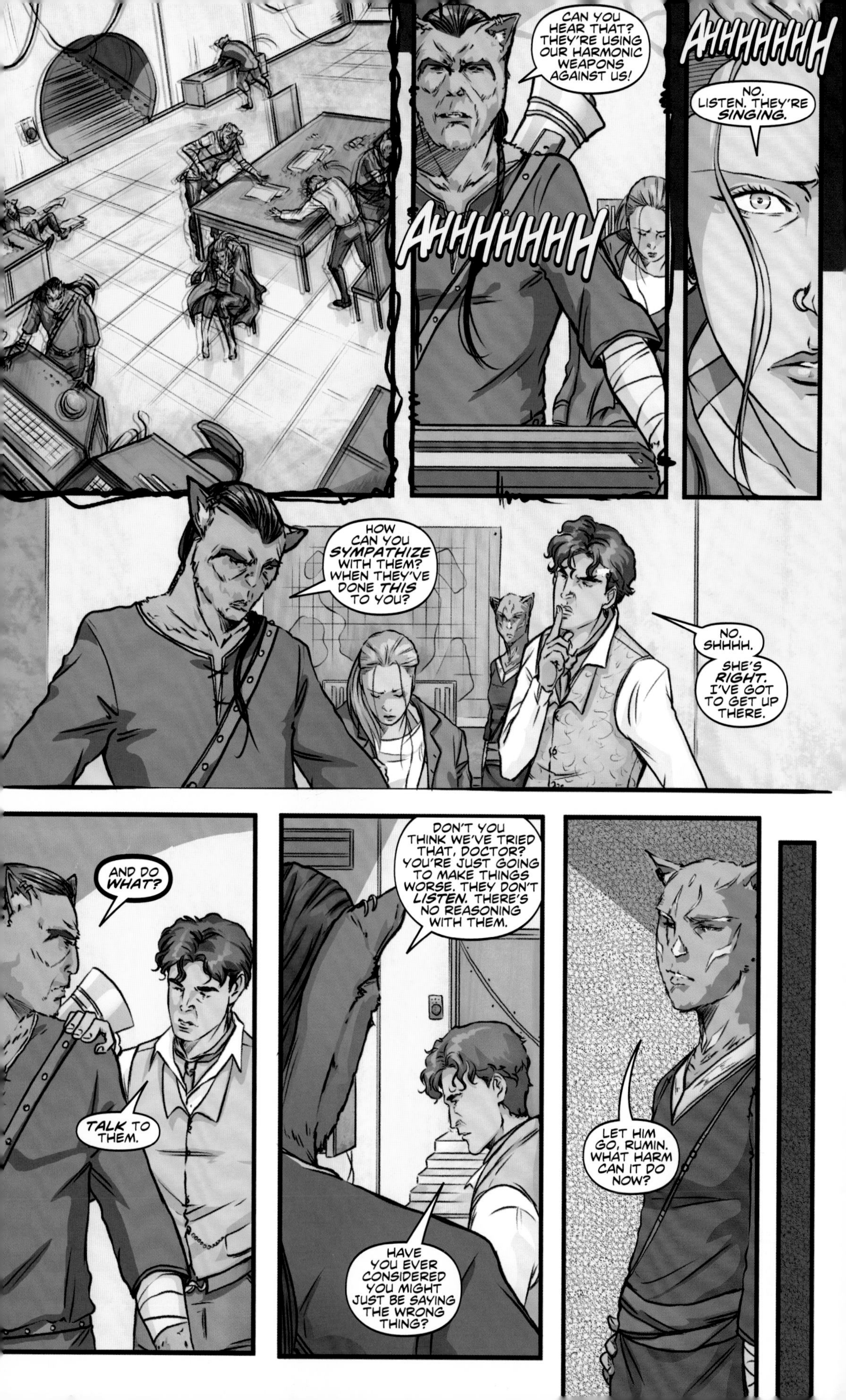
CAN YOU HEAR THAT? THEY'RE USING OUR HARMONIC WEAPONS AGAINST US!
AHHHHHHH
AHHHHHHH
NO. LISTEN. THEY'RE *SINGING.*
HOW CAN YOU *SYMPATHIZE* WITH THEM? WHEN THEY'VE DONE *THIS* TO YOU?
NO. SHHHH.
SHE'S *RIGHT.* I'VE GOT TO GET UP THERE.
AND DO *WHAT?*
TALK TO THEM.
DON'T YOU THINK WE'VE TRIED THAT, DOCTOR? YOU'RE JUST GOING TO MAKE THINGS WORSE. THEY DON'T *LISTEN.* THERE'S NO REASONING WITH THEM.
HAVE YOU EVER CONSIDERED YOU MIGHT JUST BE SAYING THE WRONG THING?
LET HIM GO, RUMIN. WHAT HARM CAN IT DO NOW?

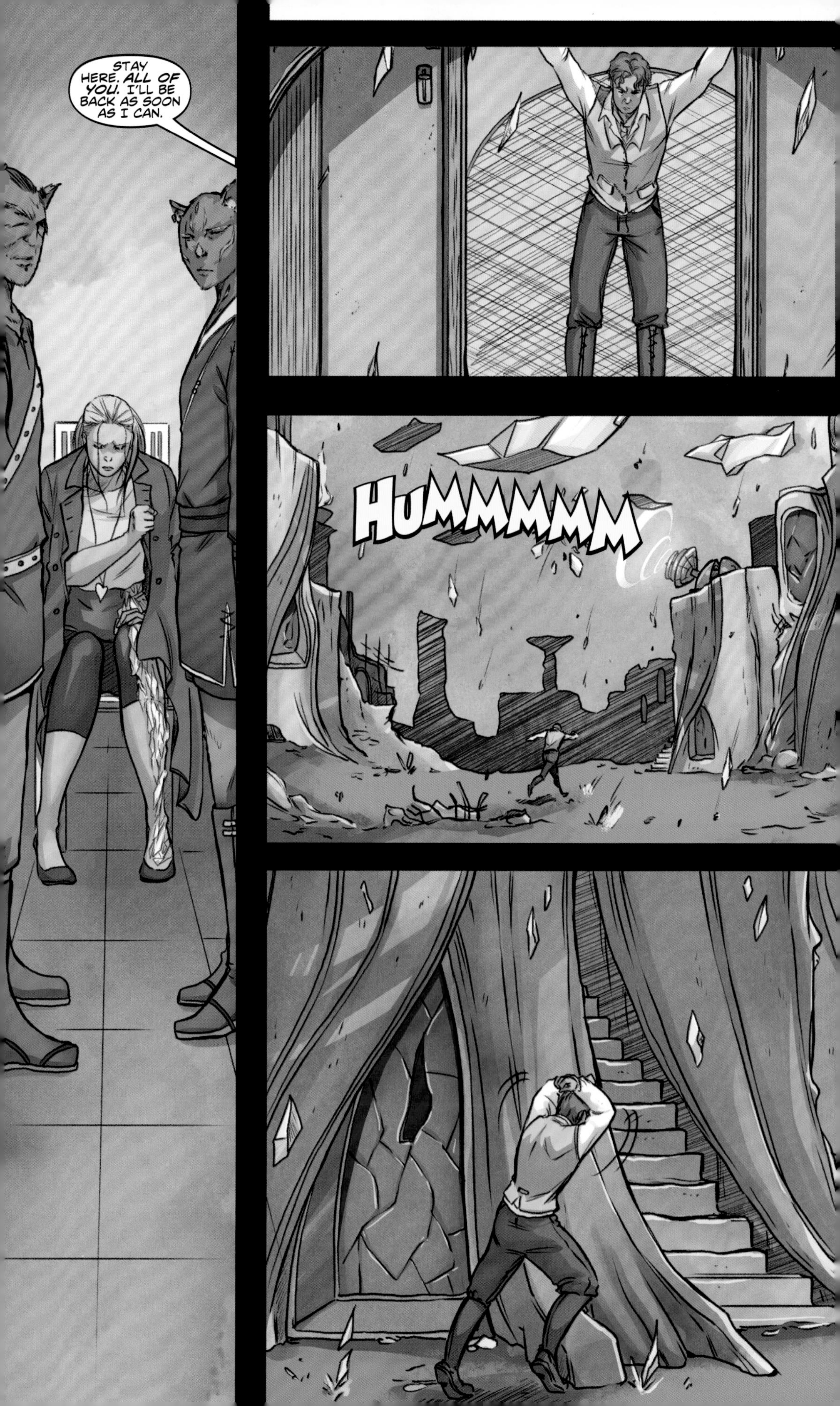
STAY HERE. ALL OF YOU. I'LL BE BACK AS SOON AS I CAN.
HUMMMMM

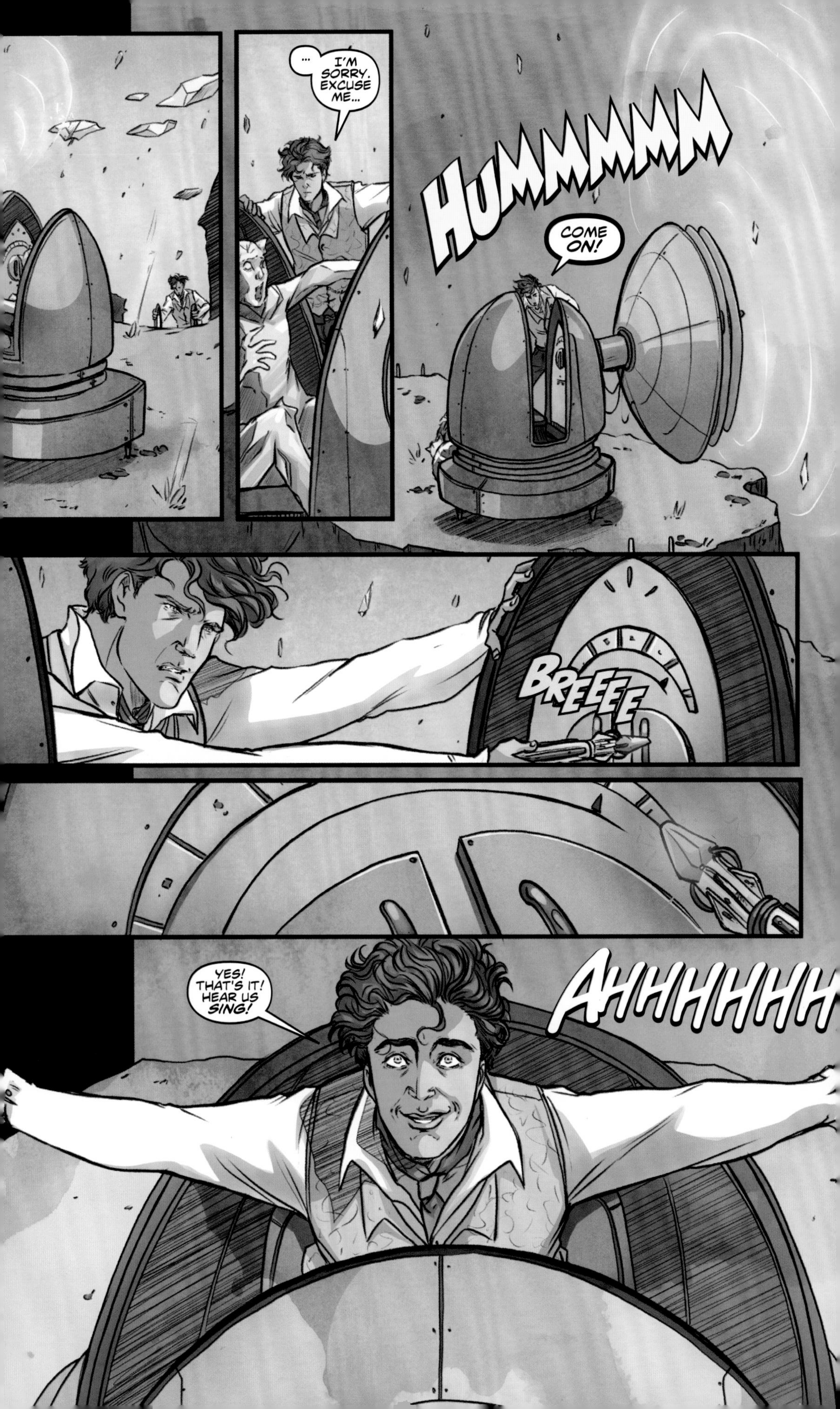
... I'M SORRY. EXCUSE ME...
HUMMMMM
COME ON!
BREEEE
YES! THAT'S IT! HEAR US SING!
AHHHHHH

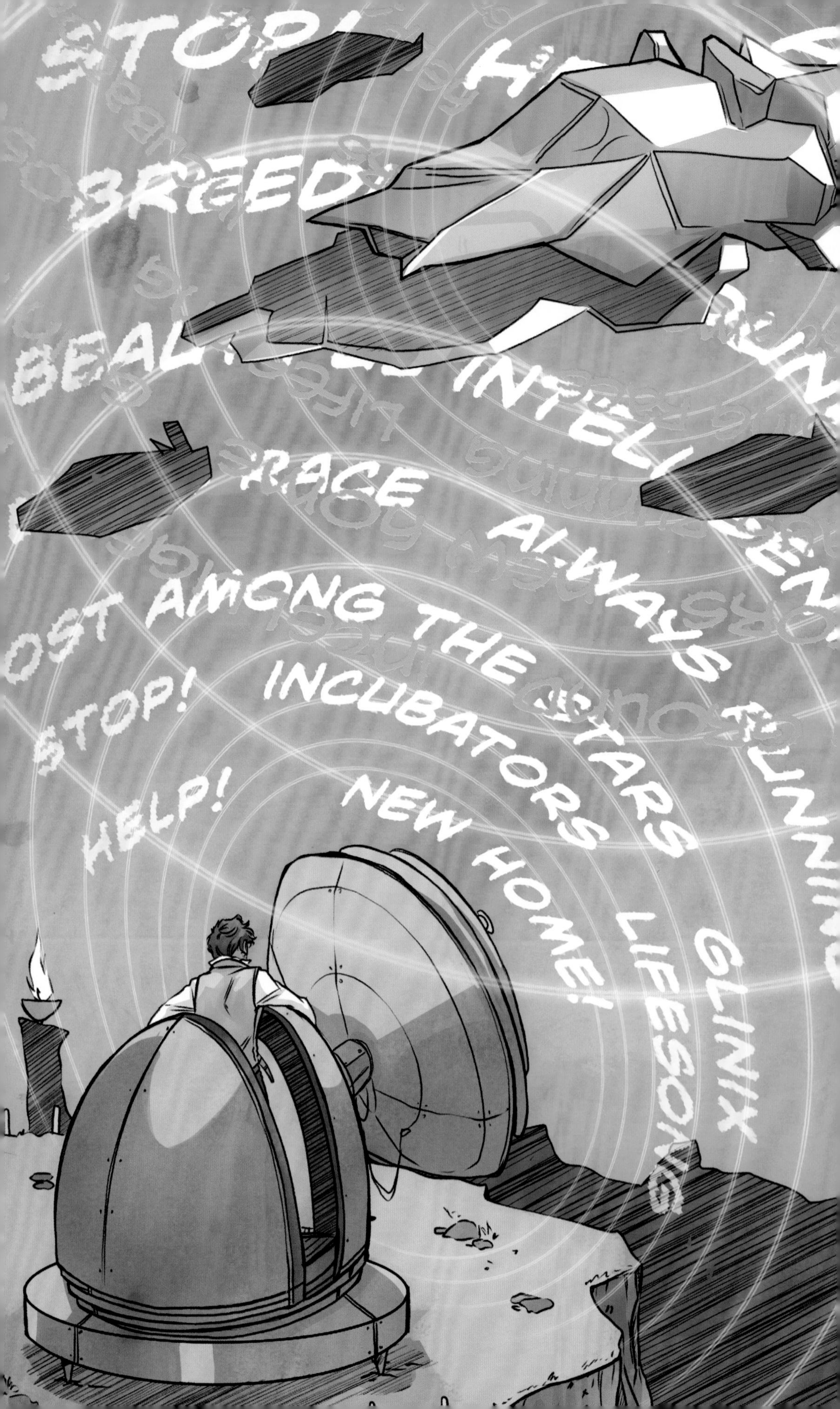
STOP!
BREED!
RACE
ALWAYS
AMONG THE STARS
STOP!
INCUBATORS
HELP!
NEW HOME!
LIFESONG
GLINIX

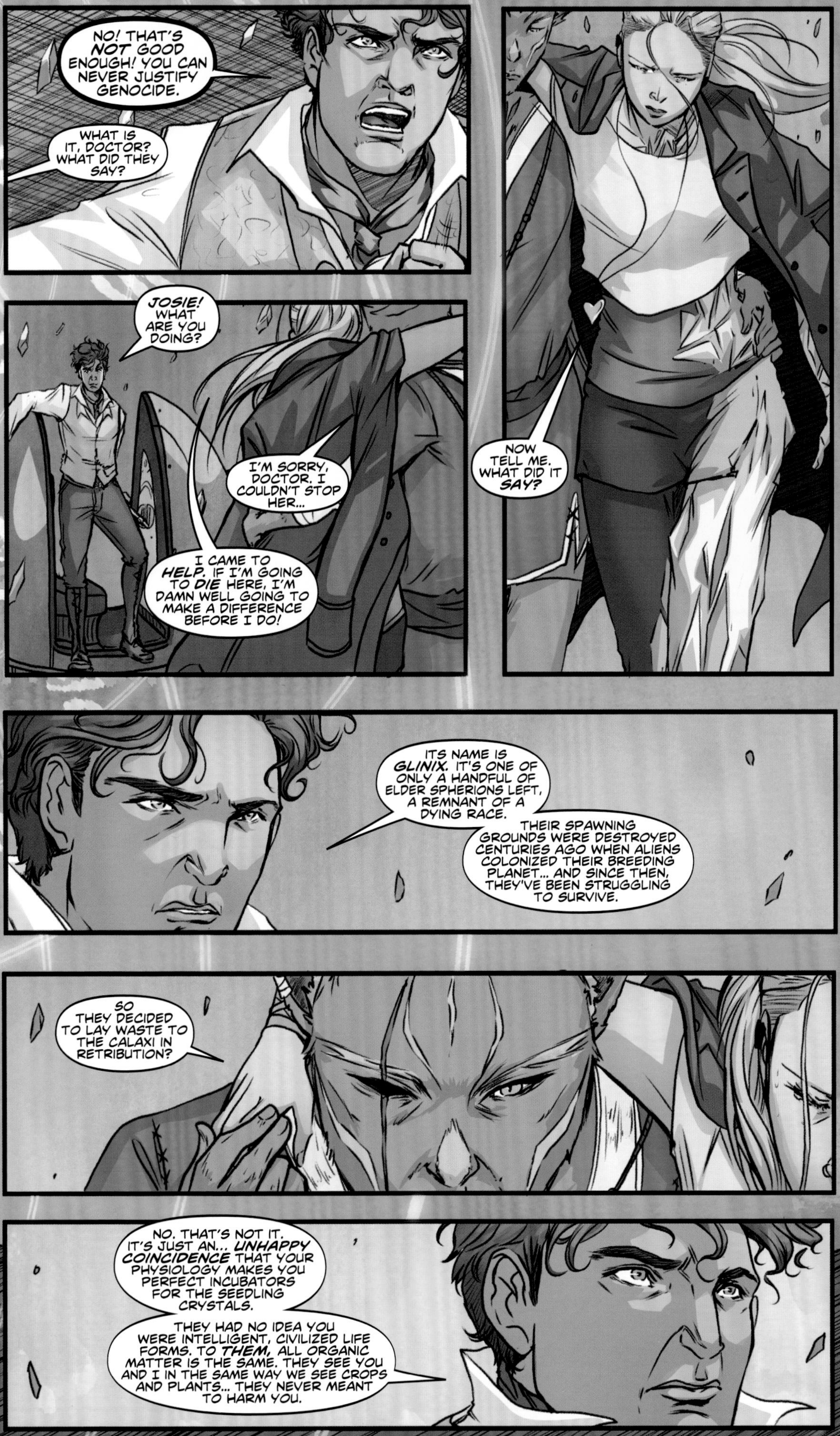
NO! THAT'S NOT GOOD ENOUGH! YOU CAN NEVER JUSTIFY GENOCIDE.
WHAT IS IT, DOCTOR? WHAT DID THEY SAY?
JOSIE! WHAT ARE YOU DOING?
I'M SORRY, DOCTOR. I COULDN'T STOP HER...
I CAME TO HELP. IF I'M GOING TO DIE HERE, I'M DAMN WELL GOING TO MAKE A DIFFERENCE BEFORE I DO!
NOW TELL ME. WHAT DID IT SAY?
ITS NAME IS GLINIX. IT'S ONE OF ONLY A HANDFUL OF ELDER SPHERIONS LEFT, A REMNANT OF A DYING RACE.
THEIR SPAWNING GROUNDS WERE DESTROYED CENTURIES AGO WHEN ALIENS COLONIZED THEIR BREEDING PLANET... AND SINCE THEN, THEY'VE BEEN STRUGGLING TO SURVIVE.
SO THEY DECIDED TO LAY WASTE TO THE CALAXI IN RETRIBUTION?
NO. THAT'S NOT IT. IT'S JUST AN... UNHAPPY COINCIDENCE THAT YOUR PHYSIOLOGY MAKES YOU PERFECT INCUBATORS FOR THE SEEDLING CRYSTALS.
THEY HAD NO IDEA YOU WERE INTELLIGENT, CIVILIZED LIFE FORMS. TO THEM, ALL ORGANIC MATTER IS THE SAME. THEY SEE YOU AND I IN THE SAME WAY WE SEE CROPS AND PLANTS... THEY NEVER MEANT TO HARM YOU.

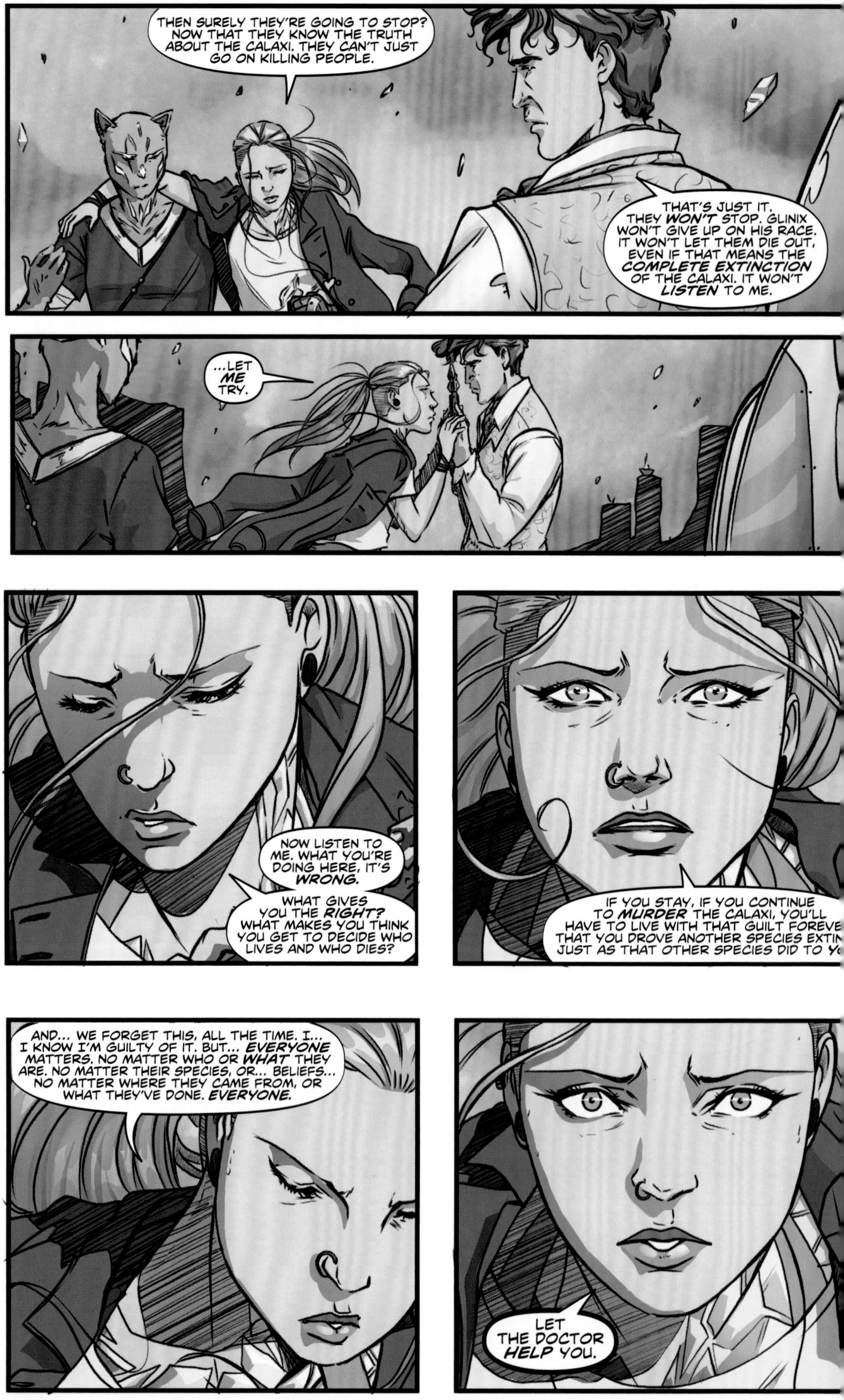
THEN SURELY THEY'RE GOING TO STOP? NOW THAT THEY KNOW THE TRUTH ABOUT THE CALAXI. THEY CAN'T JUST GO ON KILLING PEOPLE.
THAT'S JUST IT. THEY **WON'T** STOP. GLINIX WON'T GIVE UP ON HIS RACE. IT WON'T LET THEM DIE OUT, EVEN IF THAT MEANS THE **COMPLETE EXTINCTION** OF THE CALAXI. IT WON'T **LISTEN** TO ME.
...LET **ME** TRY.
NOW LISTEN TO ME. WHAT YOU'RE DOING HERE, IT'S **WRONG.**
WHAT GIVES YOU THE **RIGHT?** WHAT MAKES YOU THINK YOU GET TO DECIDE WHO LIVES AND WHO DIES?
IF YOU STAY, IF YOU CONTINUE TO **MURDER** THE CALAXI, YOU'LL HAVE TO LIVE WITH THAT GUILT FOREVE THAT YOU DROVE ANOTHER SPECIES EXTIN JUST AS THAT OTHER SPECIES DID TO YO
AND... WE FORGET THIS, ALL THE TIME. I... I KNOW I'M GUILTY OF IT. BUT... **EVERYONE** MATTERS. NO MATTER WHO OR **WHAT** THEY ARE. NO MATTER THEIR SPECIES, OR... BELIEFS... NO MATTER WHERE THEY CAME FROM, OR WHAT THEY'VE DONE. **EVERYONE.**
LET THE DOCTOR **HELP** YOU.

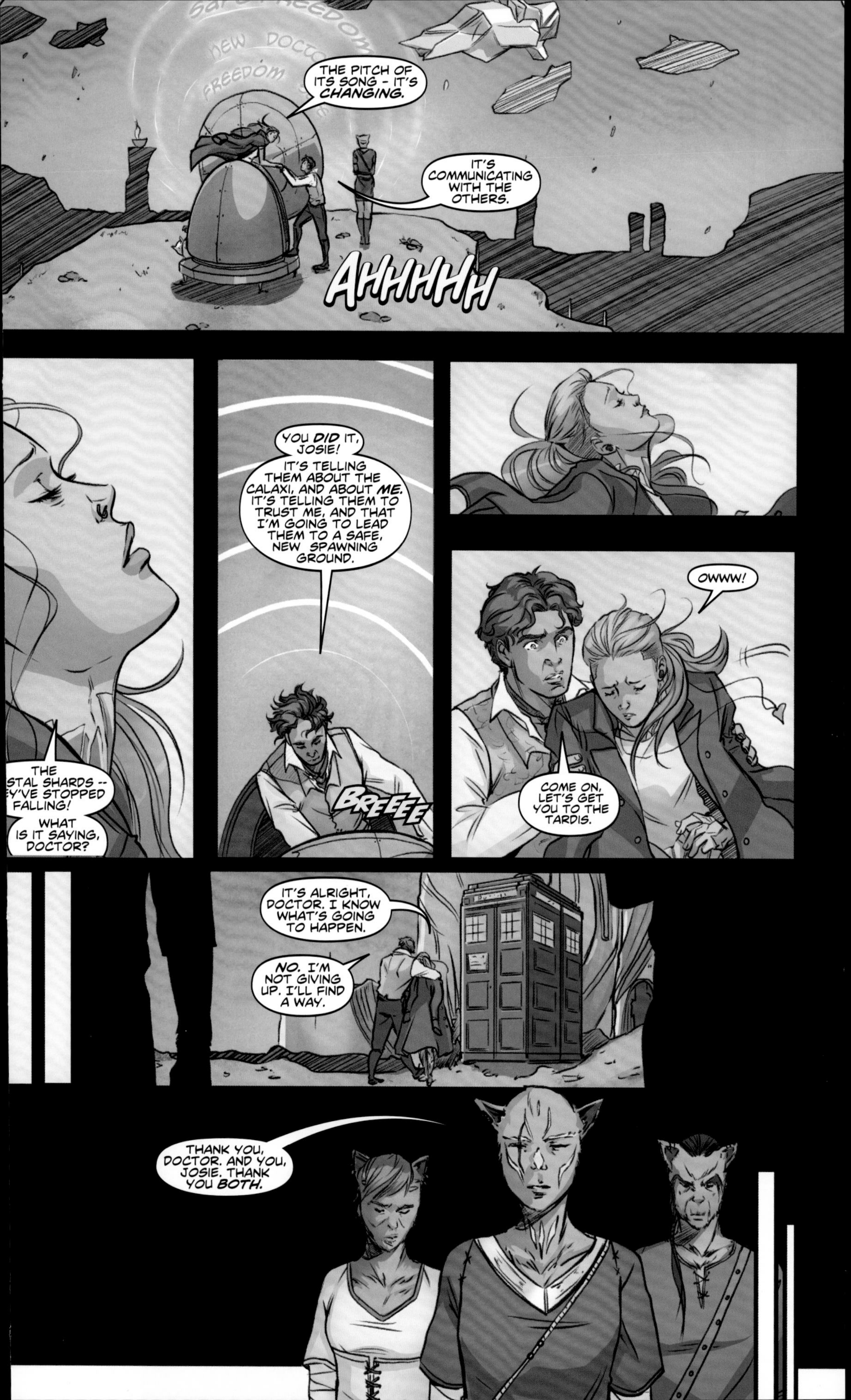

THE PITCH OF ITS SONG – IT'S CHANGING.
IT'S COMMUNICATING WITH THE OTHERS.
AHHHHH
THE STAL SHARDS -- EY'VE STOPPED FALLING!
WHAT IS IT SAYING, DOCTOR?
YOU DID IT, JOSIE!
IT'S TELLING THEM ABOUT THE CALAXI, AND ABOUT ME. IT'S TELLING THEM TO TRUST ME, AND THAT I'M GOING TO LEAD THEM TO A SAFE, NEW SPAWNING GROUND.
BREEEE
OWWW!
COME ON, LET'S GET YOU TO THE TARDIS.
IT'S ALRIGHT, DOCTOR. I KNOW WHAT'S GOING TO HAPPEN.
NO. I'M NOT GIVING UP. I'LL FIND A WAY.
THANK YOU, DOCTOR. AND YOU, JOSIE. THANK YOU BOTH.

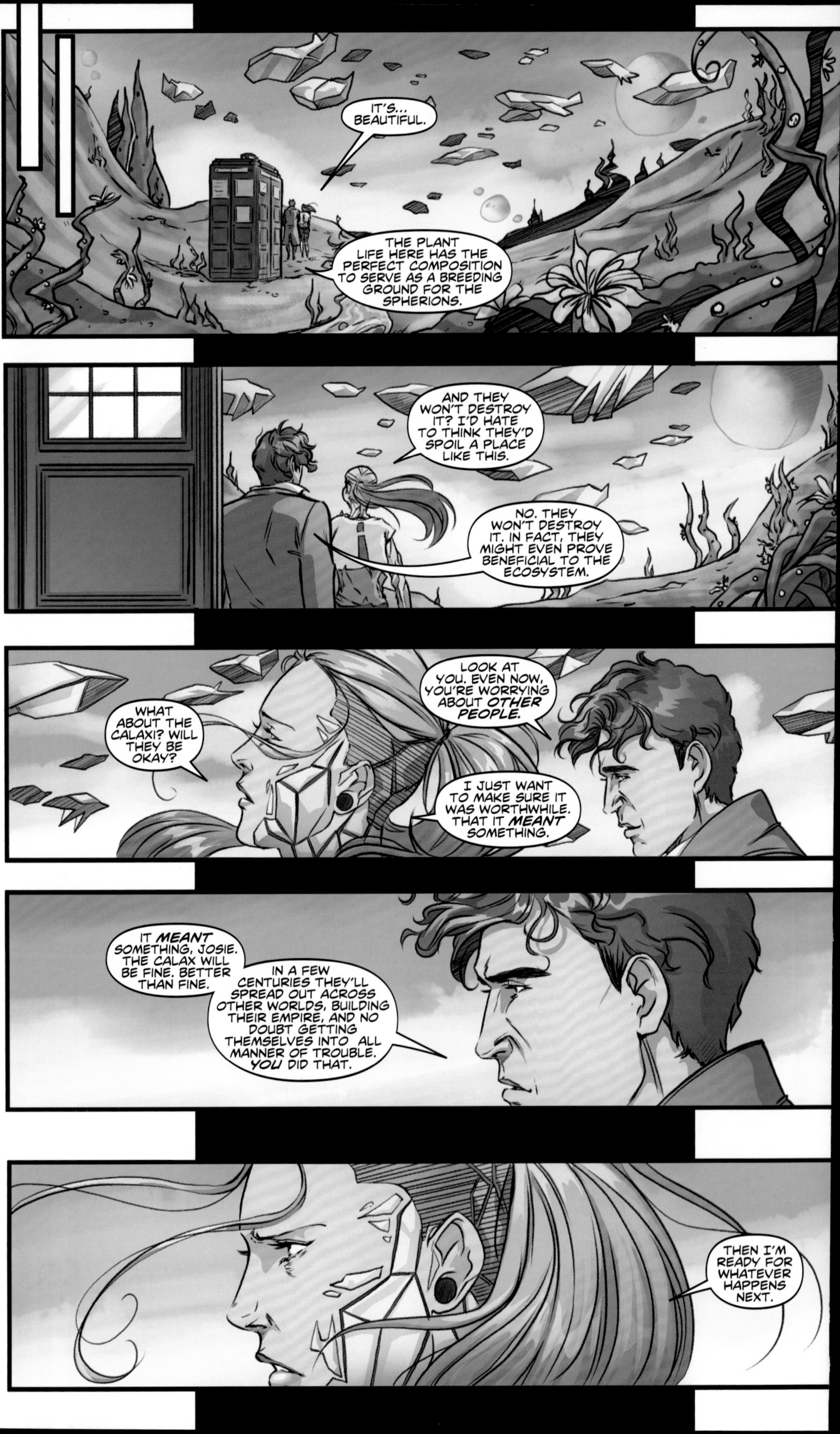
IT'S... BEAUTIFUL.
THE PLANT LIFE HERE HAS THE PERFECT COMPOSITION TO SERVE AS A BREEDING GROUND FOR THE SPHERIONS.
AND THEY WON'T DESTROY IT? I'D HATE TO THINK THEY'D SPOIL A PLACE LIKE THIS.
NO. THEY WON'T DESTROY IT. IN FACT, THEY MIGHT EVEN PROVE BENEFICIAL TO THE ECOSYSTEM.
WHAT ABOUT THE CALAXI? WILL THEY BE OKAY?
LOOK AT YOU. EVEN NOW, YOU'RE WORRYING ABOUT OTHER PEOPLE.
I JUST WANT TO MAKE SURE IT WAS WORTHWHILE. THAT IT MEANT SOMETHING.
IT MEANT SOMETHING, JOSIE. THE CALAX WILL BE FINE. BETTER THAN FINE.
IN A FEW CENTURIES THEY'LL SPREAD OUT ACROSS OTHER WORLDS, BUILDING THEIR EMPIRE, AND NO DOUBT GETTING THEMSELVES INTO ALL MANNER OF TROUBLE. YOU DID THAT.
THEN I'M READY FOR WHATEVER HAPPENS NEXT.

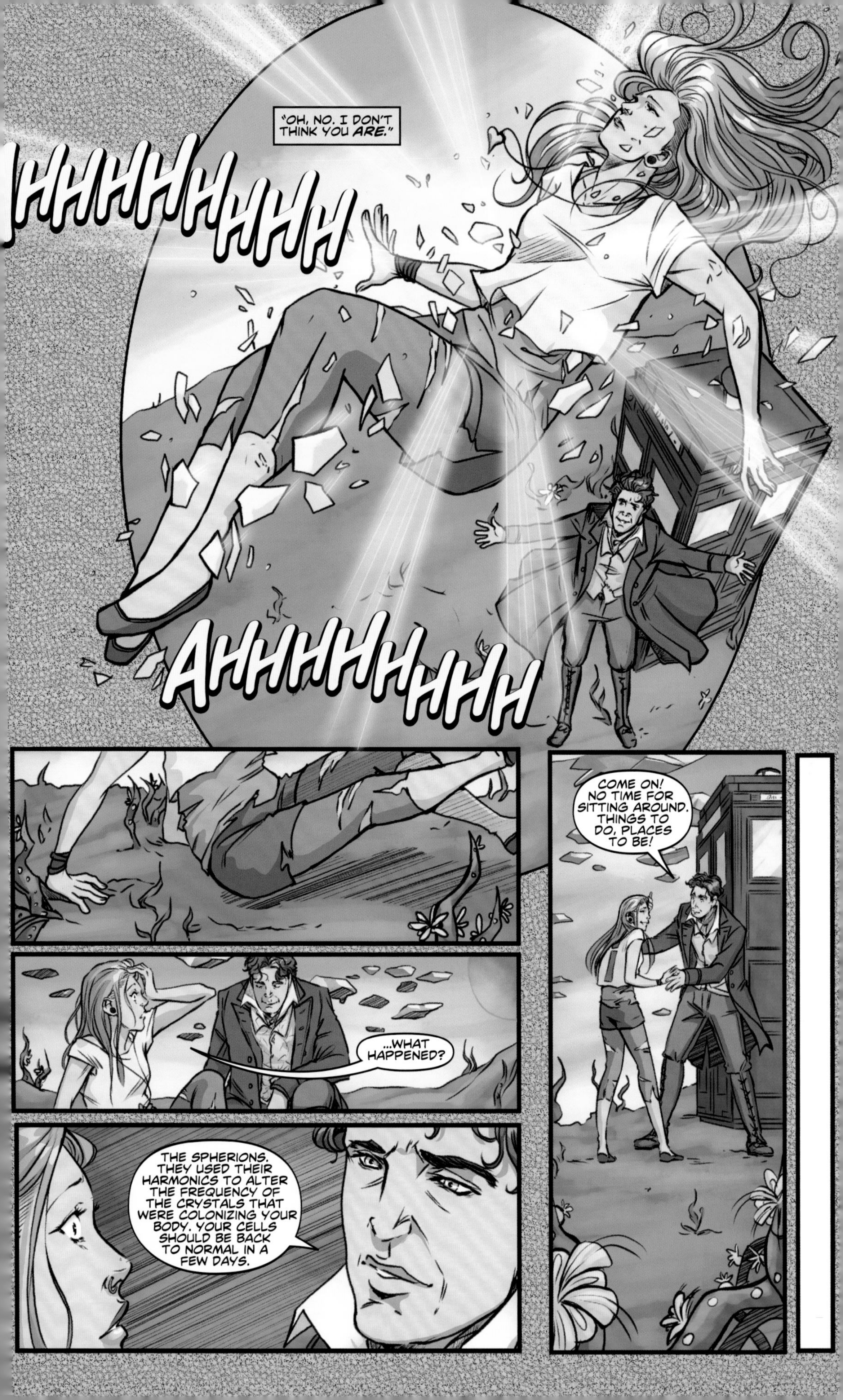
"OH, NO. I DON'T THINK YOU *ARE*."
HHHHHHHHHH
AHHHHHHHHH
COME ON! NO TIME FOR SITTING AROUND. THINGS TO DO, PLACES TO BE!
...WHAT HAPPENED?
THE SPHERIONS. THEY USED THEIR HARMONICS TO ALTER THE FREQUENCY OF THE CRYSTALS THAT WERE COLONIZING YOUR BODY. YOUR CELLS SHOULD BE BACK TO NORMAL IN A FEW DAYS.

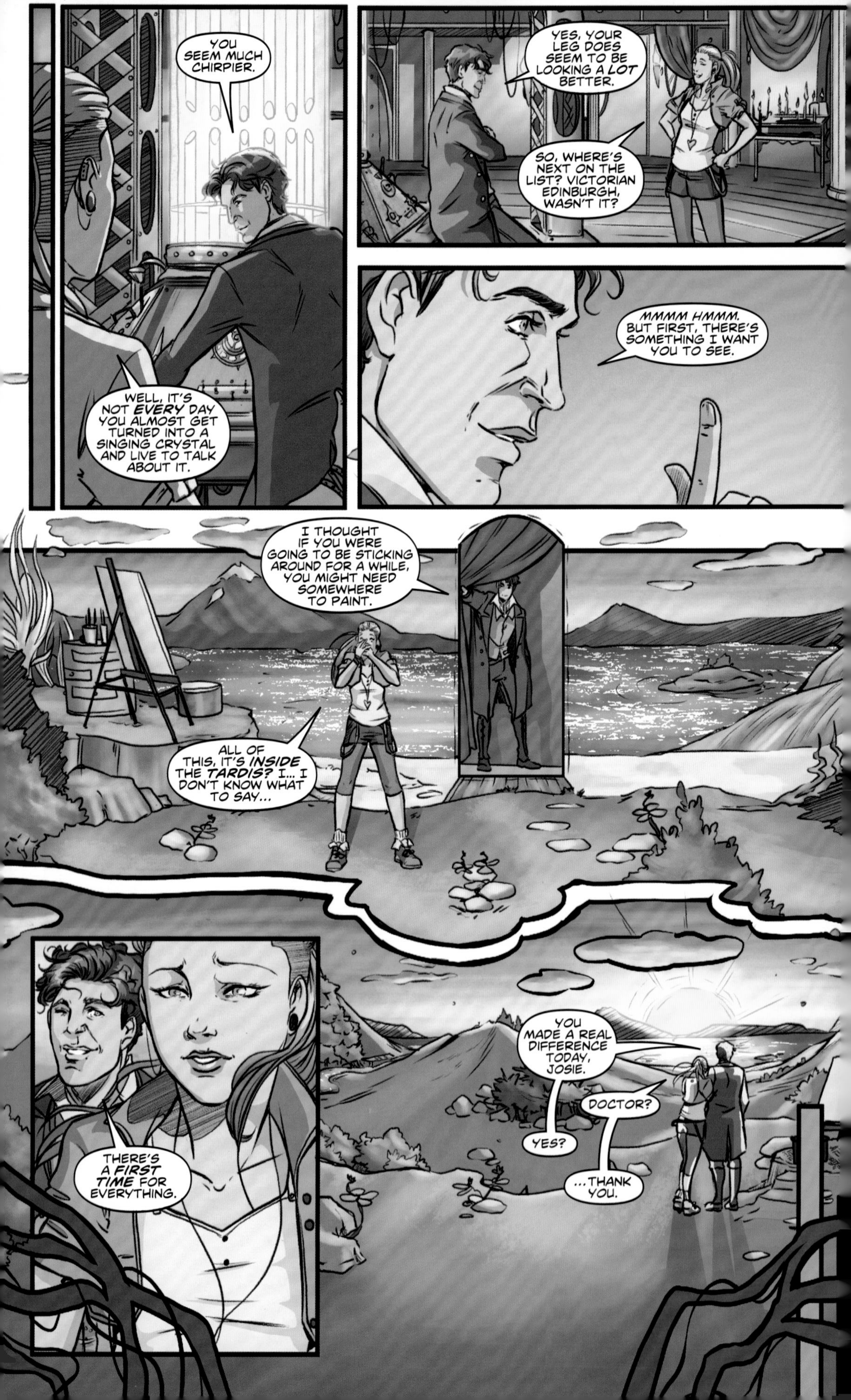
YOU SEEM MUCH CHIRPIER.
WELL, IT'S NOT EVERY DAY YOU ALMOST GET TURNED INTO A SINGING CRYSTAL AND LIVE TO TALK ABOUT IT.
YES, YOUR LEG DOES SEEM TO BE LOOKING A LOT BETTER.
SO, WHERE'S NEXT ON THE LIST? VICTORIAN EDINBURGH, WASN'T IT?
MMMM HMMM. BUT FIRST, THERE'S SOMETHING I WANT YOU TO SEE.
I THOUGHT IF YOU WERE GOING TO BE STICKING AROUND FOR A WHILE, YOU MIGHT NEED SOMEWHERE TO PAINT.
ALL OF THIS, IT'S INSIDE THE TARDIS? I... I DON'T KNOW WHAT TO SAY...
THERE'S A FIRST TIME FOR EVERYTHING.
YOU MADE A REAL DIFFERENCE TODAY, JOSIE.
DOCTOR?
YES?
...THANK YOU.

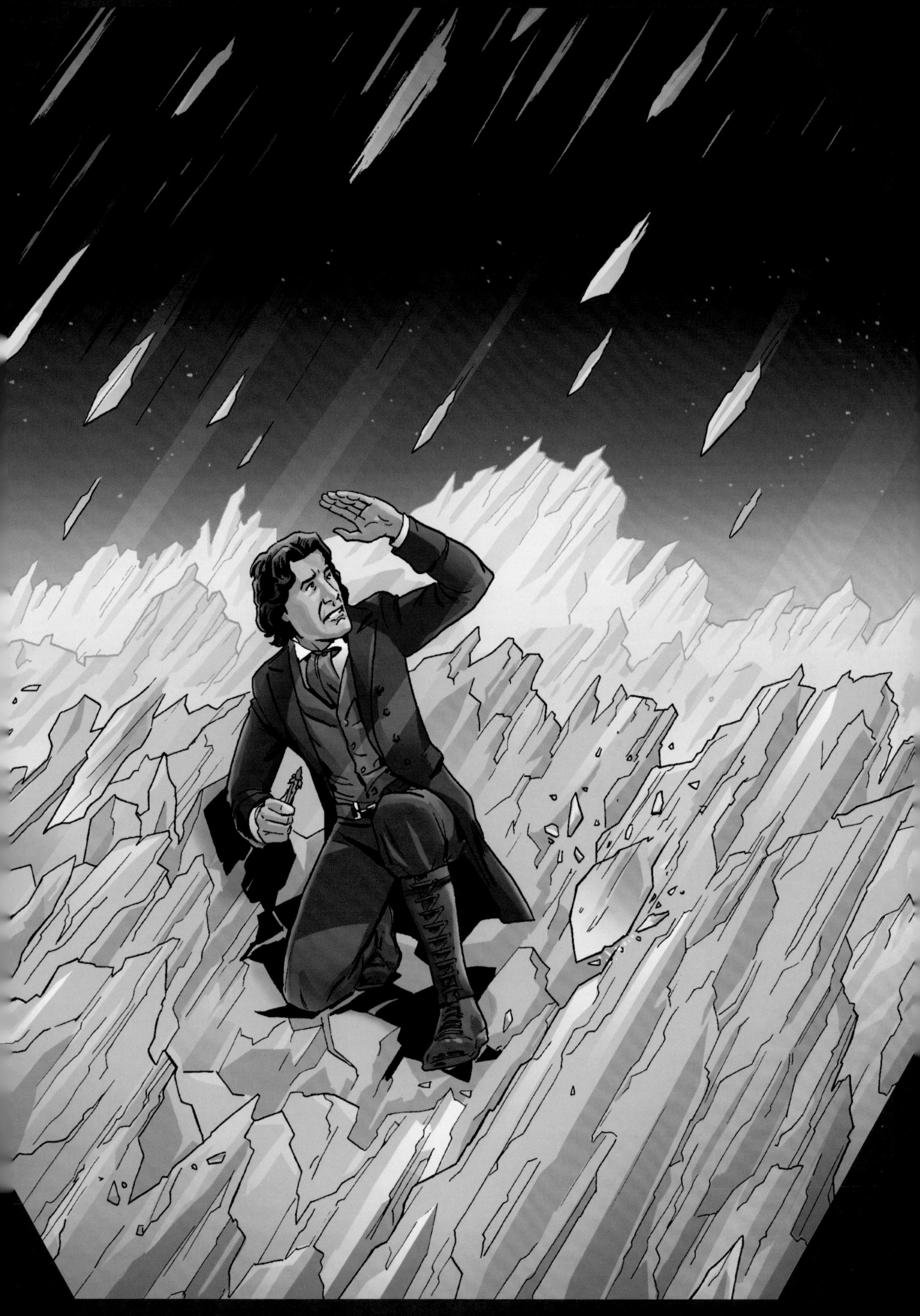

8D #2 Cover C: WARREN PLEECE

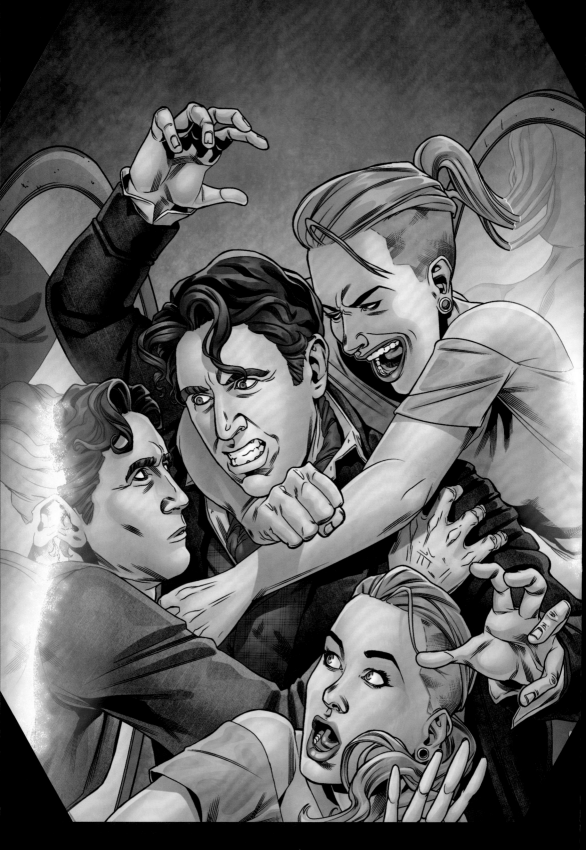

8D #3 Cover A: RACHAEL STOTT & HI-FI

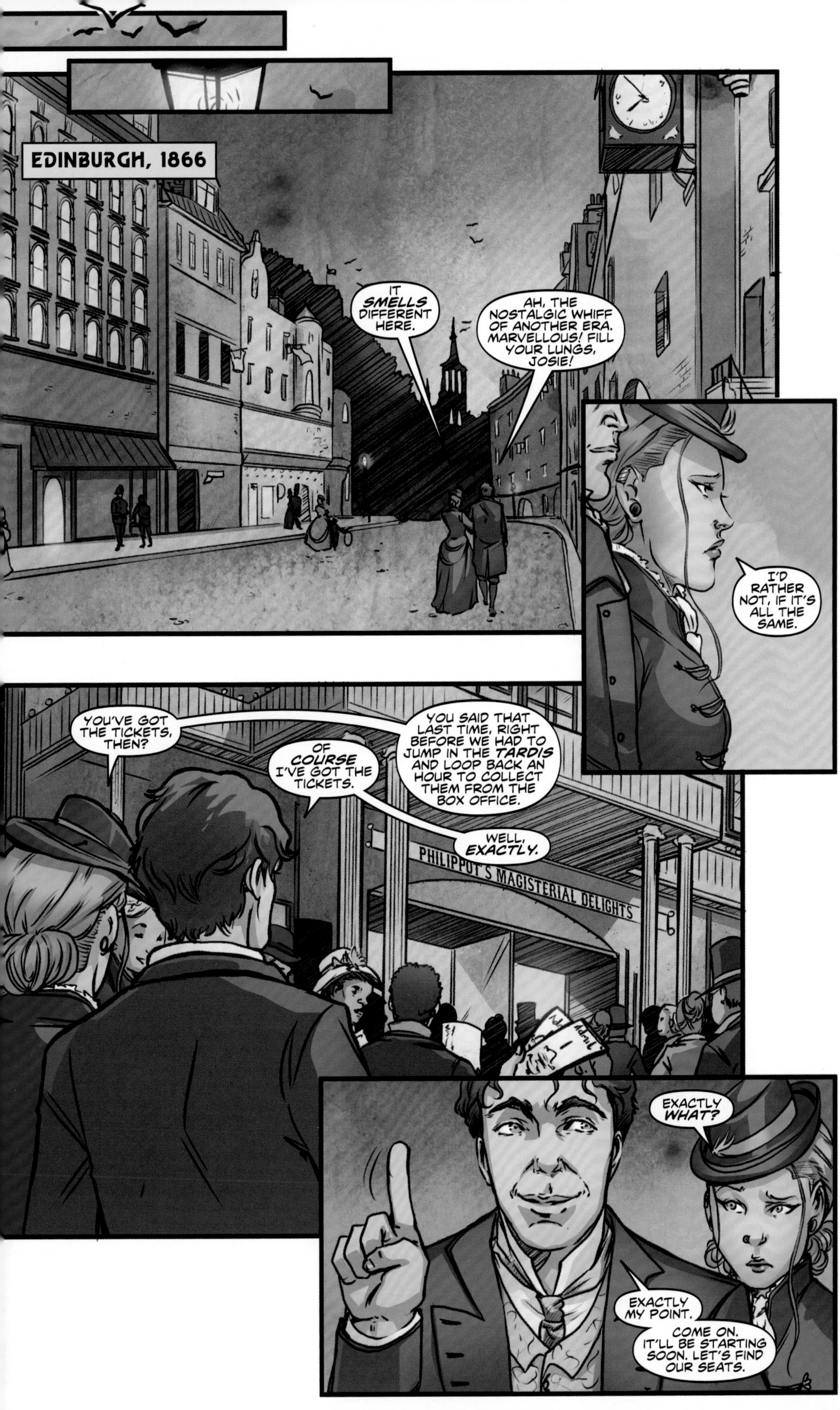
EDINBURGH, 1866
IT SMELLS DIFFERENT HERE.
AH, THE NOSTALGIC WHIFF OF ANOTHER ERA. MARVELLOUS! FILL YOUR LUNGS, JOSIE!
I'D RATHER NOT, IF IT'S ALL THE SAME.
YOU'VE GOT THE TICKETS, THEN?
OF COURSE I'VE GOT THE TICKETS.
YOU SAID THAT LAST TIME, RIGHT BEFORE WE HAD TO JUMP IN THE TARDIS AND LOOP BACK AN HOUR TO COLLECT THEM FROM THE BOX OFFICE.
WELL, EXACTLY.
PHILIPPOT'S MAGISTERIAL DELIGHTS
EXACTLY WHAT?
EXACTLY MY POINT.
COME ON. IT'LL BE STARTING SOON. LET'S FIND OUR SEATS.

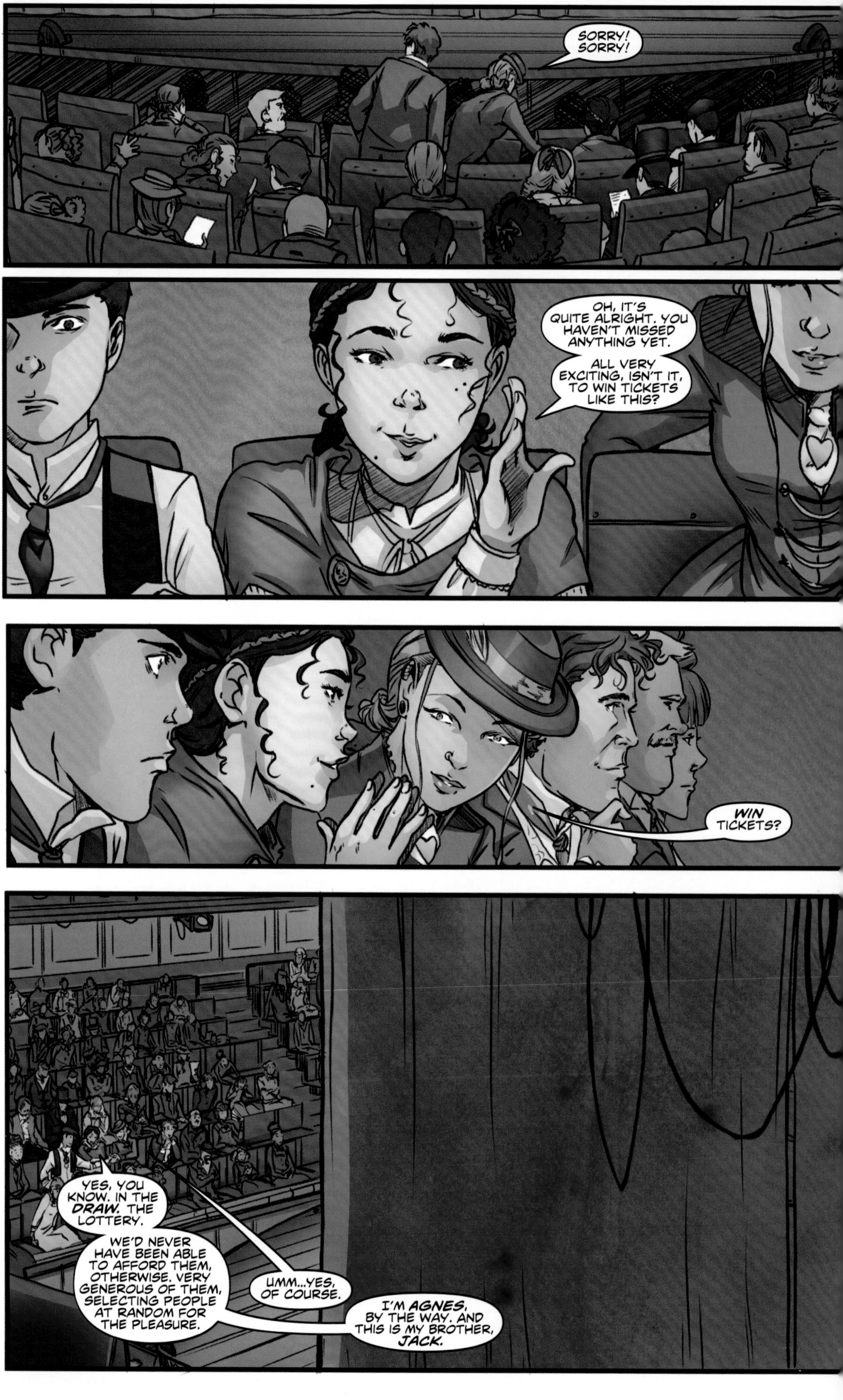
SORRY! SORRY!
OH, IT'S QUITE ALRIGHT. YOU HAVEN'T MISSED ANYTHING YET.
ALL VERY EXCITING, ISN'T IT, TO WIN TICKETS LIKE THIS?
WIN TICKETS?
YES, YOU KNOW. IN THE DRAW. THE LOTTERY.
WE'D NEVER HAVE BEEN ABLE TO AFFORD THEM, OTHERWISE. VERY GENEROUS OF THEM, SELECTING PEOPLE AT RANDOM FOR THE PLEASURE.
UMM...YES, OF COURSE.
I'M AGNES, BY THE WAY. AND THIS IS MY BROTHER, JACK.

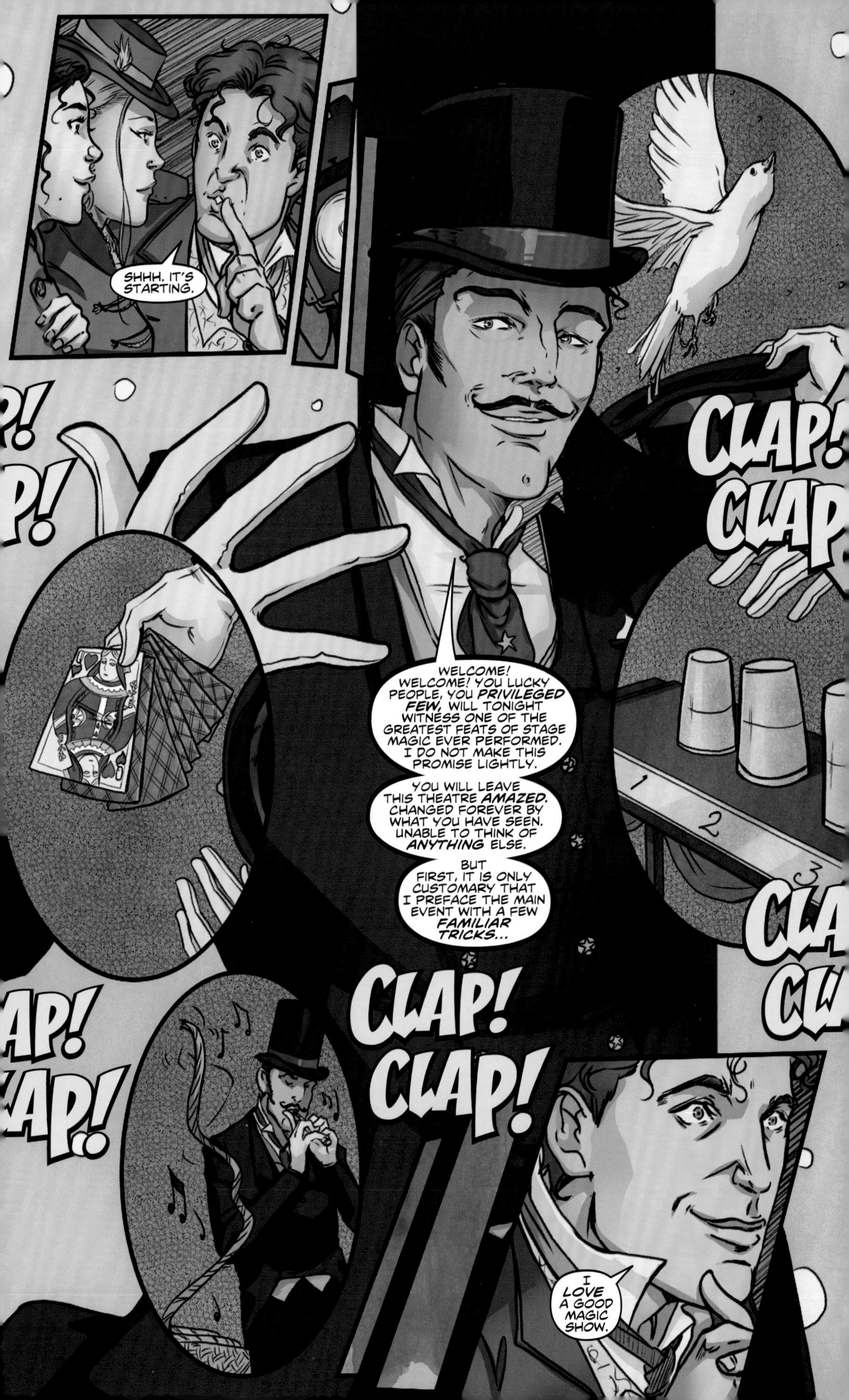

SHHH. IT'S STARTING.
WELCOME! WELCOME! YOU LUCKY PEOPLE, YOU PRIVILEGED FEW, WILL TONIGHT WITNESS ONE OF THE GREATEST FEATS OF STAGE MAGIC EVER PERFORMED. I DO NOT MAKE THIS PROMISE LIGHTLY.
YOU WILL LEAVE THIS THEATRE AMAZED. CHANGED FOREVER BY WHAT YOU HAVE SEEN. UNABLE TO THINK OF ANYTHING ELSE.
BUT FIRST, IT IS ONLY CUSTOMARY THAT I PREFACE THE MAIN EVENT WITH A FEW FAMILIAR TRICKS...
CLAP! CLAP!
CLAP! CLAP!
I LOVE A GOOD MAGIC SHOW.

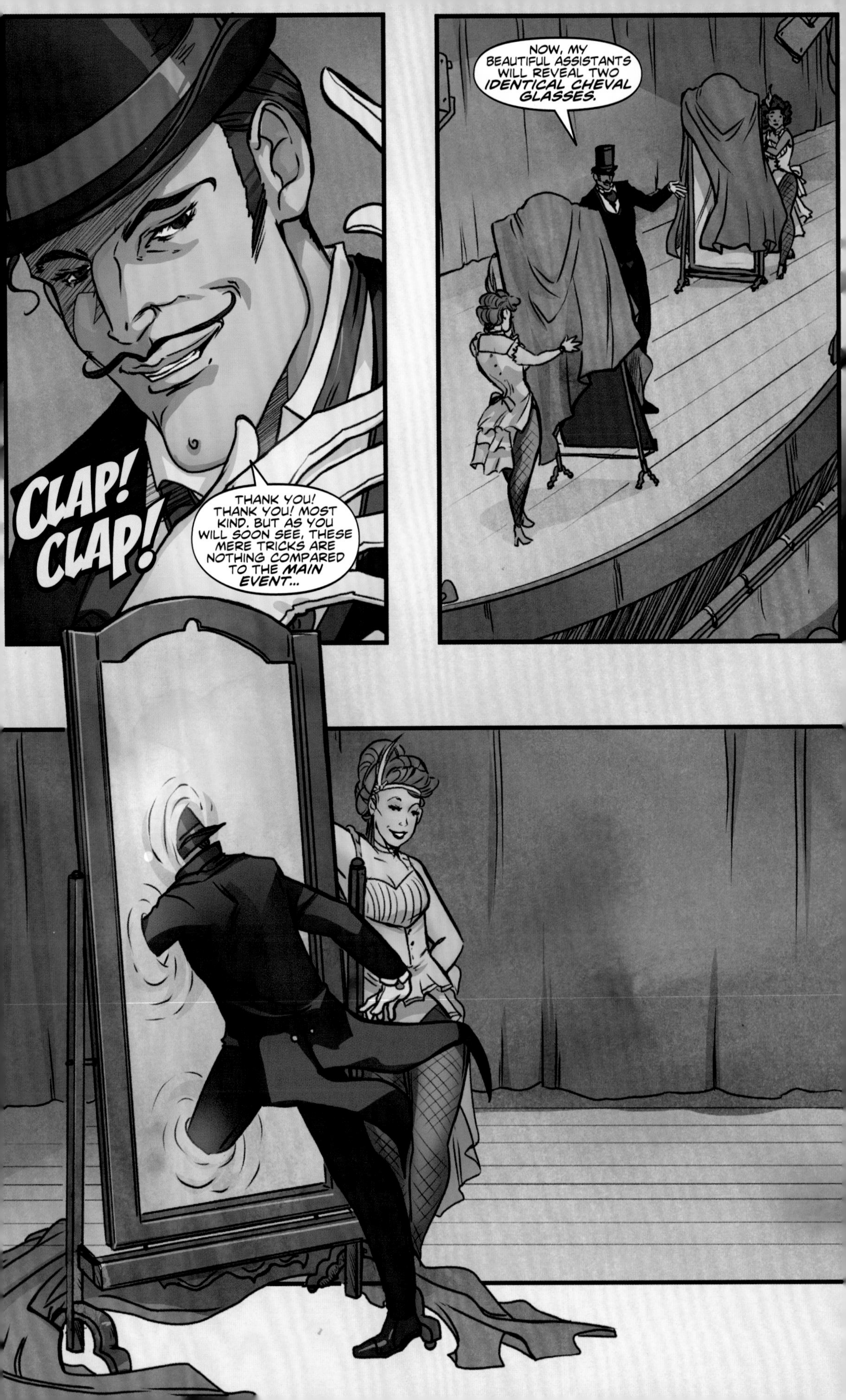
CLAP! CLAP!
THANK YOU! THANK YOU! MOST KIND. BUT AS YOU WILL SOON SEE, THESE MERE TRICKS ARE NOTHING COMPARED TO THE MAIN EVENT...
NOW, MY BEAUTIFUL ASSISTANTS WILL REVEAL TWO IDENTICAL CHEVAL GLASSES.

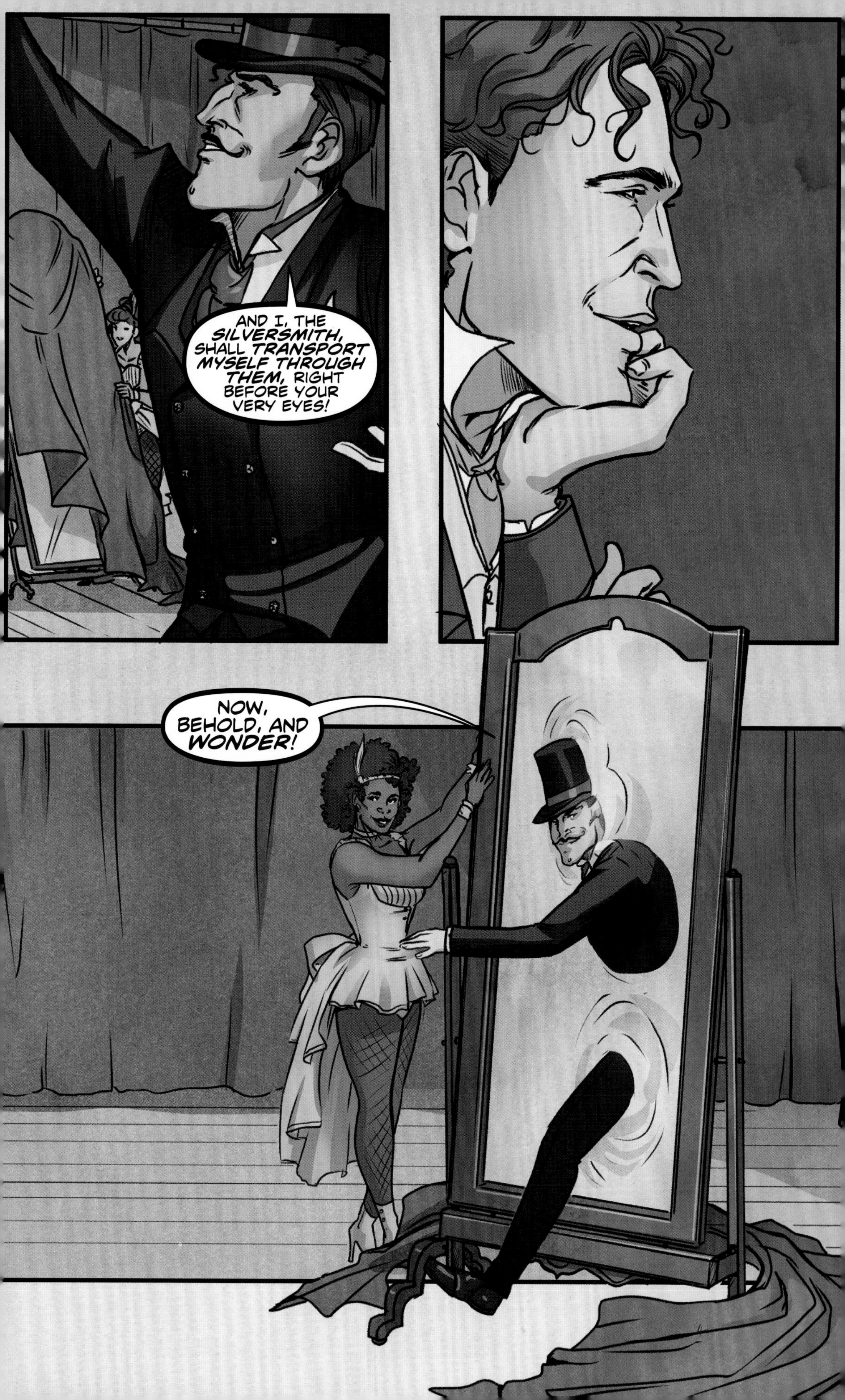
AND I, THE SILVERSMITH, SHALL TRANSPORT MYSELF THROUGH THEM, RIGHT BEFORE YOUR VERY EYES!
NOW, BEHOLD, AND WONDER!

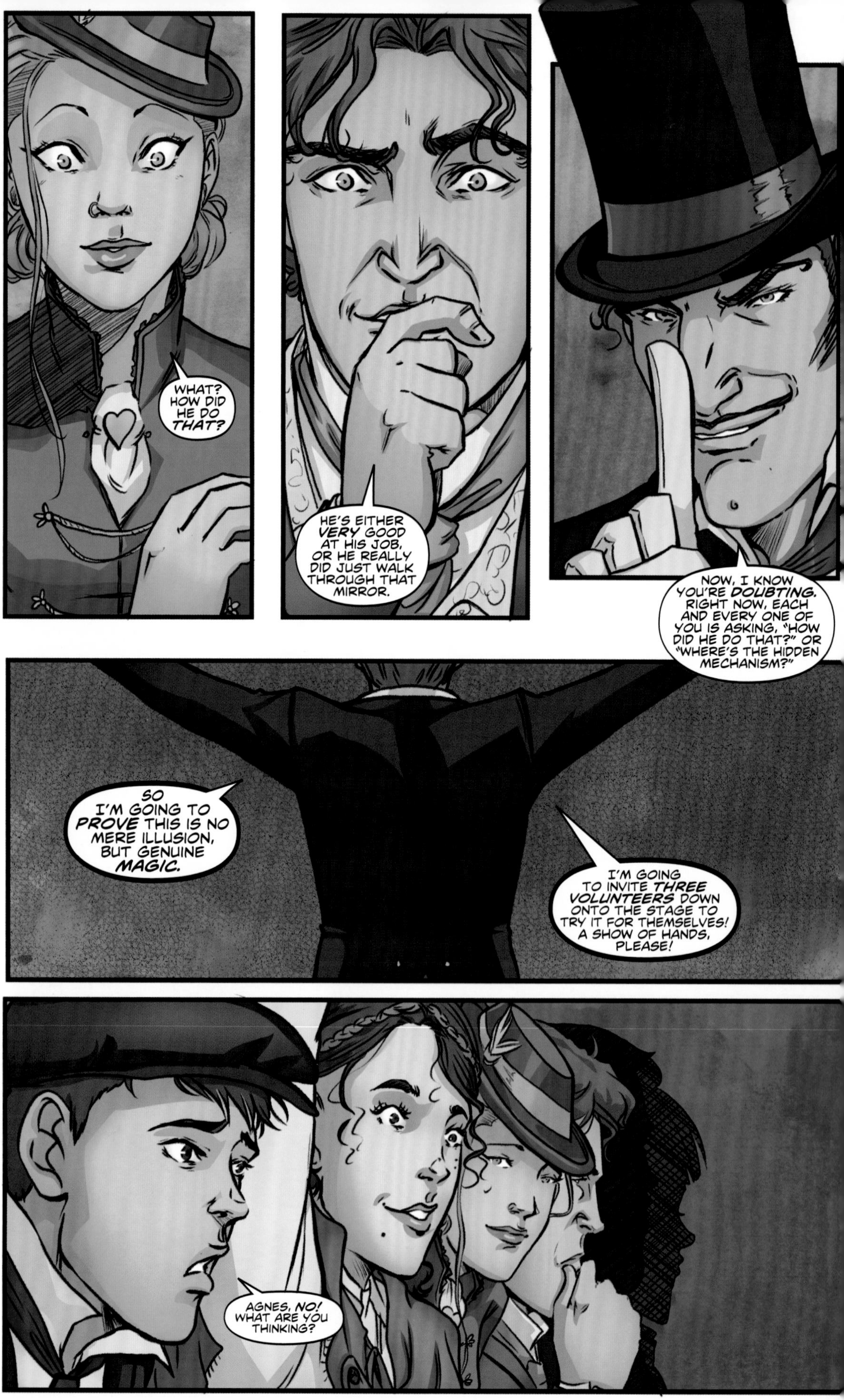
WHAT? HOW DID HE DO *THAT?*
HE'S EITHER *VERY* GOOD AT HIS JOB, OR HE REALLY DID JUST WALK THROUGH THAT MIRROR.
NOW, I KNOW YOU'RE *DOUBTING.* RIGHT NOW, EACH AND EVERY ONE OF YOU IS ASKING, "HOW DID HE DO THAT?" OR "WHERE'S THE HIDDEN MECHANISM?"
SO I'M GOING TO *PROVE* THIS IS NO MERE ILLUSION, BUT GENUINE *MAGIC.*
I'M GOING TO INVITE *THREE VOLUNTEERS* DOWN ONTO THE STAGE TO TRY IT FOR THEMSELVES! A SHOW OF HANDS, PLEASE!
AGNES, *NO!* WHAT ARE YOU THINKING?

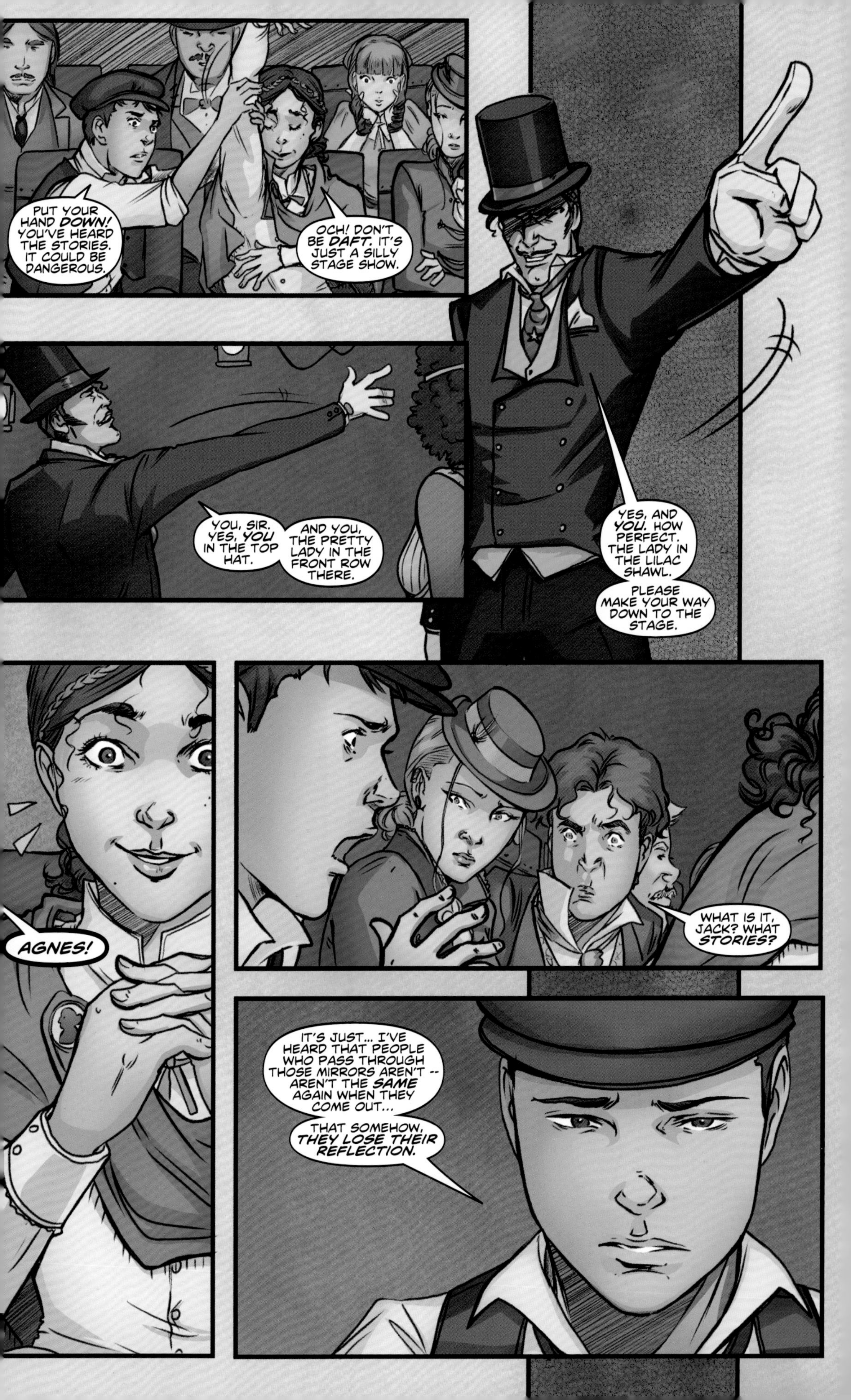
PUT YOUR HAND DOWN! YOU'VE HEARD THE STORIES. IT COULD BE DANGEROUS.
OCH! DON'T BE DAFT. IT'S JUST A SILLY STAGE SHOW.
YOU, SIR. YES, YOU IN THE TOP HAT.
AND YOU, THE PRETTY LADY IN THE FRONT ROW THERE.
YES, AND YOU. HOW PERFECT. THE LADY IN THE LILAC SHAWL.
PLEASE MAKE YOUR WAY DOWN TO THE STAGE.
AGNES!
WHAT IS IT, JACK? WHAT STORIES?
IT'S JUST... I'VE HEARD THAT PEOPLE WHO PASS THROUGH THOSE MIRRORS AREN'T -- AREN'T THE SAME AGAIN WHEN THEY COME OUT...
THAT SOMEHOW, THEY LOSE THEIR REFLECTION.

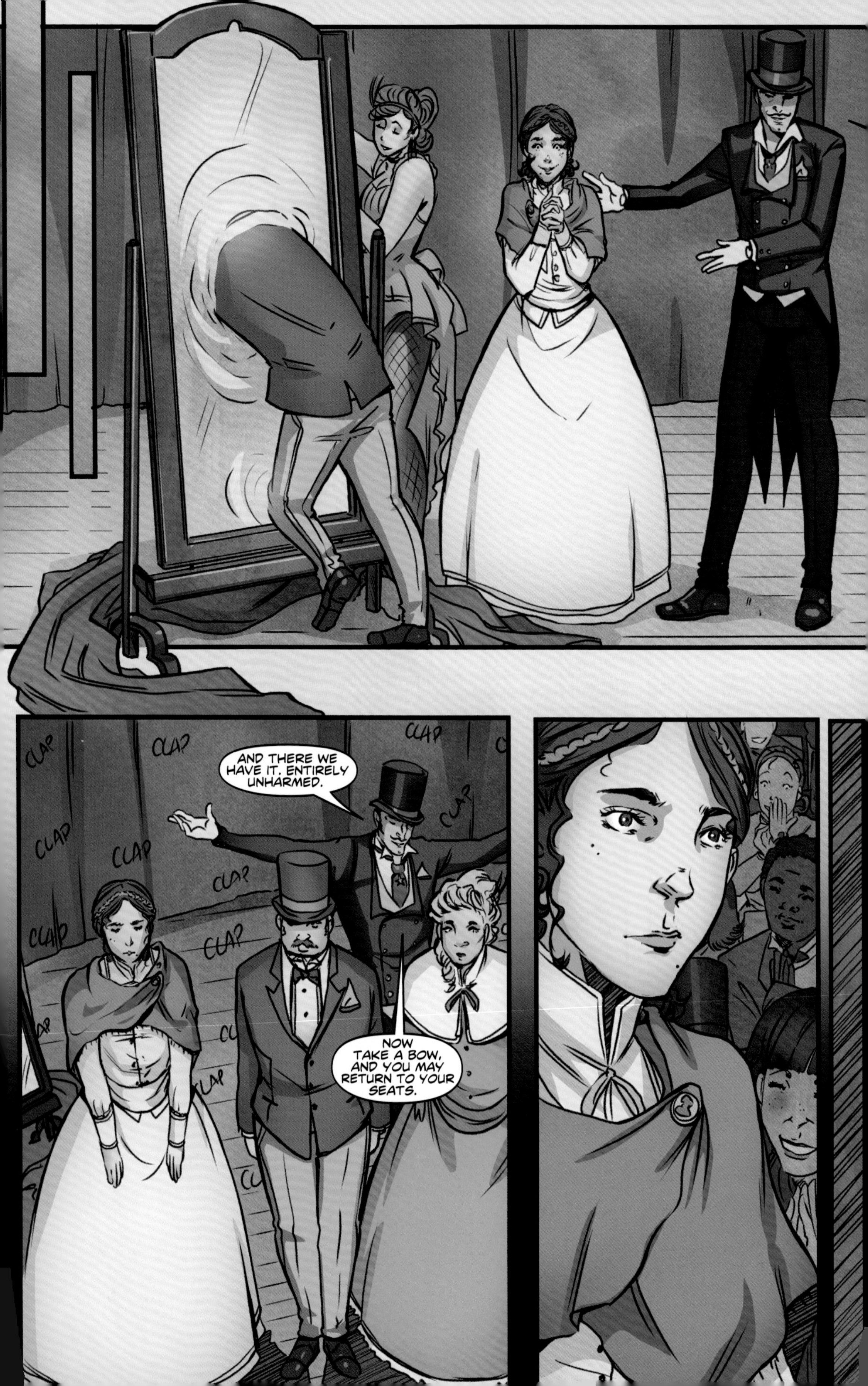
CLAP
CLAP
CLAP
AND THERE WE HAVE IT. ENTIRELY UNHARMED.
CLAP
CLAP
CLAP
CLAP
CLAP
CLAP
NOW TAKE A BOW, AND YOU MAY RETURN TO YOUR SEATS.

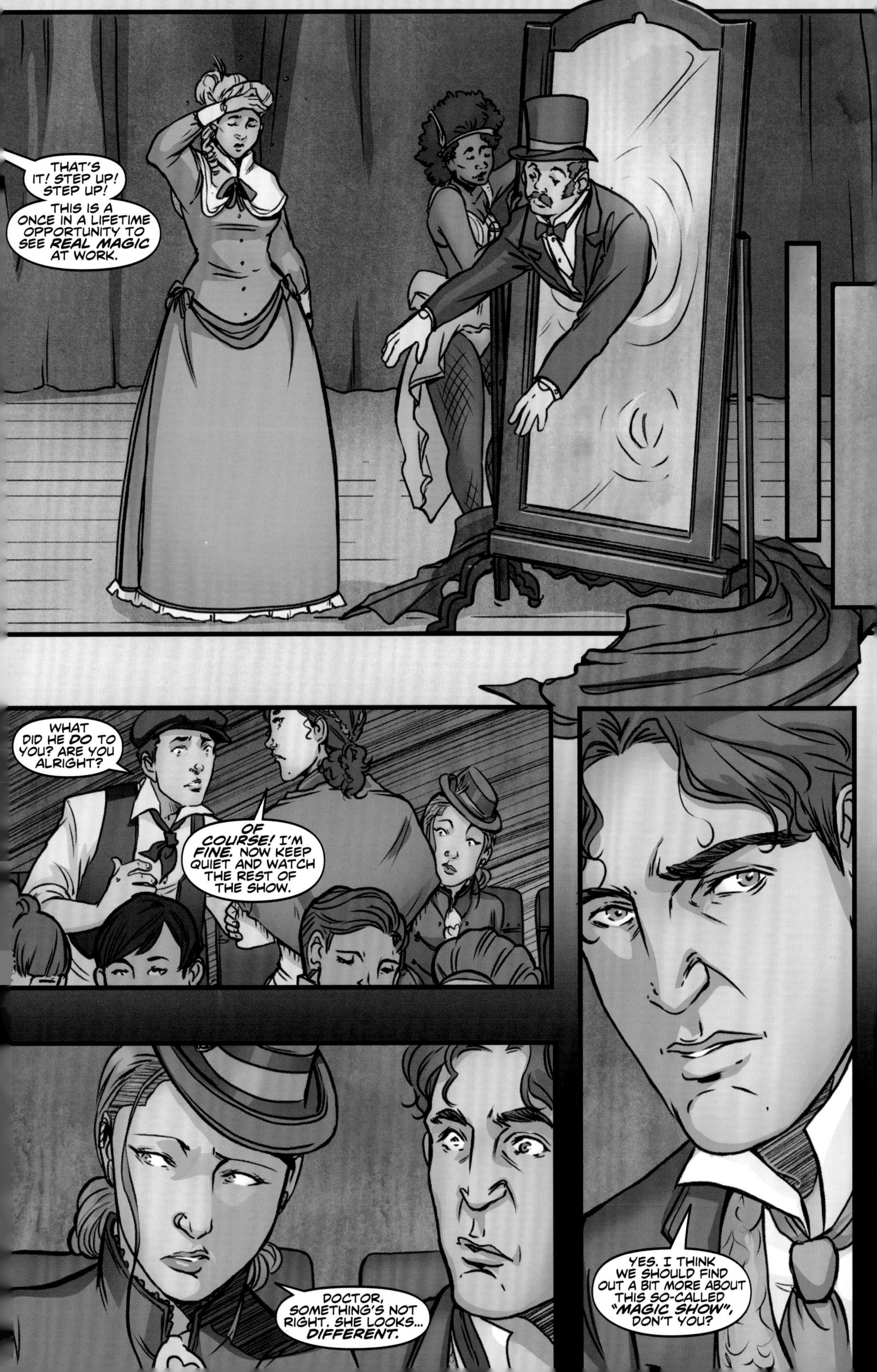
THAT'S IT! STEP UP! STEP UP!
THIS IS A ONCE IN A LIFETIME OPPORTUNITY TO SEE REAL MAGIC AT WORK.
WHAT DID HE DO TO YOU? ARE YOU ALRIGHT?
OF COURSE! I'M FINE. NOW KEEP QUIET AND WATCH THE REST OF THE SHOW.
DOCTOR, SOMETHING'S NOT RIGHT. SHE LOOKS... DIFFERENT.
YES. I THINK WE SHOULD FIND OUT A BIT MORE ABOUT THIS SO-CALLED "MAGIC SHOW", DON'T YOU?

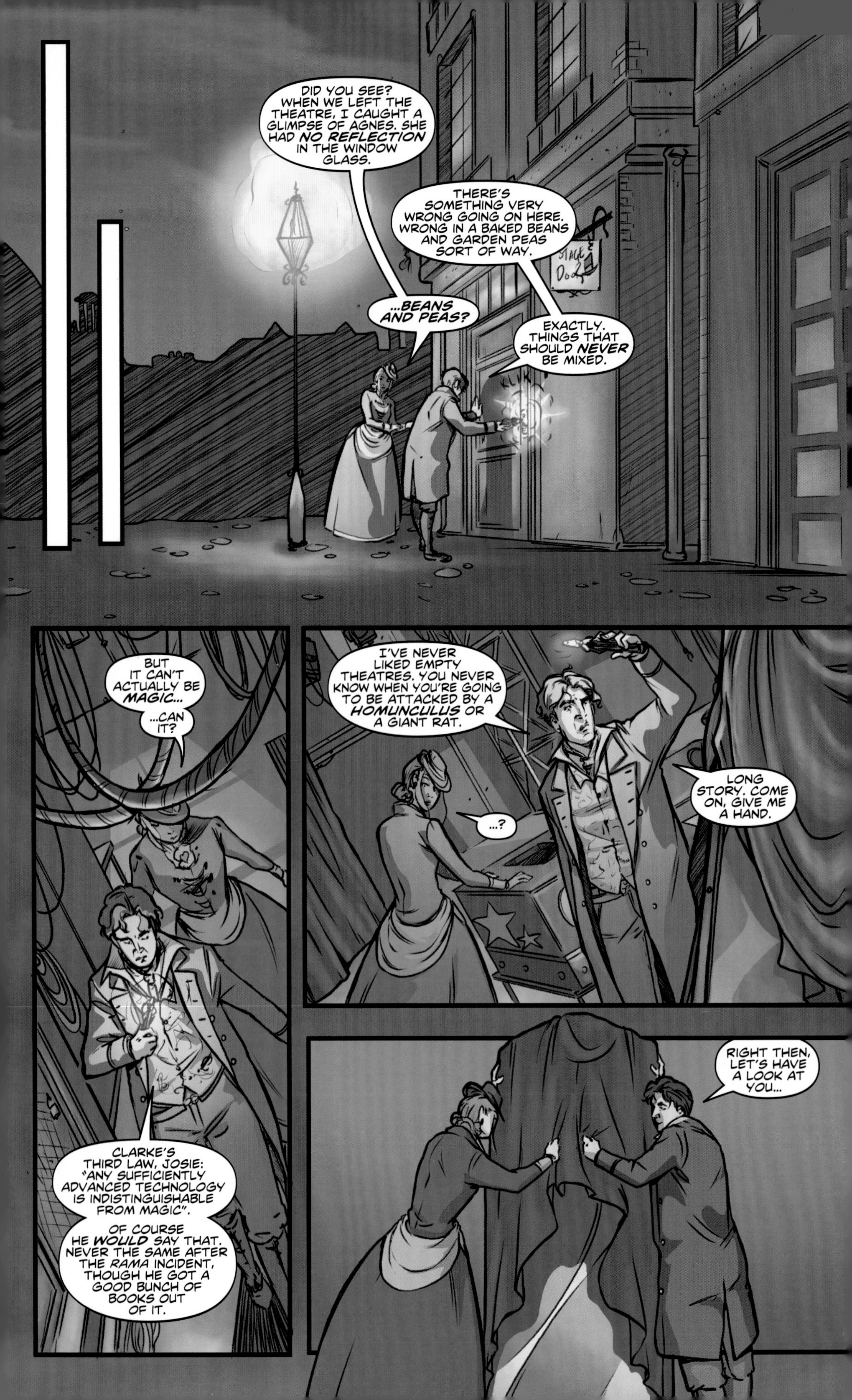
DID YOU SEE? WHEN WE LEFT THE THEATRE, I CAUGHT A GLIMPSE OF AGNES. SHE HAD NO REFLECTION IN THE WINDOW GLASS.
THERE'S SOMETHING VERY WRONG GOING ON HERE. WRONG IN A BAKED BEANS AND GARDEN PEAS SORT OF WAY.
STAGE DOOR
...BEANS AND PEAS?
EXACTLY. THINGS THAT SHOULD NEVER BE MIXED.
KLUK
BUT IT CAN'T ACTUALLY BE MAGIC...
...CAN IT?
CLARKE'S THIRD LAW, JOSIE: "ANY SUFFICIENTLY ADVANCED TECHNOLOGY IS INDISTINGUISHABLE FROM MAGIC".
OF COURSE HE WOULD SAY THAT. NEVER THE SAME AFTER THE RAMA INCIDENT, THOUGH HE GOT A GOOD BUNCH OF BOOKS OUT OF IT.
I'VE NEVER LIKED EMPTY THEATRES. YOU NEVER KNOW WHEN YOU'RE GOING TO BE ATTACKED BY A HOMUNCULUS OR A GIANT RAT.
...?
LONG STORY. COME ON, GIVE ME A HAND.
RIGHT THEN, LET'S HAVE A LOOK AT YOU...

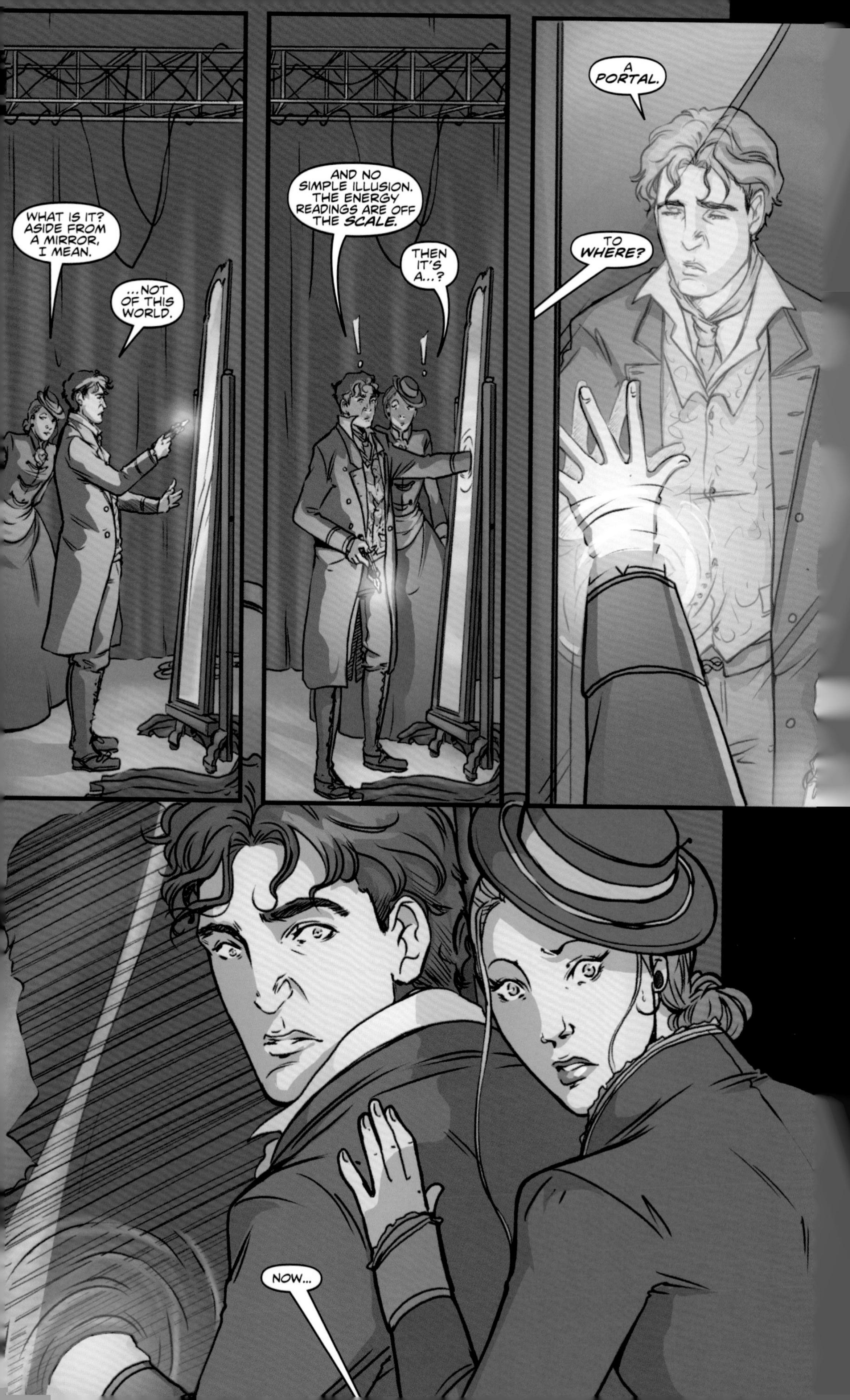
WHAT IS IT? ASIDE FROM A MIRROR, I MEAN.
...NOT OF THIS WORLD.
AND NO SIMPLE ILLUSION. THE ENERGY READINGS ARE OFF THE SCALE.
THEN IT'S A...?
!
!
A PORTAL.
TO WHERE?
NOW...

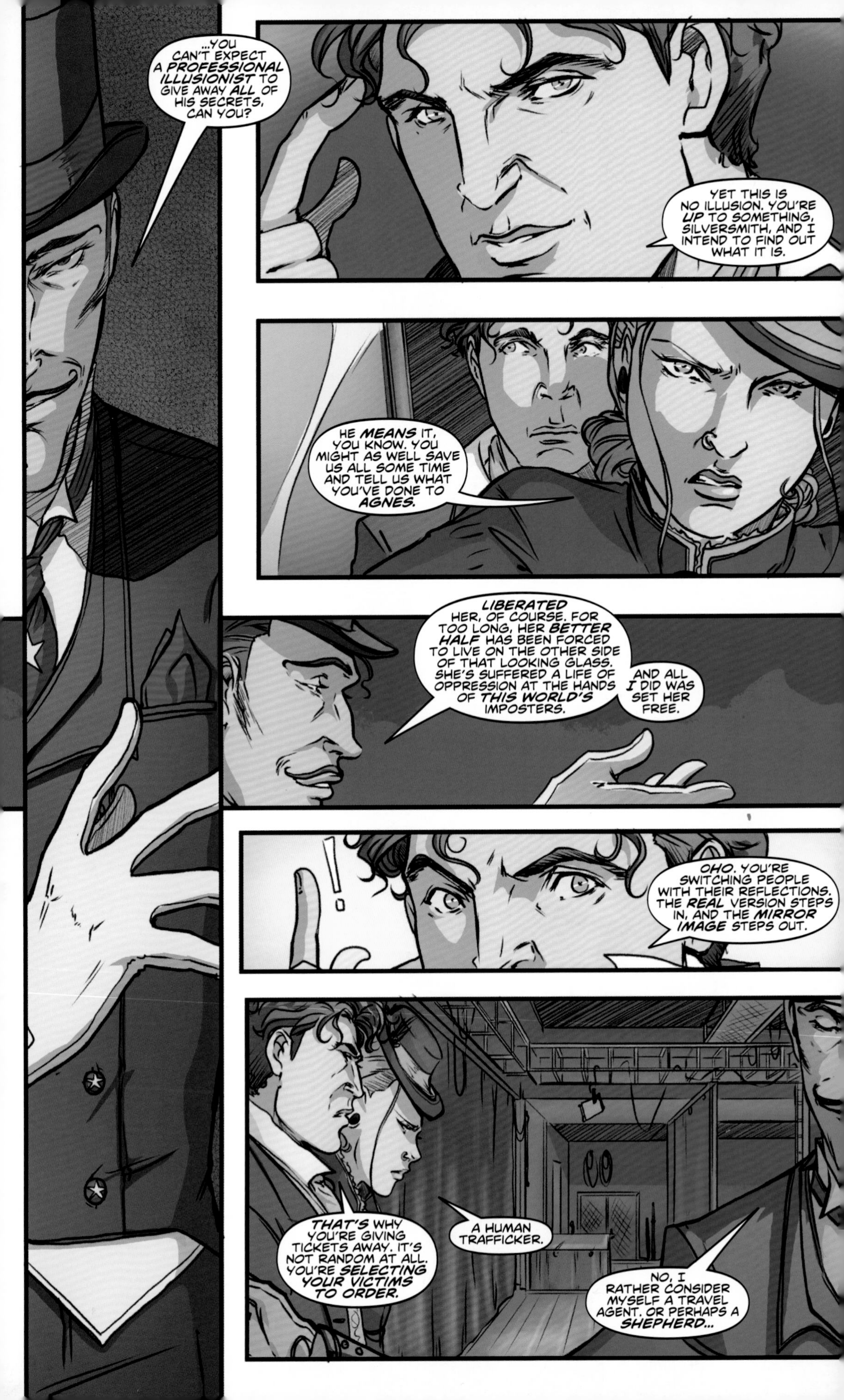
...YOU CAN'T EXPECT A PROFESSIONAL ILLUSIONIST TO GIVE AWAY ALL OF HIS SECRETS, CAN YOU?
YET THIS IS NO ILLUSION. YOU'RE UP TO SOMETHING, SILVERSMITH, AND I INTEND TO FIND OUT WHAT IT IS.
HE MEANS IT, YOU KNOW. YOU MIGHT AS WELL SAVE US ALL SOME TIME AND TELL US WHAT YOU'VE DONE TO AGNES.
LIBERATED HER, OF COURSE. FOR TOO LONG, HER BETTER HALF HAS BEEN FORCED TO LIVE ON THE OTHER SIDE OF THAT LOOKING GLASS. SHE'S SUFFERED A LIFE OF OPPRESSION AT THE HANDS OF THIS WORLD'S IMPOSTERS.
AND ALL I DID WAS SET HER FREE.
!
OHO. YOU'RE SWITCHING PEOPLE WITH THEIR REFLECTIONS. THE REAL VERSION STEPS IN, AND THE MIRROR IMAGE STEPS OUT.
THAT'S WHY YOU'RE GIVING TICKETS AWAY. IT'S NOT RANDOM AT ALL. YOU'RE SELECTING YOUR VICTIMS TO ORDER.
A HUMAN TRAFFICKER.
NO, I RATHER CONSIDER MYSELF A TRAVEL AGENT. OR PERHAPS A SHEPHERD...

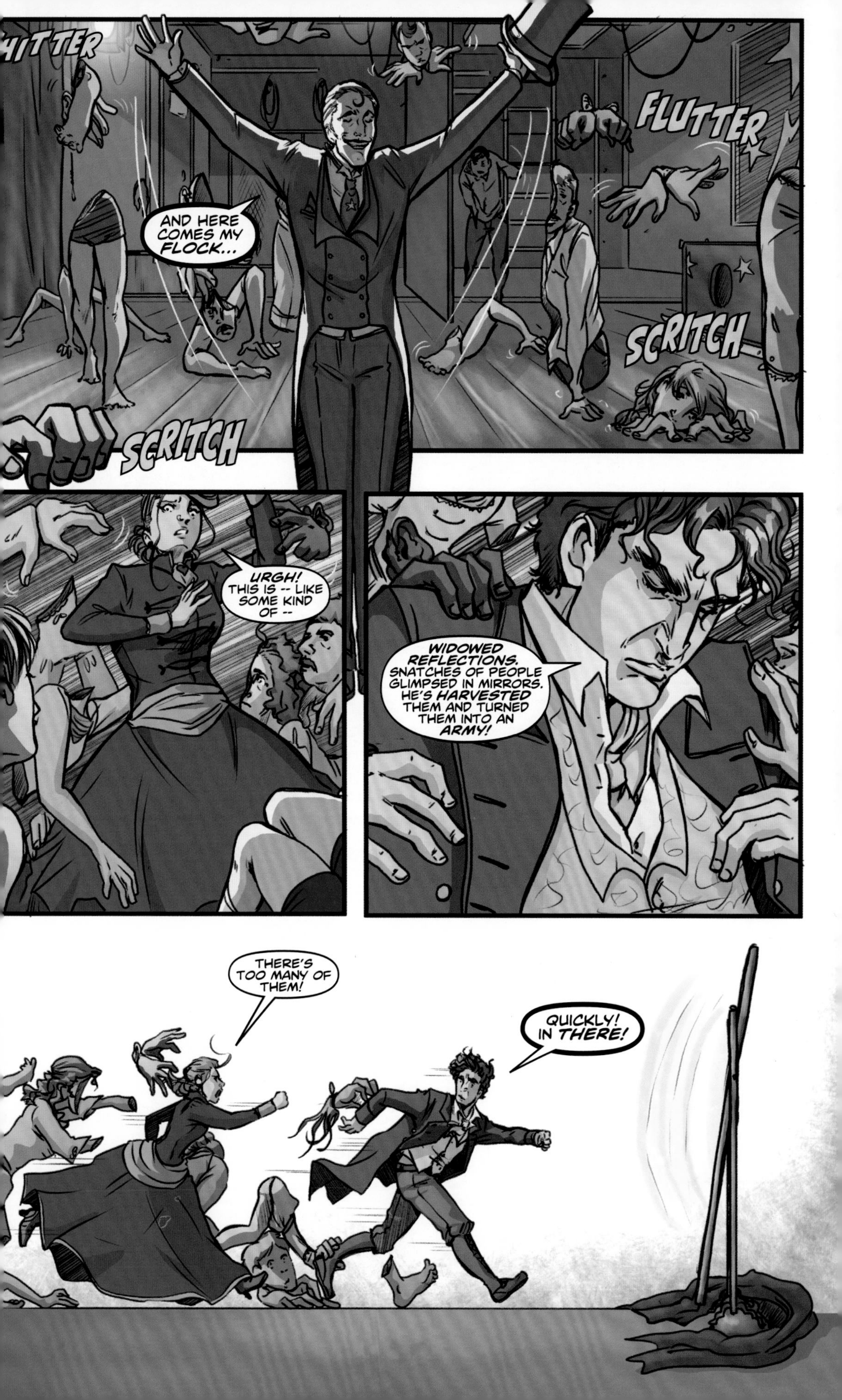

HITTER
AND HERE COMES MY FLOCK...
FLUTTER
SCRITCH
SCRITCH
URGH! THIS IS -- LIKE SOME KIND OF --
WIDOWED REFLECTIONS. SNATCHES OF PEOPLE GLIMPSED IN MIRRORS. HE'S HARVESTED THEM AND TURNED THEM INTO AN ARMY!
THERE'S TOO MANY OF THEM!
QUICKLY! IN THERE!

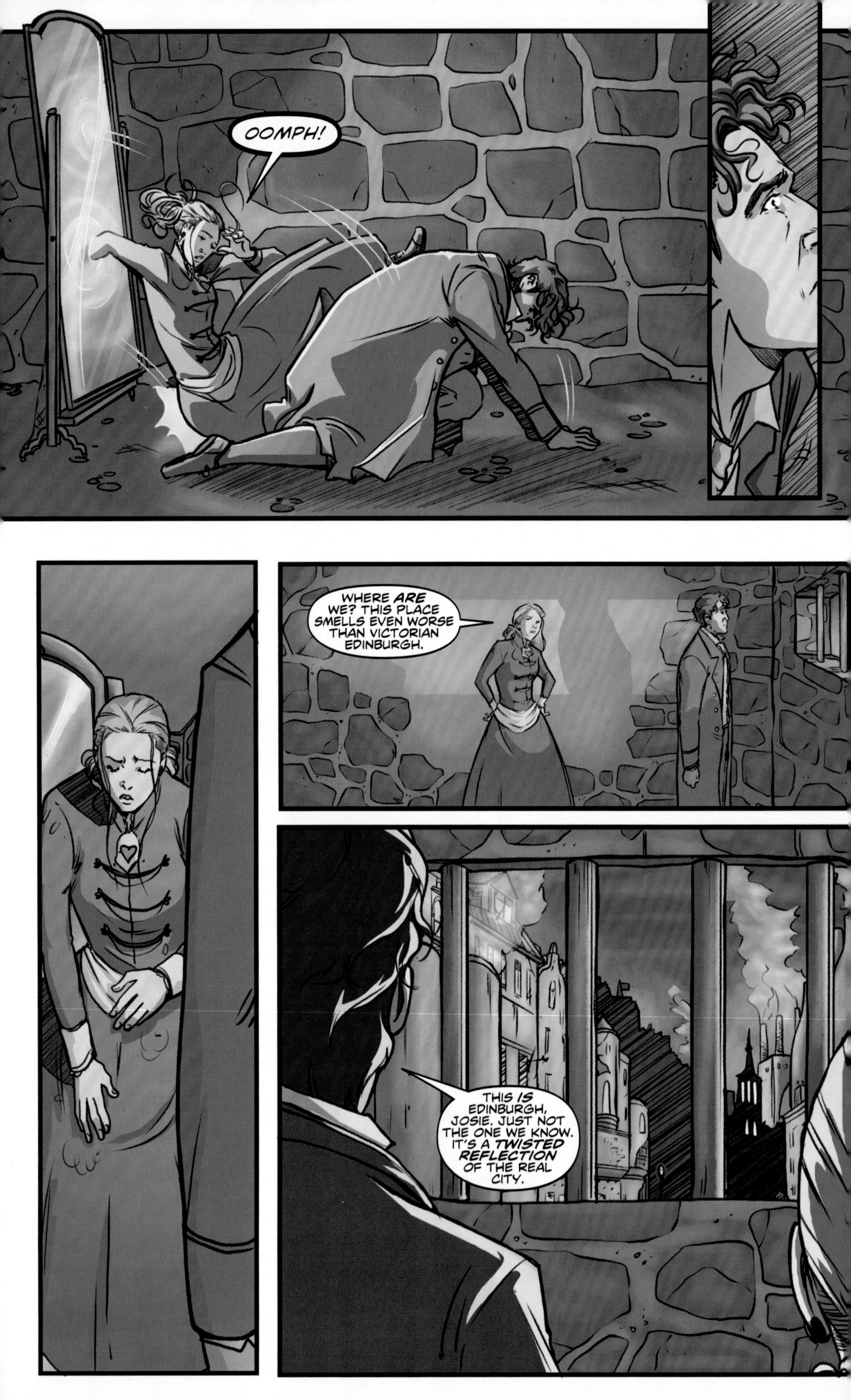
OOMPH!
WHERE *ARE* WE? THIS PLACE SMELLS EVEN WORSE THAN VICTORIAN EDINBURGH.
THIS *IS* EDINBURGH, JOSIE. JUST NOT THE ONE WE KNOW. IT'S A *TWISTED REFLECTION* OF THE REAL CITY.

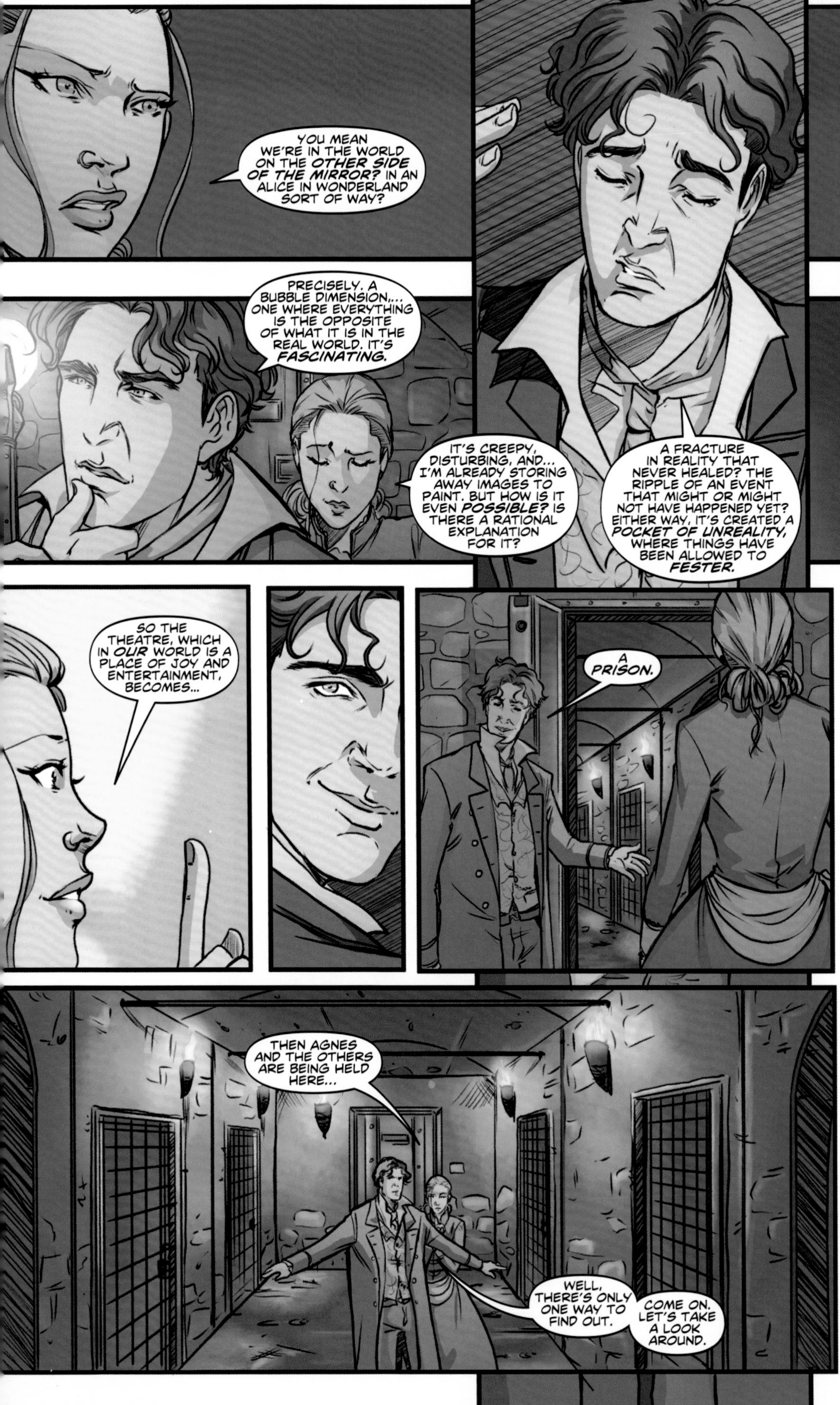

YOU MEAN WE'RE IN THE WORLD ON THE OTHER SIDE OF THE MIRROR? IN AN ALICE IN WONDERLAND SORT OF WAY?
PRECISELY. A BUBBLE DIMENSION,... ONE WHERE EVERYTHING IS THE OPPOSITE OF WHAT IT IS IN THE REAL WORLD. IT'S FASCINATING.
IT'S CREEPY, DISTURBING, AND... I'M ALREADY STORING AWAY IMAGES TO PAINT. BUT HOW IS IT EVEN POSSIBLE? IS THERE A RATIONAL EXPLANATION FOR IT?
A FRACTURE IN REALITY THAT NEVER HEALED? THE RIPPLE OF AN EVENT THAT MIGHT OR MIGHT NOT HAVE HAPPENED YET? EITHER WAY, IT'S CREATED A POCKET OF UNREALITY, WHERE THINGS HAVE BEEN ALLOWED TO FESTER.
SO THE THEATRE, WHICH IN OUR WORLD IS A PLACE OF JOY AND ENTERTAINMENT, BECOMES...
A PRISON.
THEN AGNES AND THE OTHERS ARE BEING HELD HERE...
WELL, THERE'S ONLY ONE WAY TO FIND OUT.
COME ON. LET'S TAKE A LOOK AROUND.

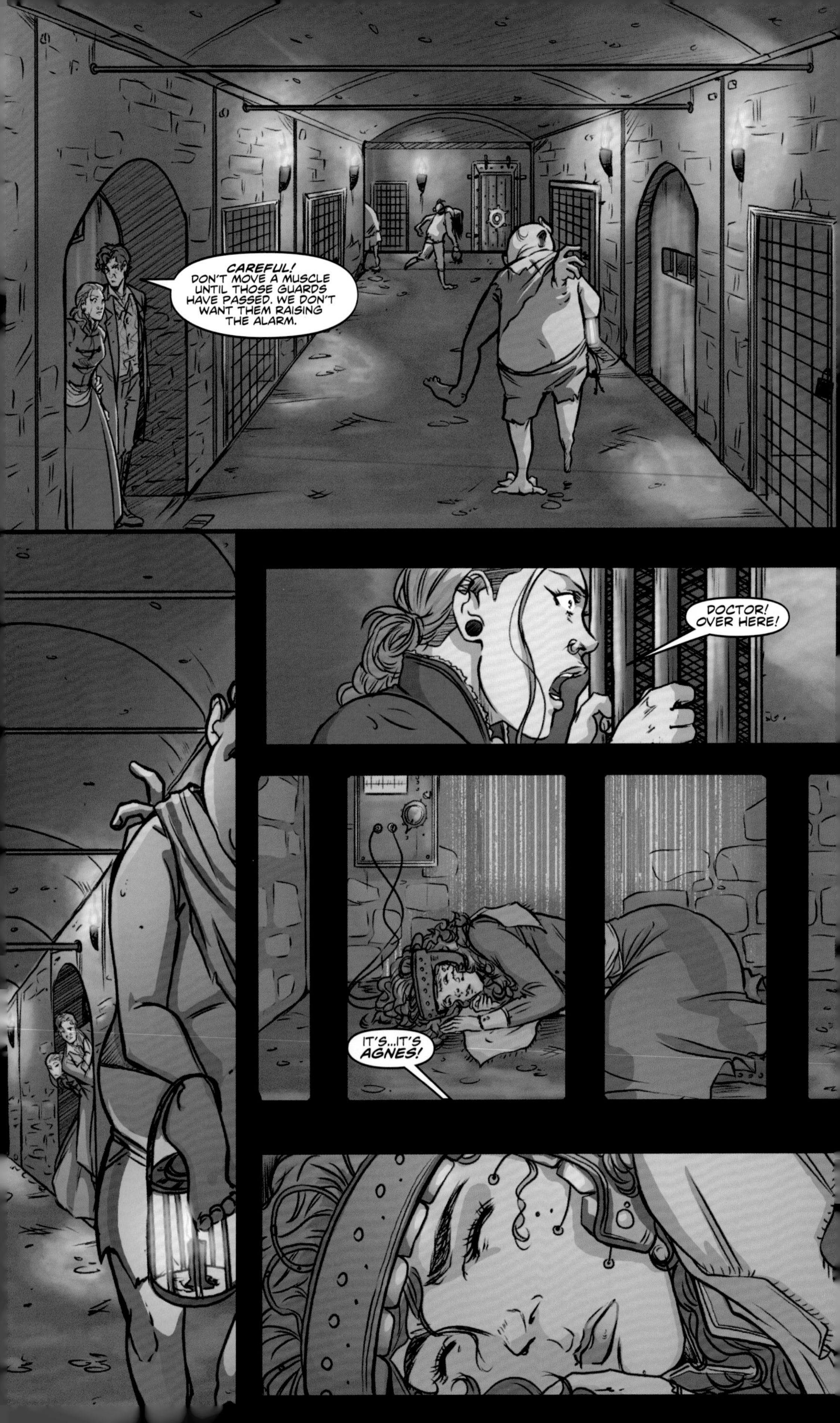
CAREFUL! DON'T MOVE A MUSCLE UNTIL THOSE GUARDS HAVE PASSED. WE DON'T WANT THEM RAISING THE ALARM.
DOCTOR! OVER HERE!
IT'S...IT'S AGNES!

HURRY UP!

OH, AGNES. WHAT HAVE THEY *DONE* TO YOU?

UNNNGG... JOSIE?

BUT-- THESE ARE FRAGMENTS OF *SPHERION* CRYSTAL! THEY STILL RETAIN SOME LOW-LEVEL PSYCHIC RESIDUE... AND THEY'RE BEING USED TO DRAW ENERGY FROM THE VICTIM'S *MINDS*.

THAT'S IT! THAT'S WHAT HE'S UP TO. THIS ISN'T A PRISON. IT'S A *PSYCHIC FARM!* THEY'RE USING THE PEOPLE TO *POWER* THE PORTALS... MAYBE EVEN THE WHOLE CITY!

OH, JOSIE. WE'VE GOT TO GET THEM OUT OF HERE. *ALL OF THEM.* BEFORE IT'S TOO LATE, AND THE PORTALS BECOME *PERMANENT.* BEFORE THE SILVERSMITH IS ABLE TO MOBILIZE A WHOLE *ARMY* OF MIRROR FOLK. COME ON!

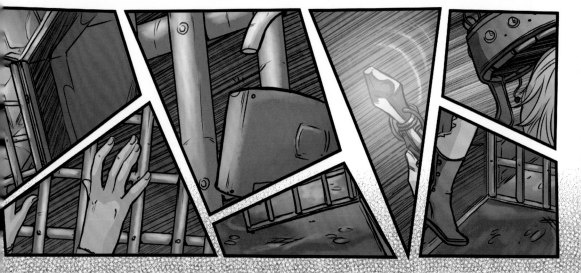

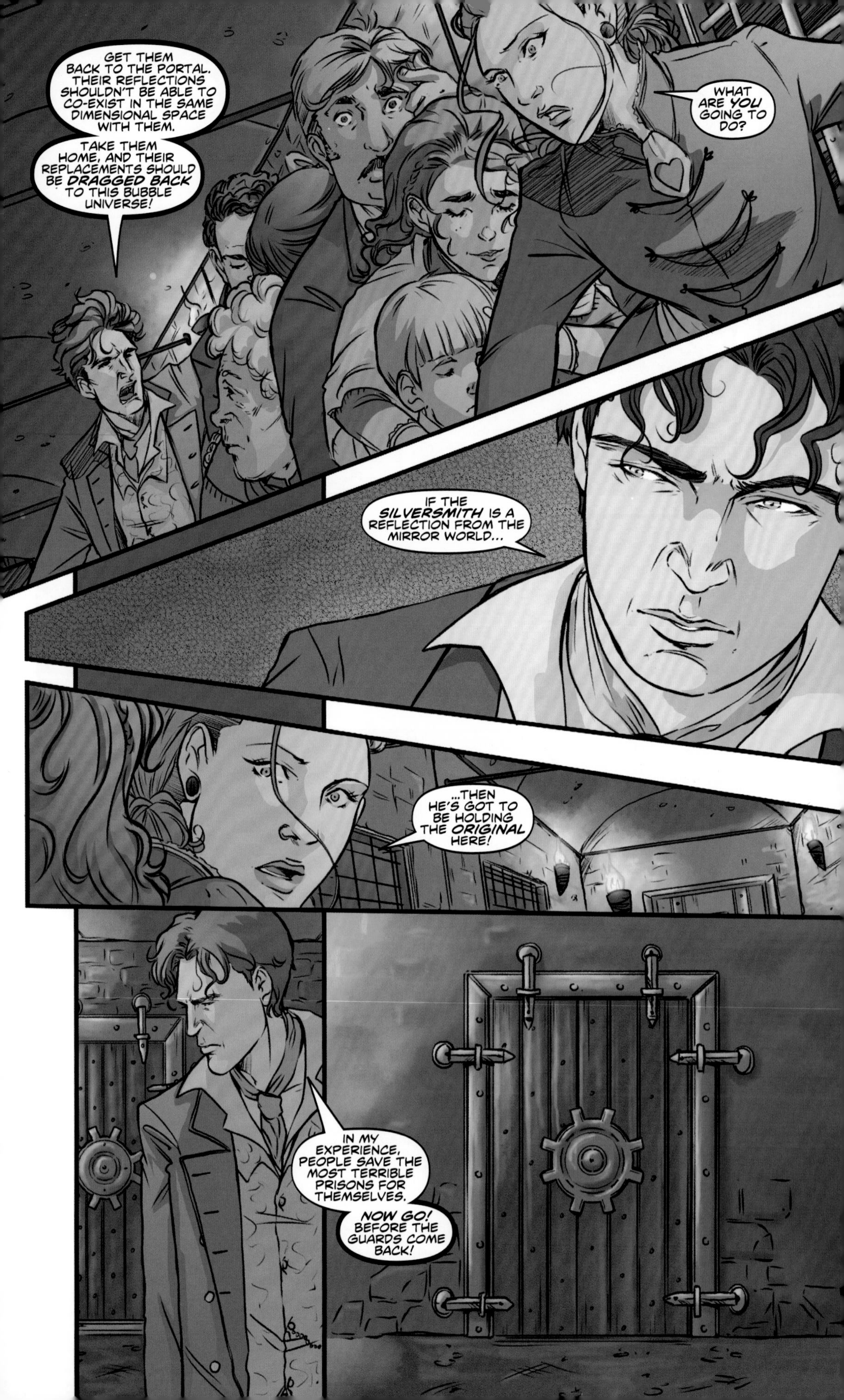
GET THEM BACK TO THE PORTAL. THEIR REFLECTIONS SHOULDN'T BE ABLE TO CO-EXIST IN THE SAME DIMENSIONAL SPACE WITH THEM.
TAKE THEM HOME, AND THEIR REPLACEMENTS SHOULD BE *DRAGGED BACK* TO THIS BUBBLE UNIVERSE!
WHAT ARE *YOU* GOING TO DO?
IF THE *SILVERSMITH* IS A REFLECTION FROM THE MIRROR WORLD...
...THEN HE'S GOT TO BE HOLDING THE *ORIGINAL* HERE!
IN MY EXPERIENCE, PEOPLE SAVE THE MOST TERRIBLE PRISONS FOR THEMSELVES.
NOW GO! BEFORE THE GUARDS COME BACK!

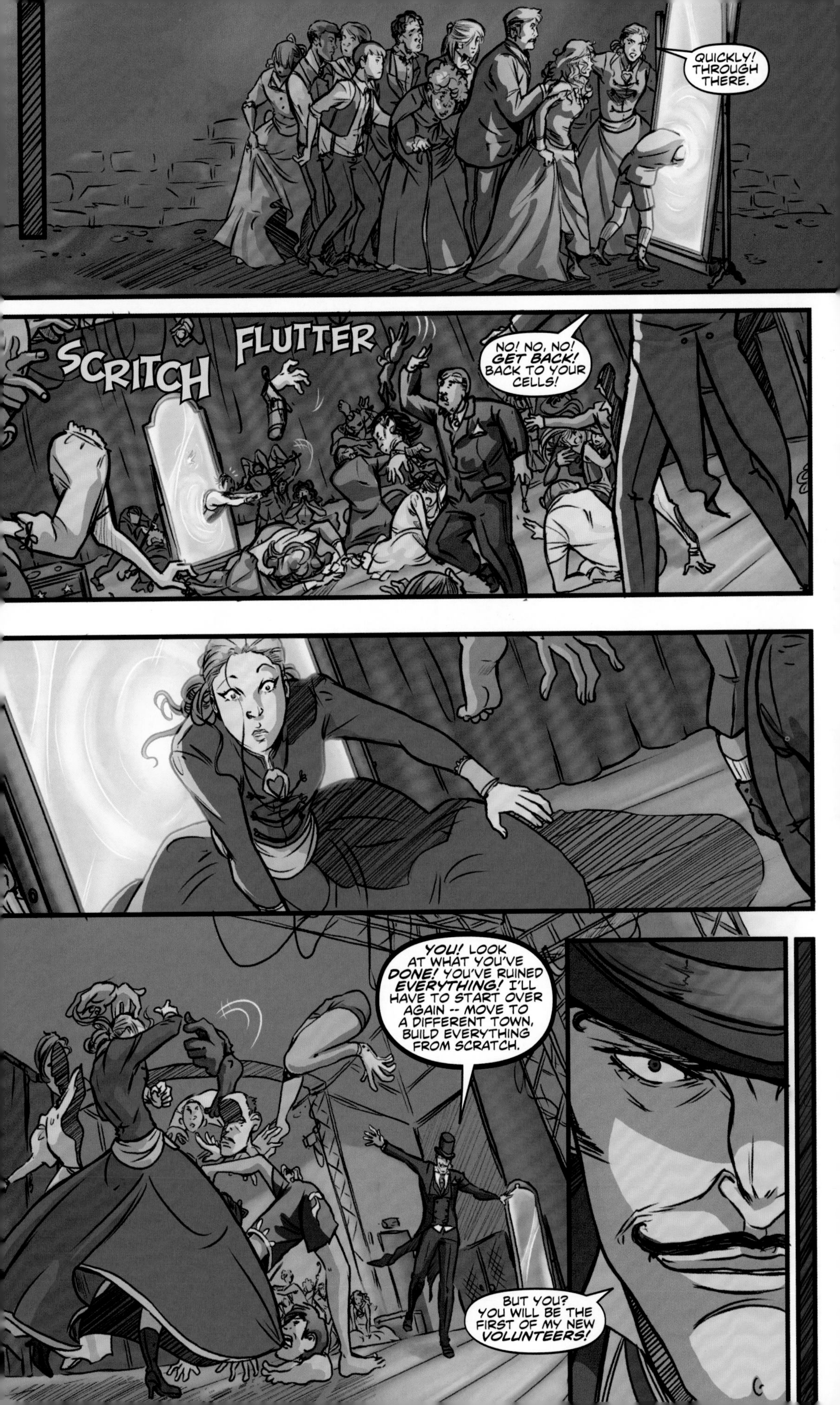
QUICKLY! THROUGH THERE.
SCRITCH
FLUTTER
NO! NO, NO! GET BACK! BACK TO YOUR CELLS!
YOU! LOOK AT WHAT YOU'VE DONE! YOU'VE RUINED EVERYTHING! I'LL HAVE TO START OVER AGAIN -- MOVE TO A DIFFERENT TOWN, BUILD EVERYTHING FROM SCRATCH.
BUT YOU? YOU WILL BE THE FIRST OF MY NEW VOLUNTEERS!

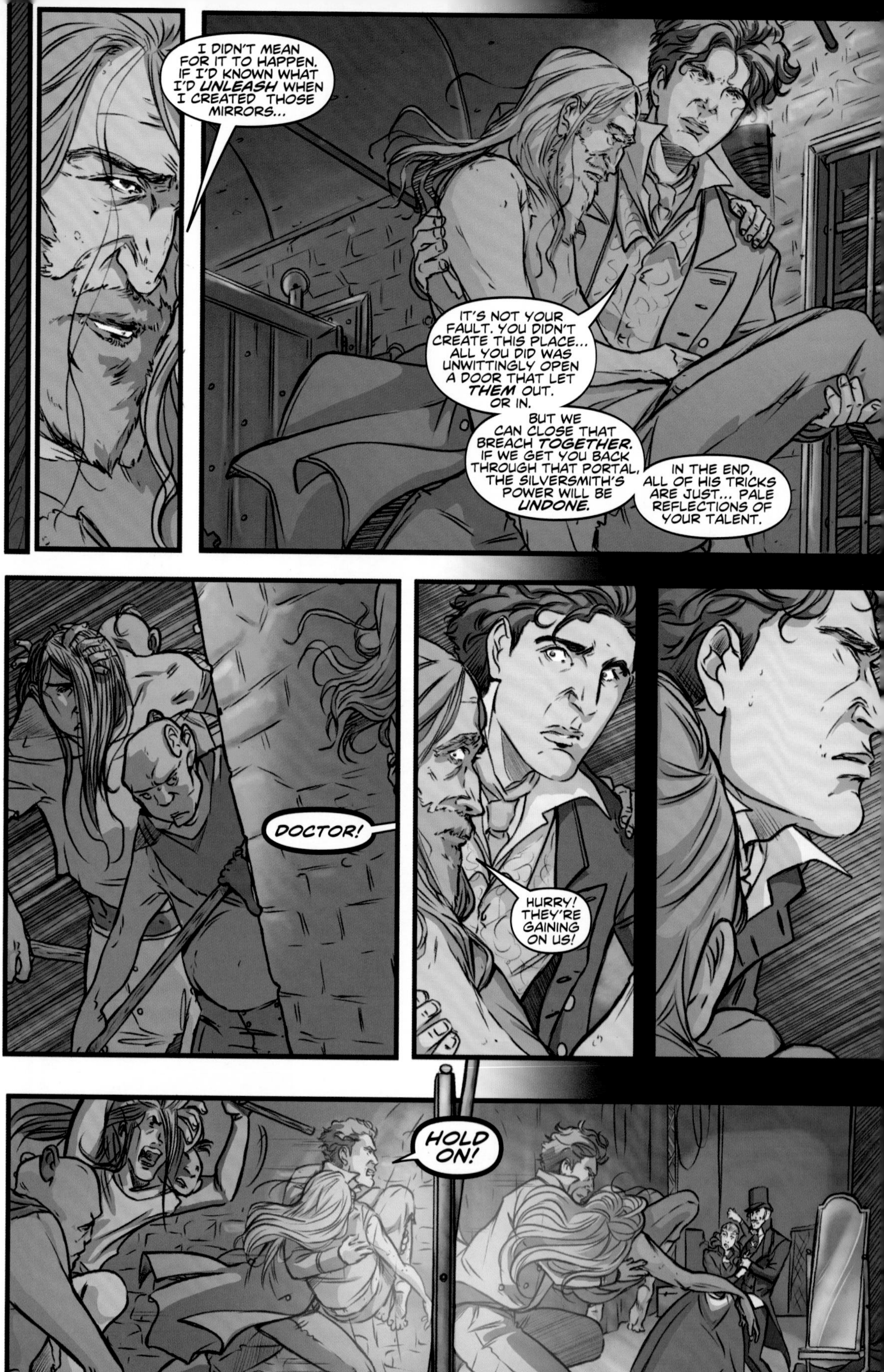
I DIDN'T MEAN FOR IT TO HAPPEN. IF I'D KNOWN WHAT I'D UNLEASH WHEN I CREATED THOSE MIRRORS...
IT'S NOT YOUR FAULT. YOU DIDN'T CREATE THIS PLACE... ALL YOU DID WAS UNWITTINGLY OPEN A DOOR THAT LET THEM OUT. OR IN.
BUT WE CAN CLOSE THAT BREACH TOGETHER. IF WE GET YOU BACK THROUGH THAT PORTAL, THE SILVERSMITH'S POWER WILL BE UNDONE.
IN THE END, ALL OF HIS TRICKS ARE JUST... PALE REFLECTIONS OF YOUR TALENT.
DOCTOR!
HURRY! THEY'RE GAINING ON US!
HOLD ON!

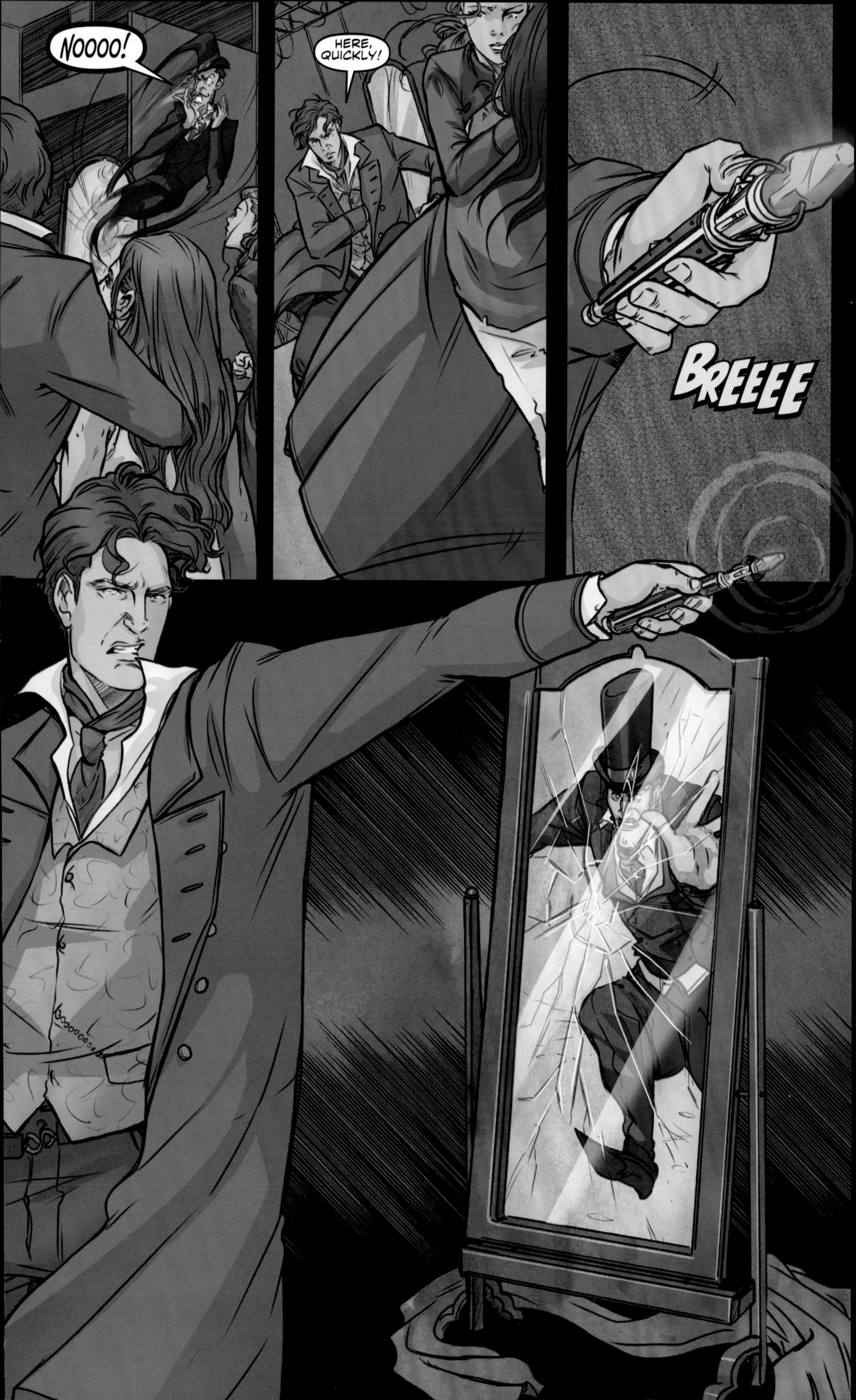
NOOOO!
HERE, QUICKLY!
BREEEE

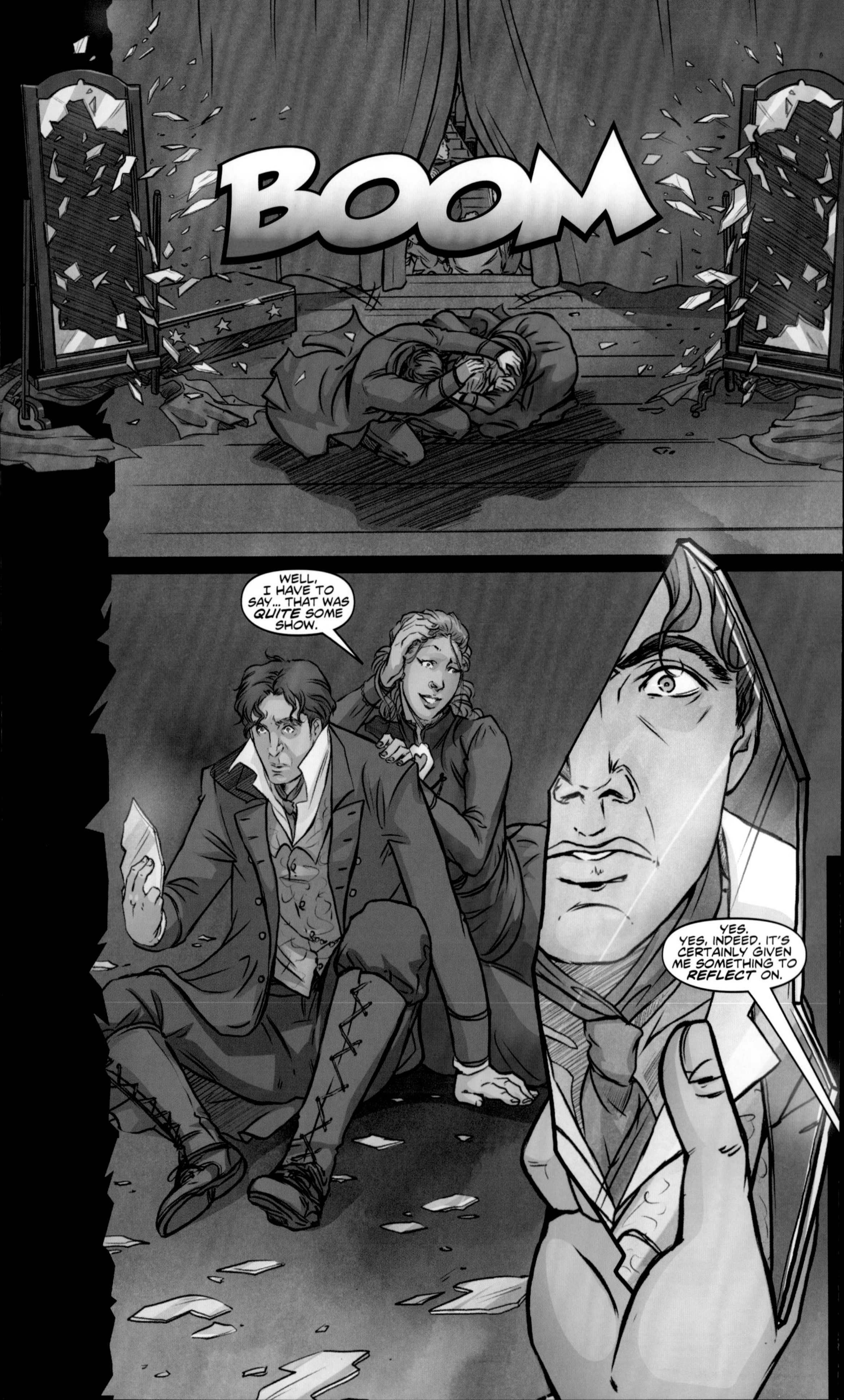
BOOM
WELL, I HAVE TO SAY... THAT WAS QUITE SOME SHOW.
YES. YES, INDEED. IT'S CERTAINLY GIVEN ME SOMETHING TO REFLECT ON.

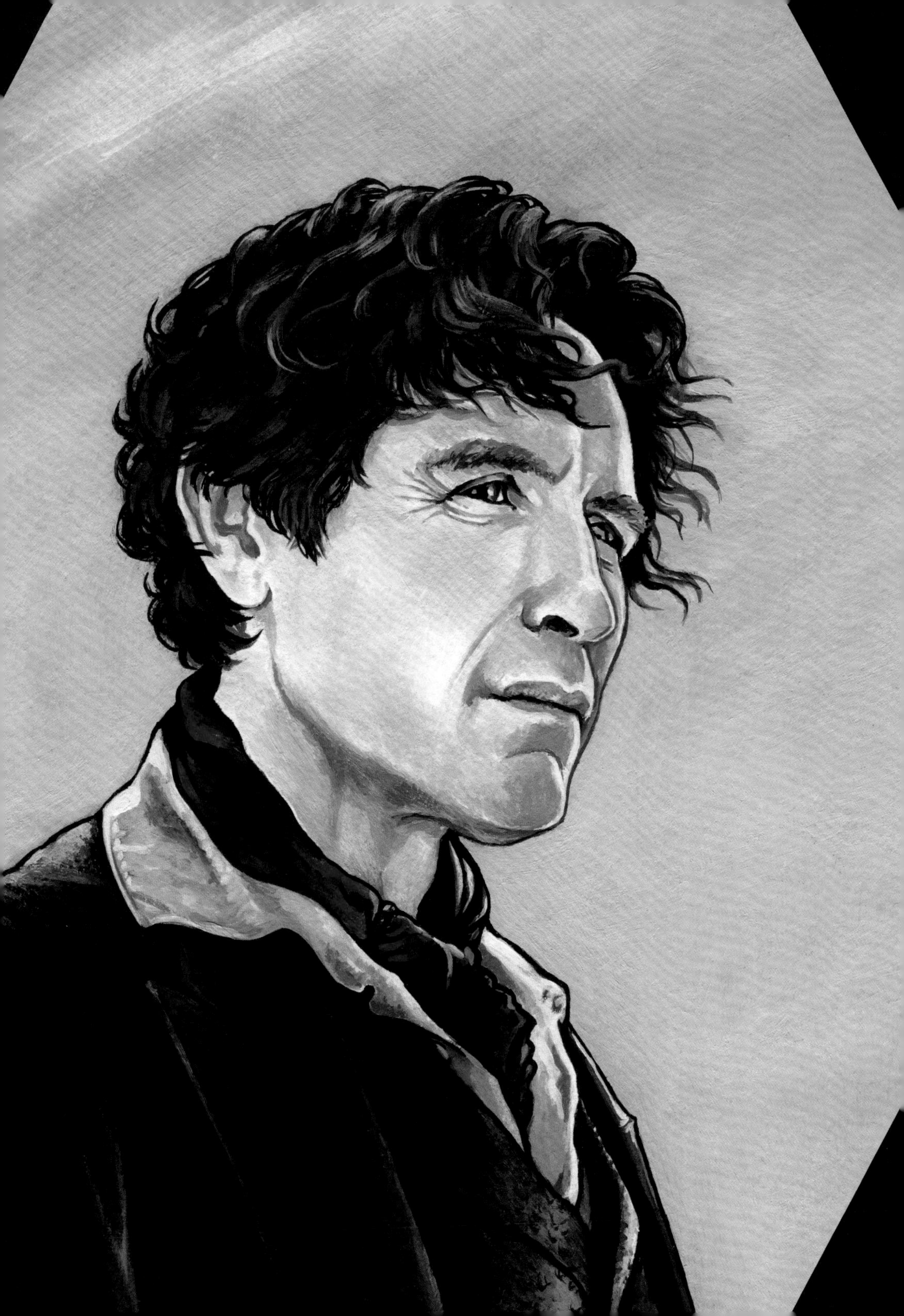

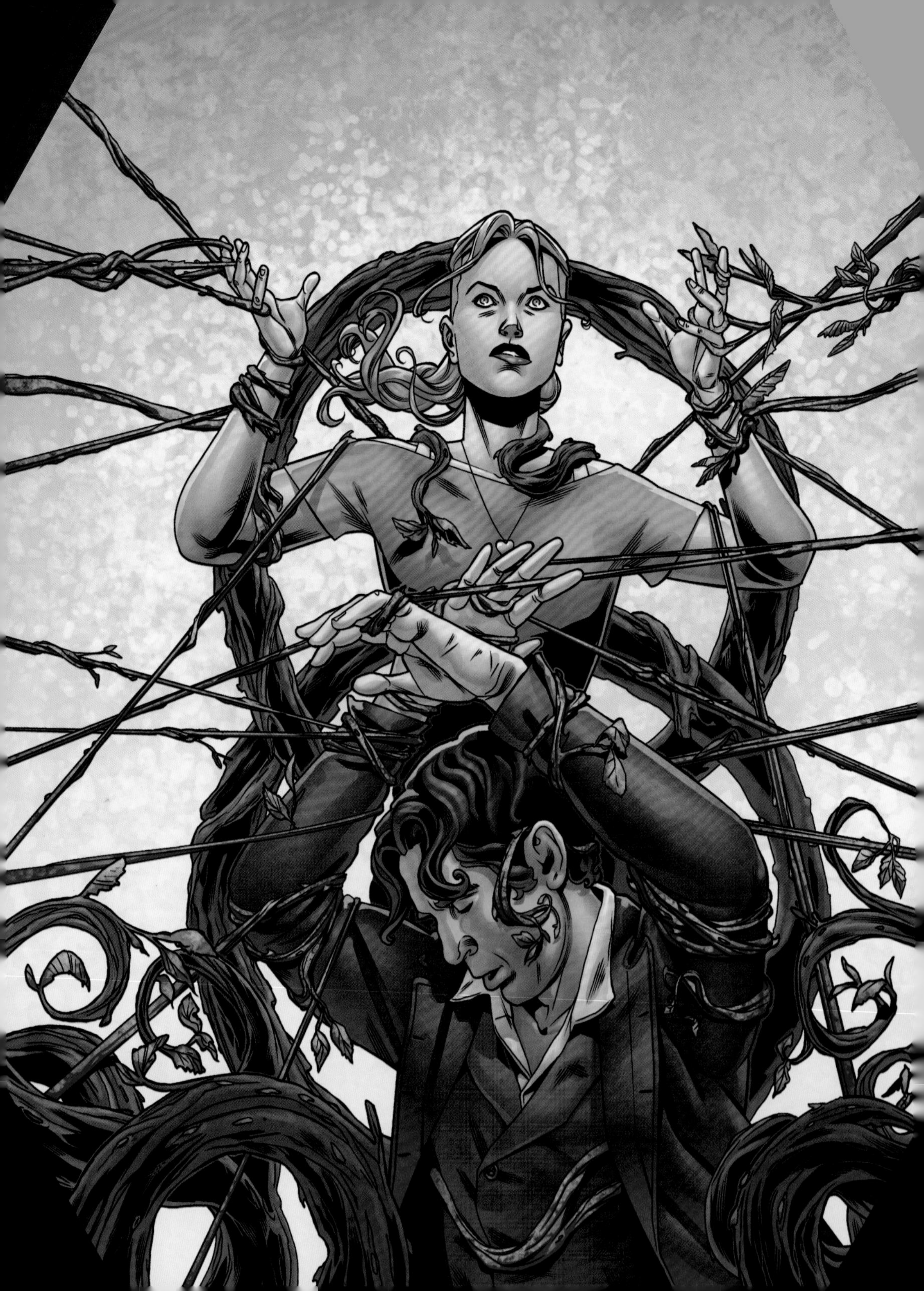

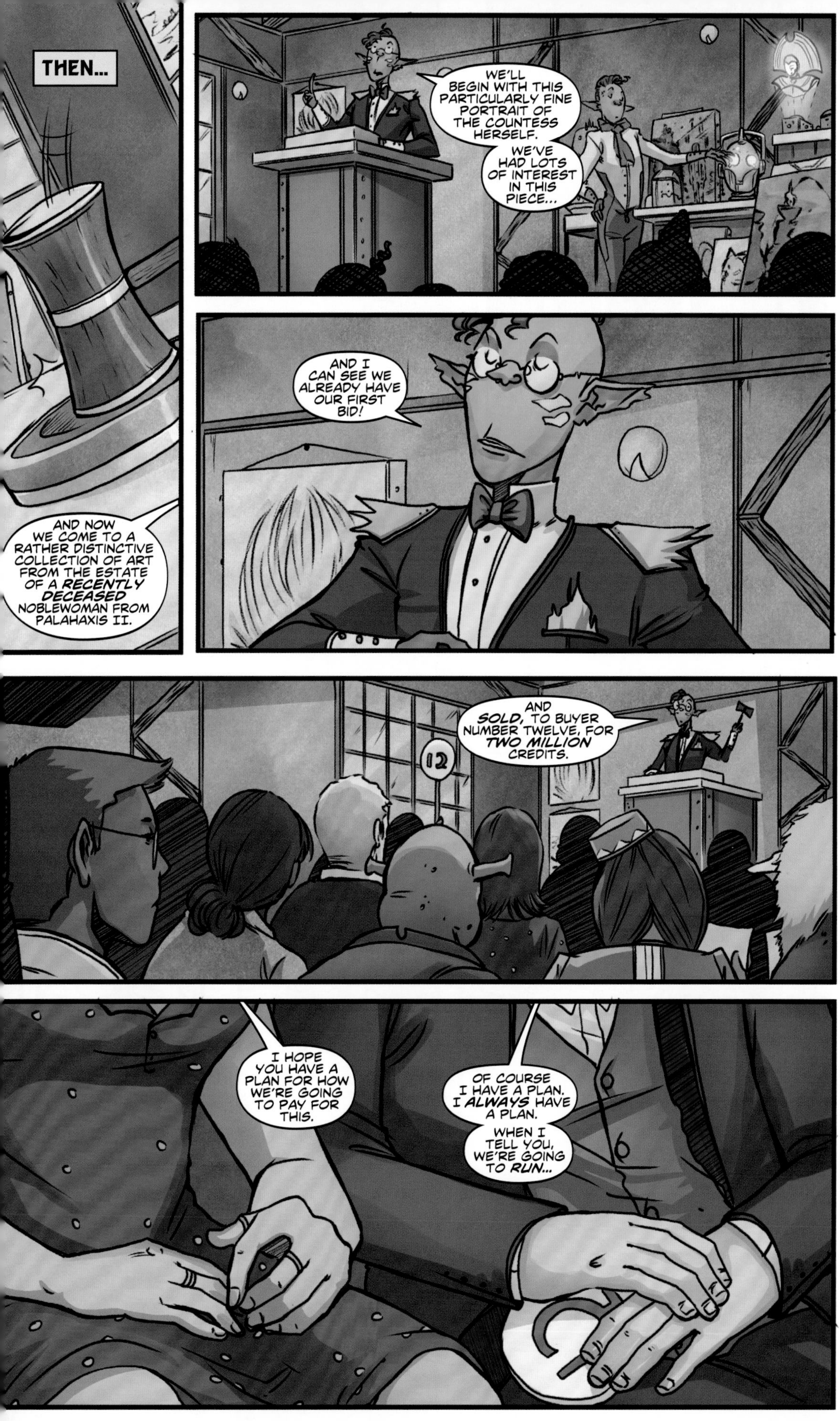
THEN...
AND NOW WE COME TO A RATHER DISTINCTIVE COLLECTION OF ART FROM THE ESTATE OF A ***RECENTLY DECEASED*** NOBLEWOMAN FROM PALAHAXIS II.
WE'LL BEGIN WITH THIS PARTICULARLY FINE PORTRAIT OF THE COUNTESS HERSELF.
WE'VE HAD LOTS OF INTEREST IN THIS PIECE...
AND I CAN SEE WE ALREADY HAVE OUR FIRST BID!
12
AND ***SOLD***, TO BUYER NUMBER TWELVE, FOR ***TWO MILLION*** CREDITS.
I HOPE YOU HAVE A PLAN FOR HOW WE'RE GOING TO PAY FOR THIS.
OF COURSE I HAVE A PLAN. I ***ALWAYS*** HAVE A PLAN.
WHEN I TELL YOU, WE'RE GOING TO ***RUN***...

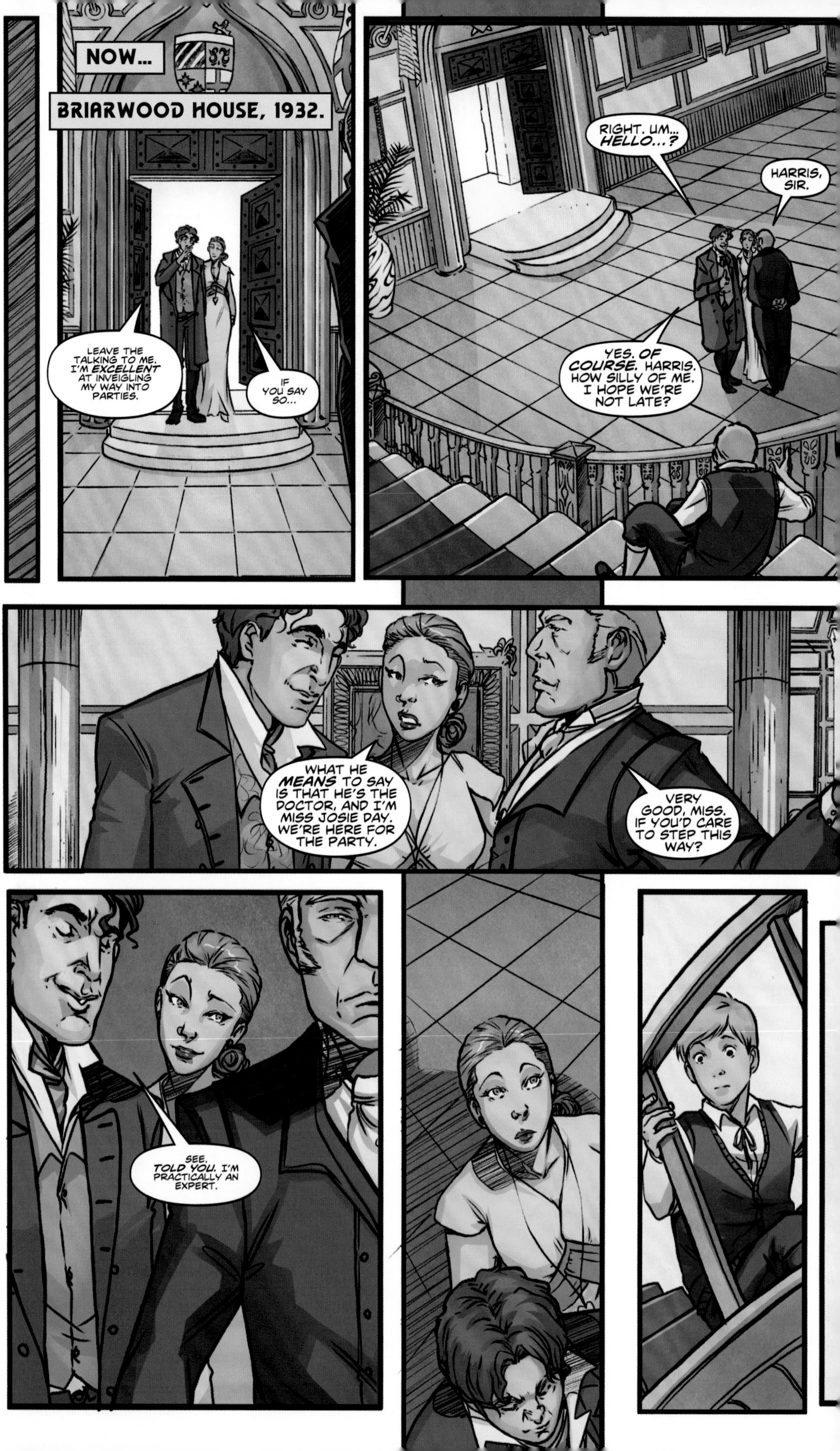
NOW...
BRIARWOOD HOUSE, 1932.
LEAVE THE TALKING TO ME. I'M EXCELLENT AT INVEIGLING MY WAY INTO PARTIES.
IF YOU SAY SO...
RIGHT. UM... HELLO...?
HARRIS, SIR.
YES. OF COURSE. HARRIS. HOW SILLY OF ME. I HOPE WE'RE NOT LATE?
WHAT HE MEANS TO SAY IS THAT HE'S THE DOCTOR, AND I'M MISS JOSIE DAY. WE'RE HERE FOR THE PARTY.
VERY GOOD, MISS. IF YOU'D CARE TO STEP THIS WAY?
SEE. TOLD YOU. I'M PRACTICALLY AN EXPERT.

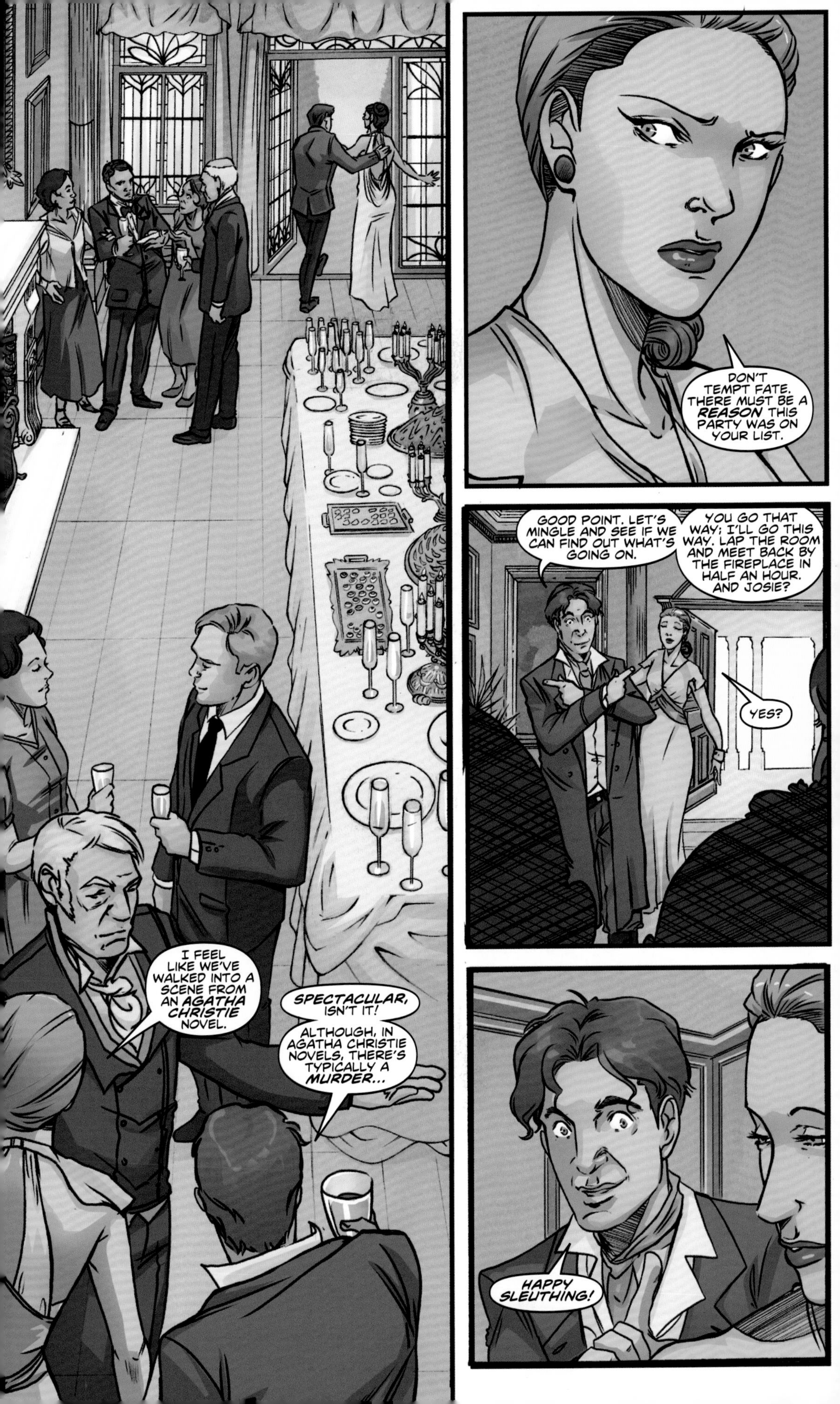

I FEEL LIKE WE'VE WALKED INTO A SCENE FROM AN AGATHA CHRISTIE NOVEL.
SPECTACULAR, ISN'T IT!
ALTHOUGH, IN AGATHA CHRISTIE NOVELS, THERE'S TYPICALLY A MURDER...
DON'T TEMPT FATE. THERE MUST BE A REASON THIS PARTY WAS ON YOUR LIST.
GOOD POINT. LET'S MINGLE AND SEE IF WE CAN FIND OUT WHAT'S GOING ON.
YOU GO THAT WAY; I'LL GO THIS WAY. LAP THE ROOM AND MEET BACK BY THE FIREPLACE IN HALF AN HOUR. AND JOSIE?
YES?
HAPPY SLEUTHING!

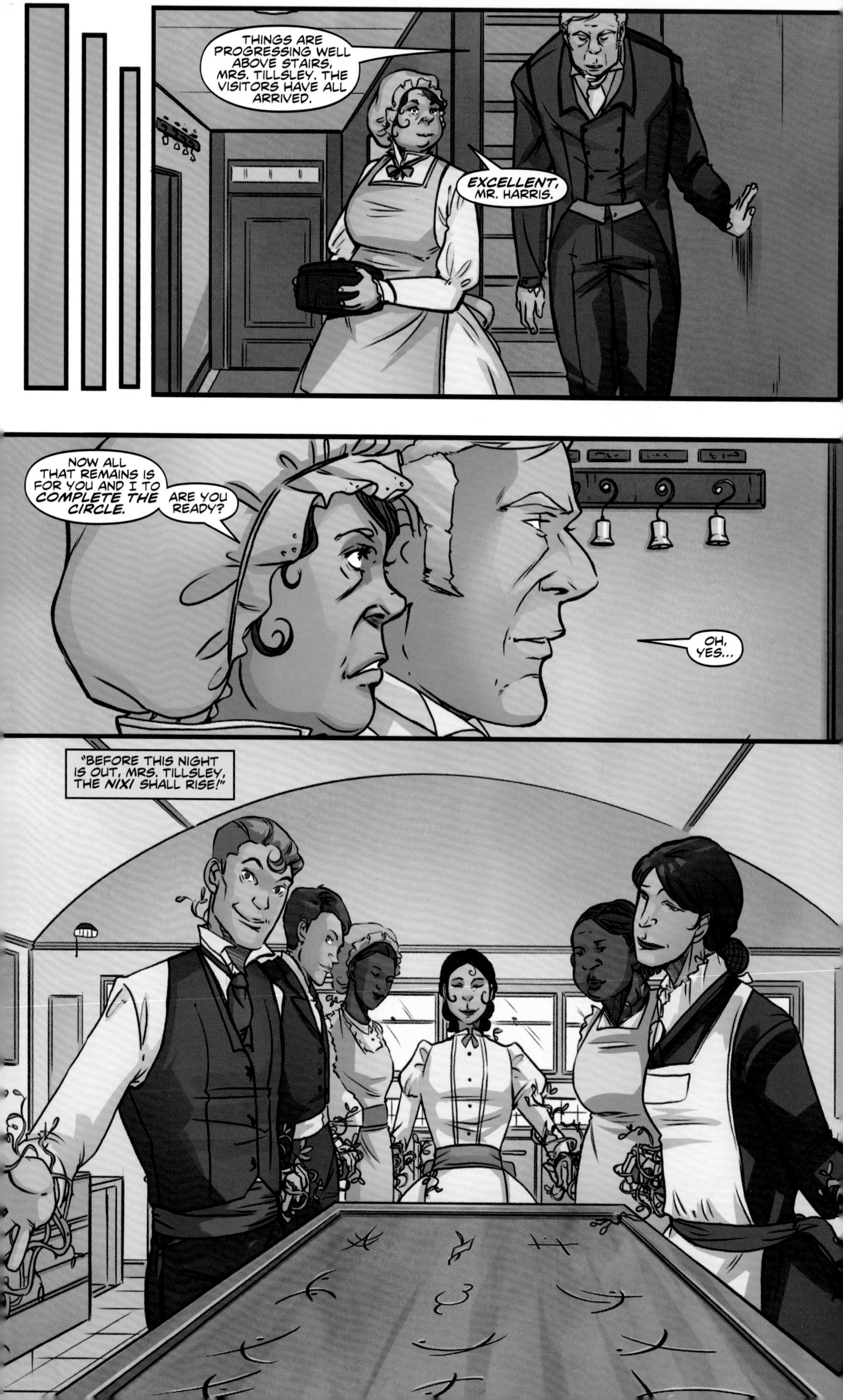
THINGS ARE PROGRESSING WELL ABOVE STAIRS, MRS. TILLSLEY. THE VISITORS HAVE ALL ARRIVED.
EXCELLENT, MR. HARRIS.
NOW ALL THAT REMAINS IS FOR YOU AND I TO COMPLETE THE CIRCLE.
ARE YOU READY?
OH, YES...
"BEFORE THIS NIGHT IS OUT, MRS. TILLSLEY, THE NIXI SHALL RISE!"

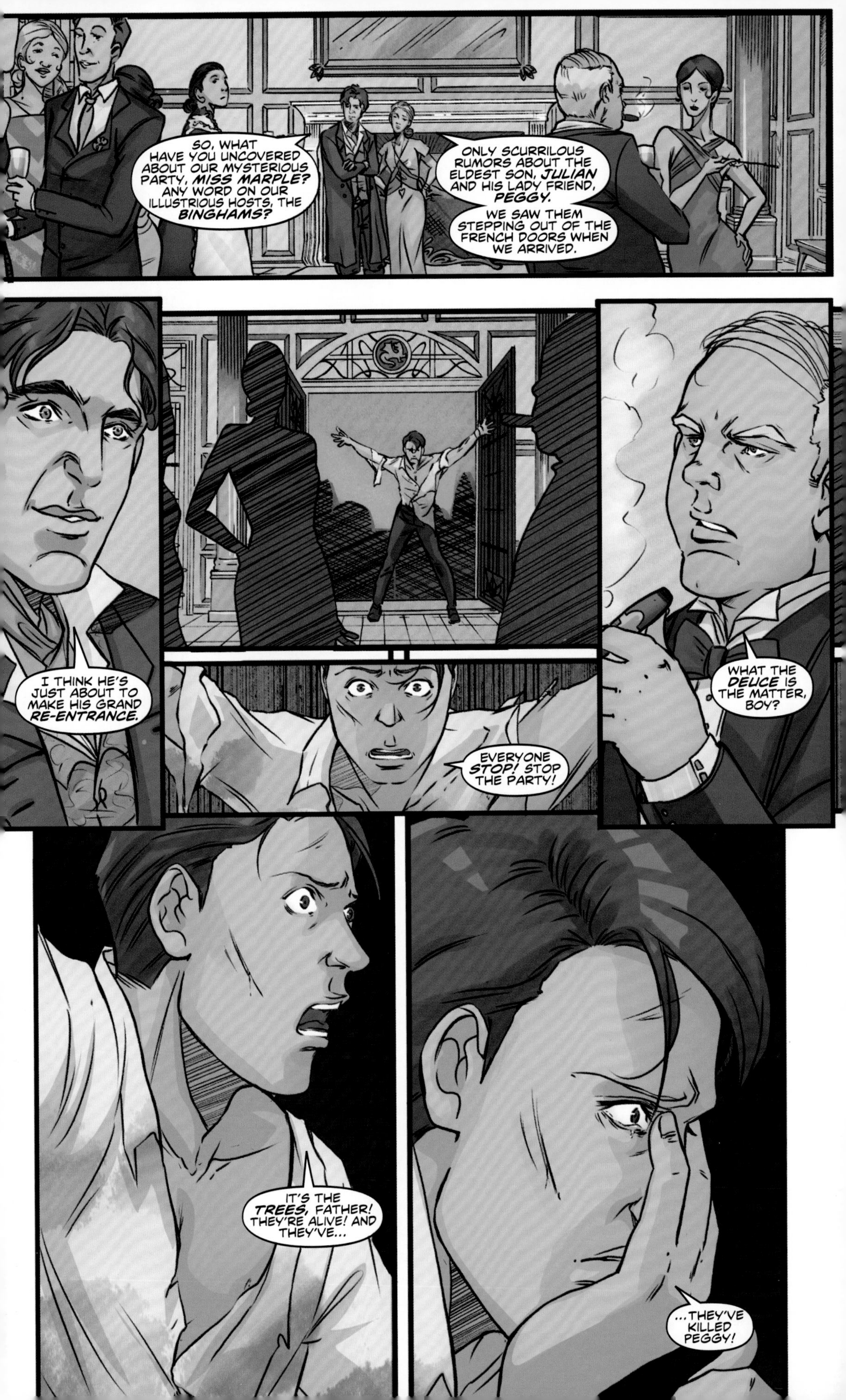
SO, WHAT HAVE YOU UNCOVERED ABOUT OUR MYSTERIOUS PARTY, MISS MARPLE? ANY WORD ON OUR ILLUSTRIOUS HOSTS, THE BINGHAMS?
ONLY SCURRILOUS RUMORS ABOUT THE ELDEST SON, JULIAN AND HIS LADY FRIEND, PEGGY.
WE SAW THEM STEPPING OUT OF THE FRENCH DOORS WHEN WE ARRIVED.
I THINK HE'S JUST ABOUT TO MAKE HIS GRAND RE-ENTRANCE.
EVERYONE STOP! STOP THE PARTY!
WHAT THE DEUCE IS THE MATTER, BOY?
IT'S THE TREES, FATHER! THEY'RE ALIVE! AND THEY'VE...
...THEY'VE KILLED PEGGY!

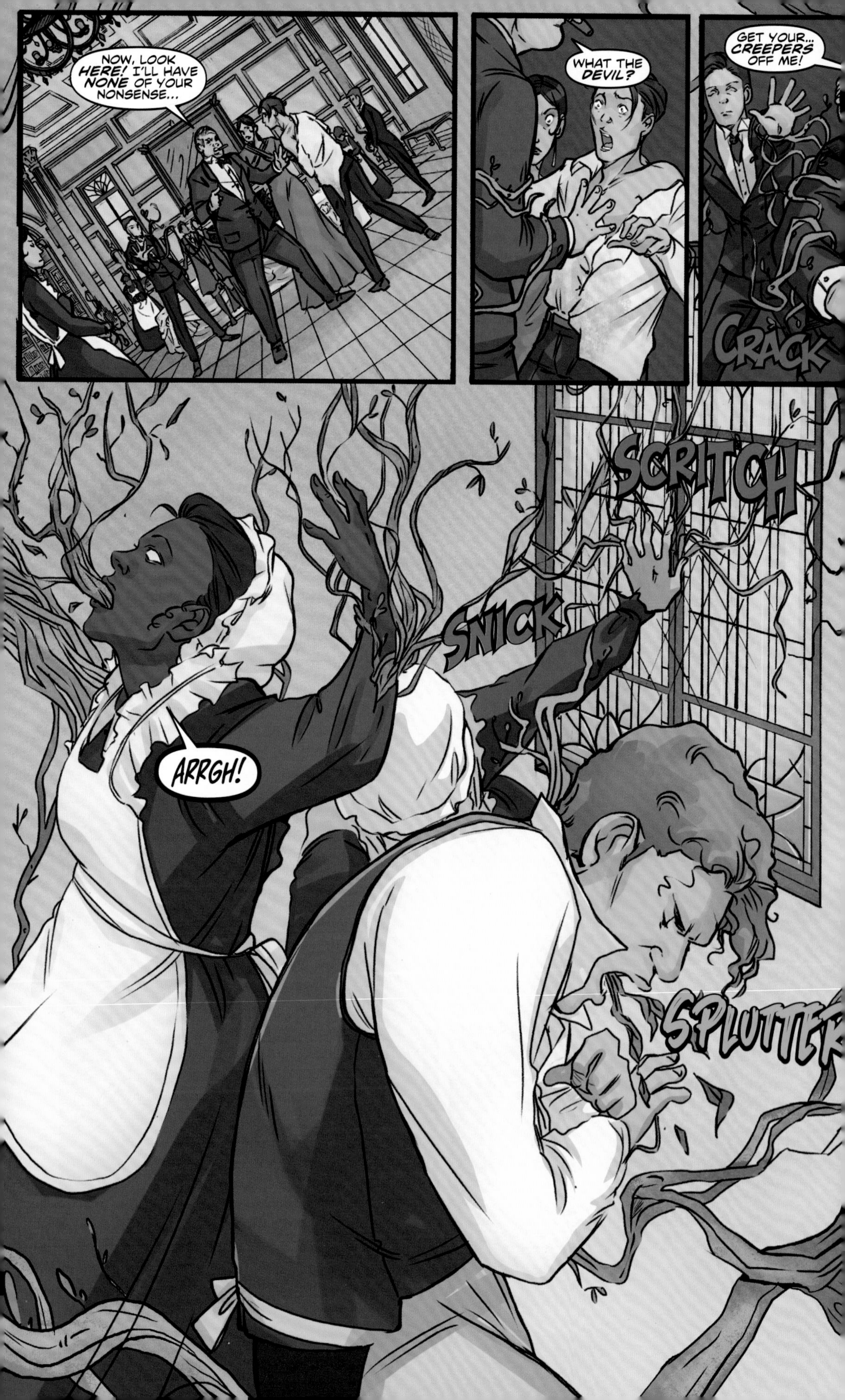
NOW, LOOK HERE! I'LL HAVE NONE OF YOUR NONSENSE...
WHAT THE DEVIL?
GET YOUR... CREEPERS OFF ME!
CRACK
SCRITCH
SNICK
ARRGH!
SPLUTTER

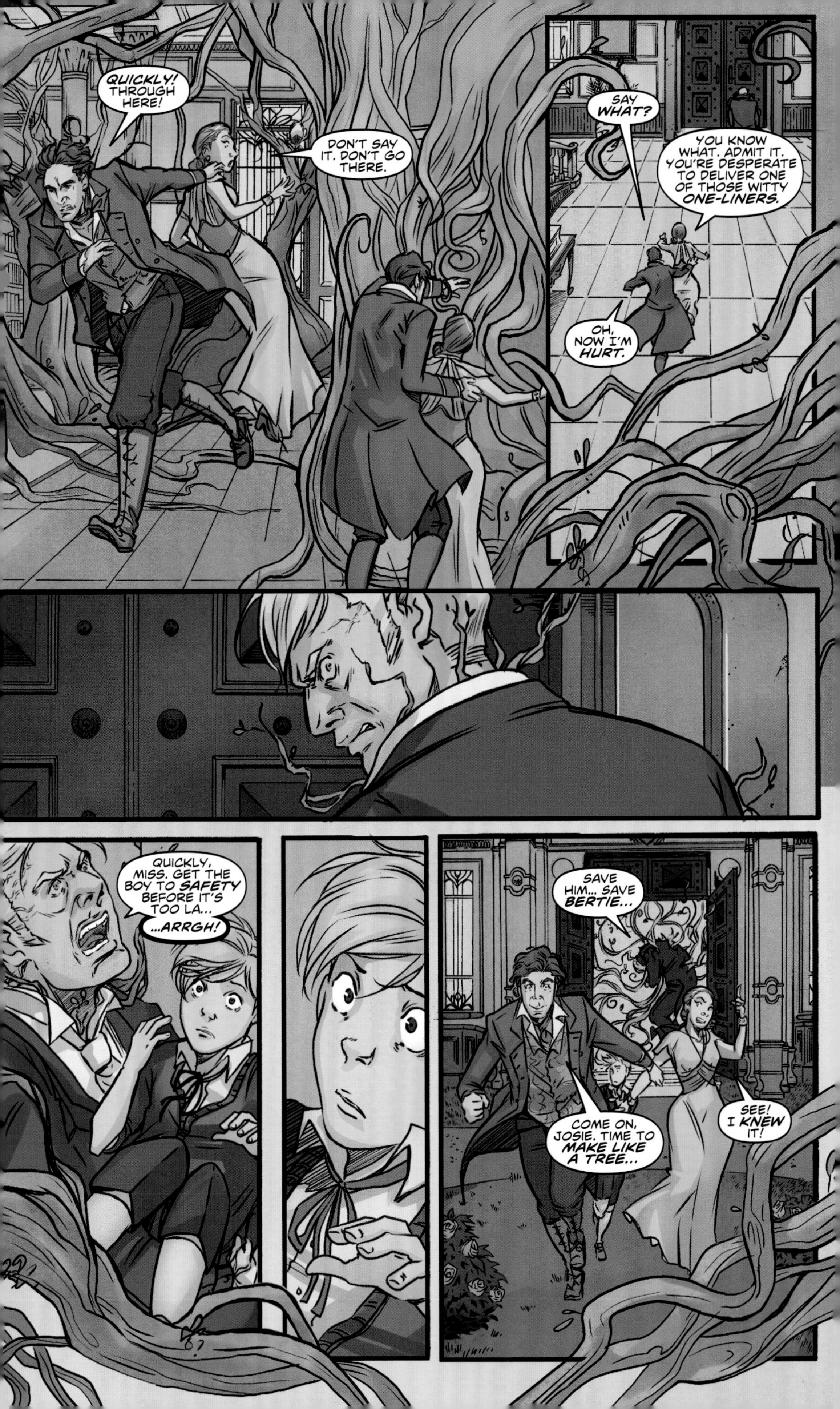
QUICKLY! THROUGH HERE!
DON'T SAY IT. DON'T GO THERE.
SAY WHAT?
YOU KNOW WHAT. ADMIT IT. YOU'RE DESPERATE TO DELIVER ONE OF THOSE WITTY ONE-LINERS.
OH, NOW I'M HURT.
QUICKLY, MISS. GET THE BOY TO SAFETY BEFORE IT'S TOO LA...
...ARRGH!
SAVE HIM... SAVE BERTIE...
COME ON, JOSIE. TIME TO MAKE LIKE A TREE...
SEE! I KNEW IT!

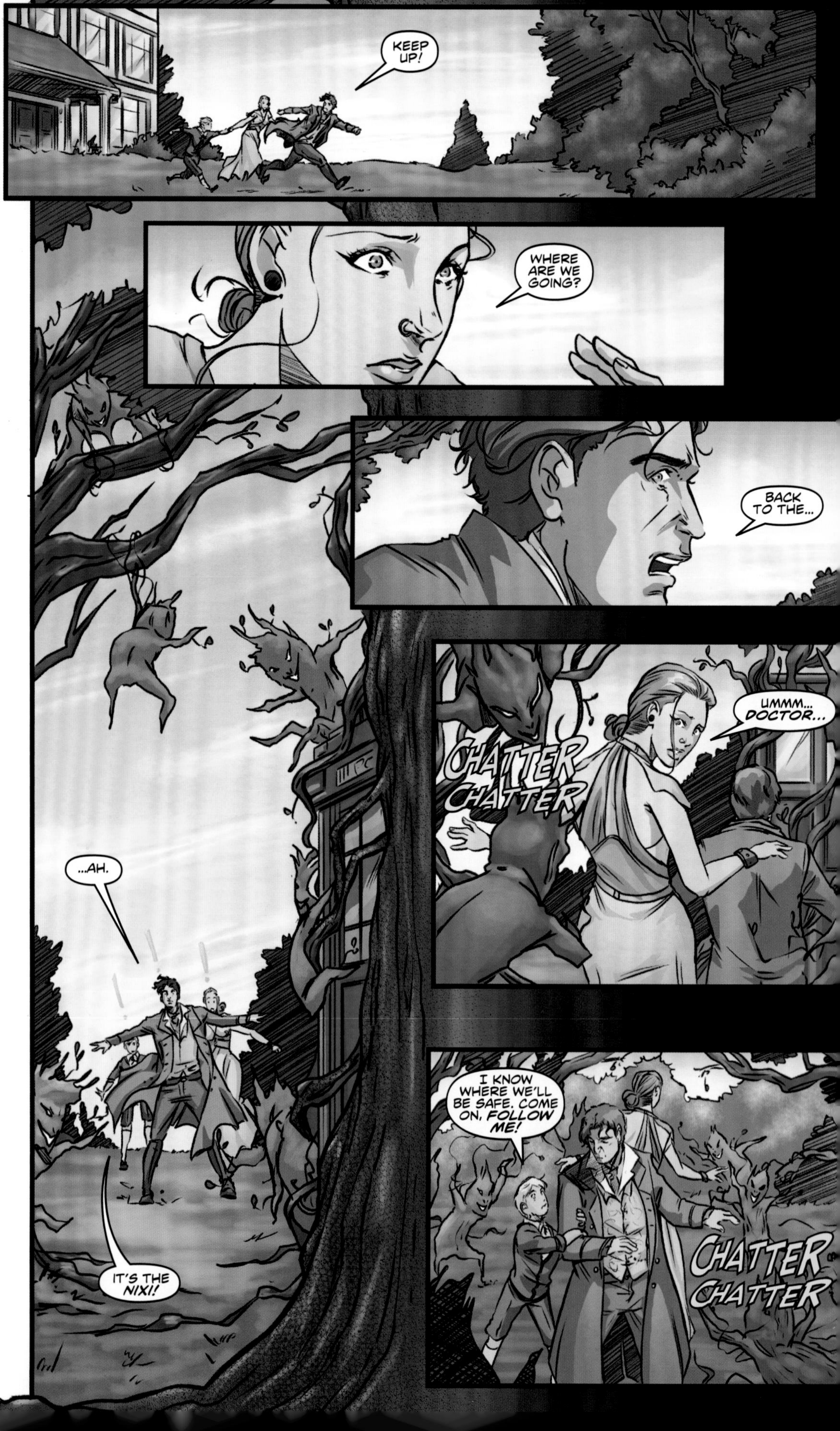
KEEP UP!
WHERE ARE WE GOING?
BACK TO THE...
UMMM... DOCTOR...
CHATTER CHATTER
...AH.
IT'S THE NIXI!
I KNOW WHERE WE'LL BE SAFE. COME ON, FOLLOW ME!
CHATTER CHATTER

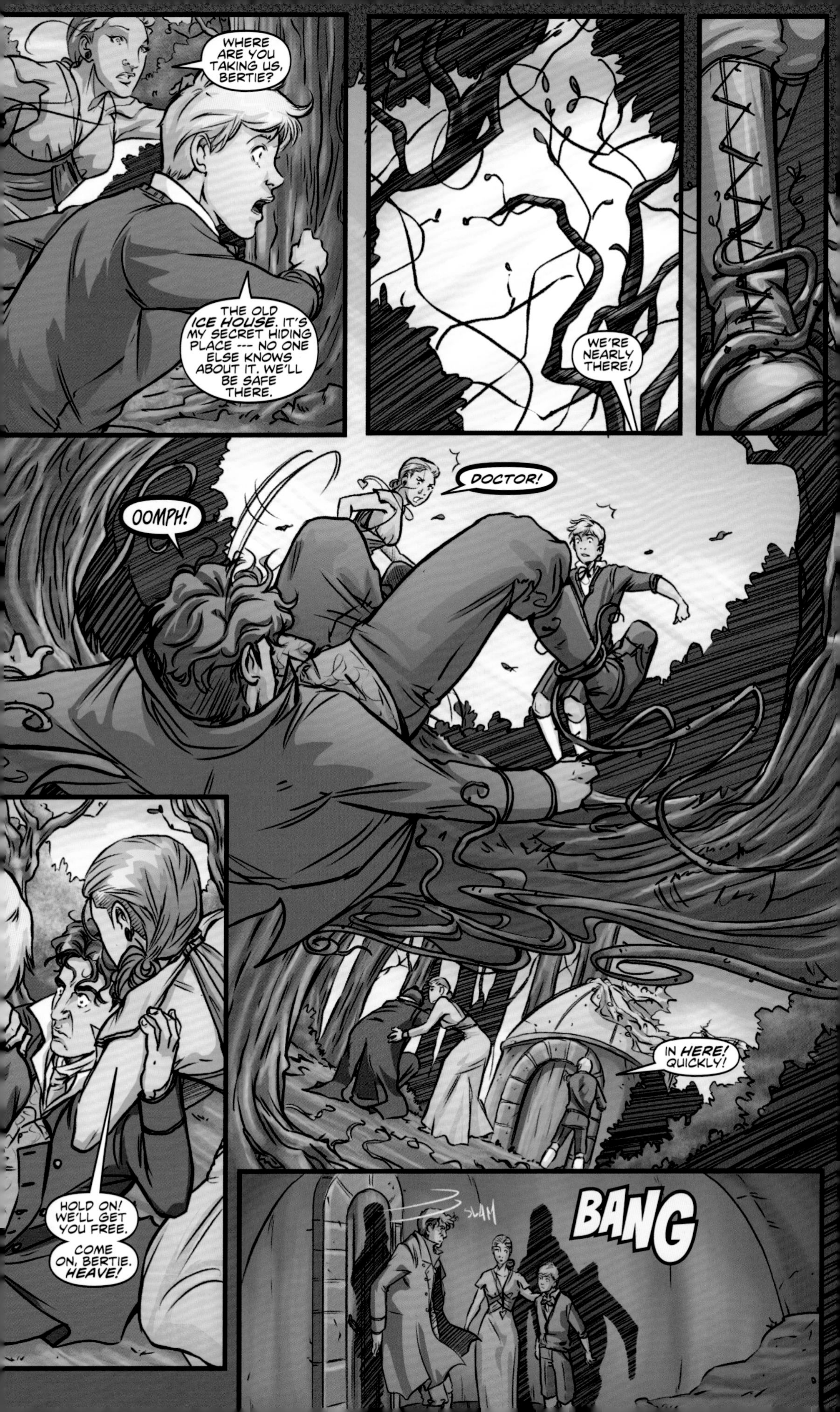
WHERE ARE YOU TAKING US, BERTIE?
THE OLD *ICE HOUSE*. IT'S MY SECRET HIDING PLACE --- NO ONE ELSE KNOWS ABOUT IT. WE'LL BE SAFE THERE.
WE'RE NEARLY THERE!
DOCTOR!
OOMPH!
HOLD ON! WE'LL GET YOU FREE.
COME ON, BERTIE. *HEAVE!*
IN *HERE!* QUICKLY!
SLAM
BANG

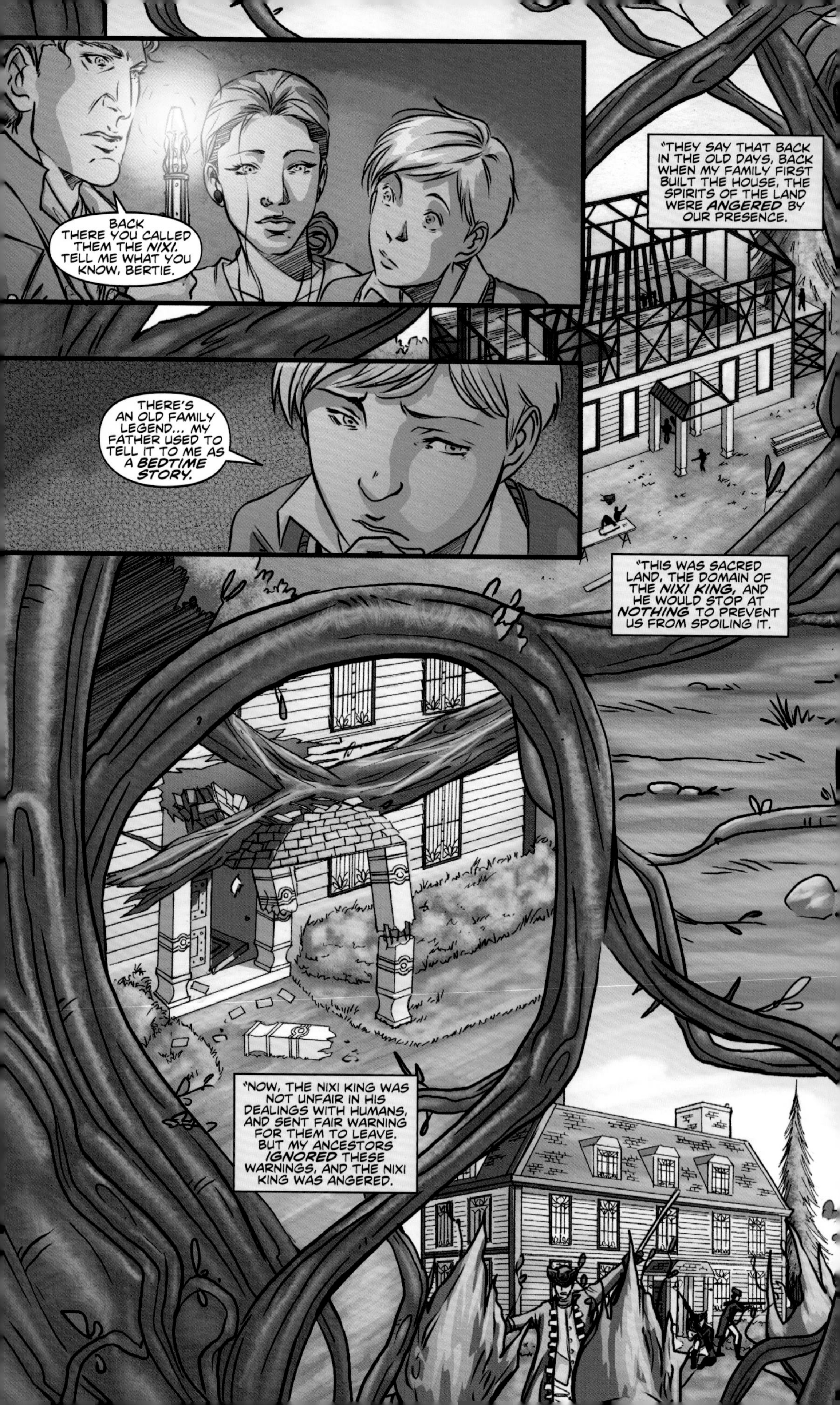
BACK THERE YOU CALLED THEM THE *NIXI*. TELL ME WHAT YOU KNOW, BERTIE.
"THEY SAY THAT BACK IN THE OLD DAYS, BACK WHEN MY FAMILY FIRST BUILT THE HOUSE, THE SPIRITS OF THE LAND WERE *ANGERED* BY OUR PRESENCE.
THERE'S AN OLD FAMILY LEGEND... MY FATHER USED TO TELL IT TO ME AS A *BEDTIME STORY*.
"THIS WAS SACRED LAND, THE DOMAIN OF THE *NIXI KING*, AND HE WOULD STOP AT *NOTHING* TO PREVENT US FROM SPOILING IT.
"NOW, THE NIXI KING WAS NOT UNFAIR IN HIS DEALINGS WITH HUMANS, AND SENT FAIR WARNING FOR THEM TO LEAVE. BUT MY ANCESTORS *IGNORED* THESE WARNINGS, AND THE NIXI KING WAS ANGERED.

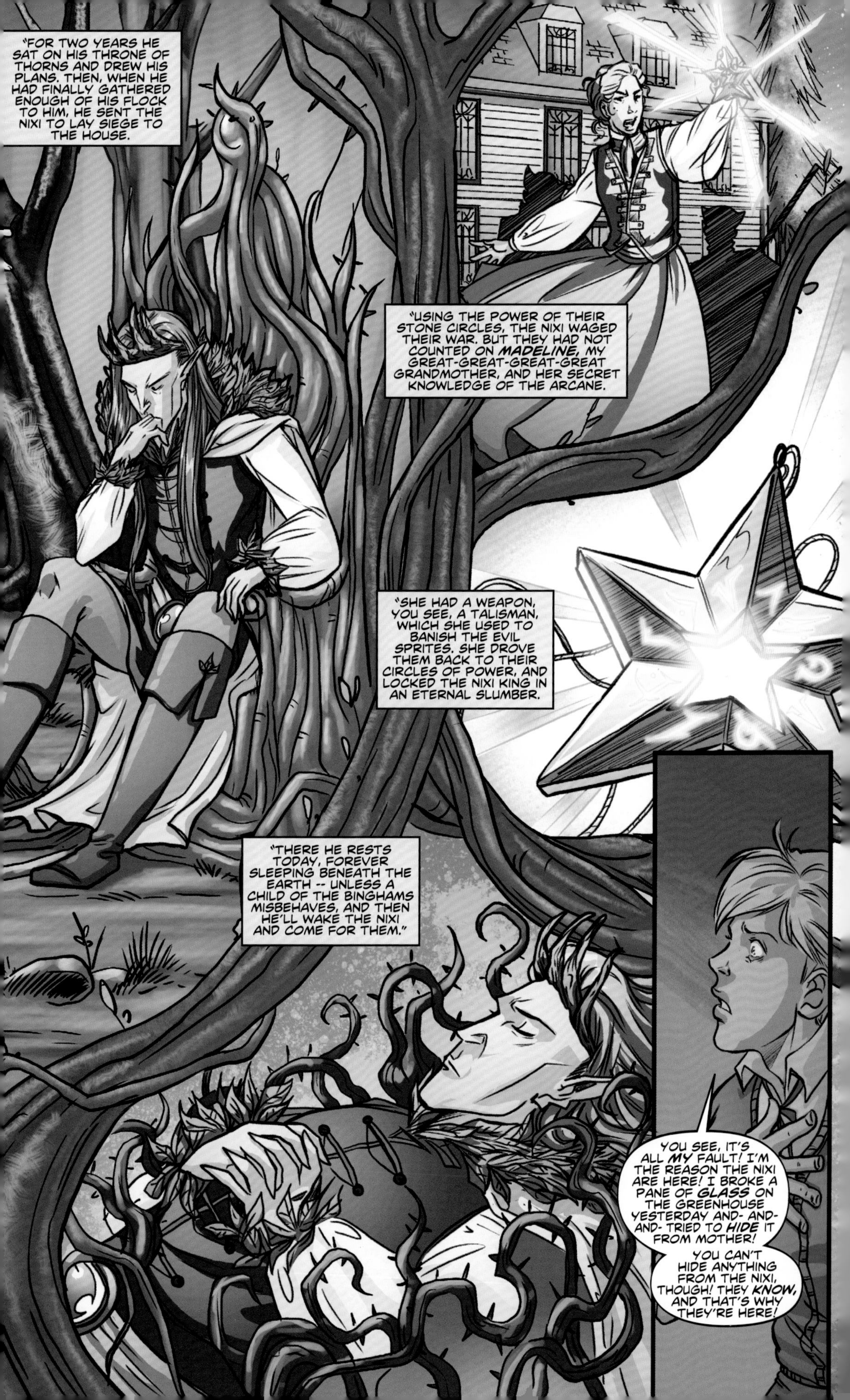
"FOR TWO YEARS HE SAT ON HIS THRONE OF THORNS AND DREW HIS PLANS. THEN, WHEN HE HAD FINALLY GATHERED ENOUGH OF HIS FLOCK TO HIM, HE SENT THE NIXI TO LAY SIEGE TO THE HOUSE.
"USING THE POWER OF THEIR STONE CIRCLES, THE NIXI WAGED THEIR WAR. BUT THEY HAD NOT COUNTED ON *MADELINE,* MY GREAT-GREAT-GREAT-GREAT GRANDMOTHER, AND HER SECRET KNOWLEDGE OF THE ARCANE.
"SHE HAD A WEAPON, YOU SEE, A TALISMAN, WHICH SHE USED TO BANISH THE EVIL SPRITES. SHE DROVE THEM BACK TO THEIR CIRCLES OF POWER, AND LOCKED THE NIXI KING IN AN ETERNAL SLUMBER.
"THERE HE RESTS TODAY, FOREVER SLEEPING BENEATH THE EARTH -- UNLESS A CHILD OF THE BINGHAMS MISBEHAVES, AND THEN HE'LL WAKE THE NIXI AND COME FOR THEM."
YOU SEE, IT'S ALL *MY* FAULT! I'M THE REASON THE NIXI ARE HERE! I BROKE A PANE OF *GLASS* ON THE GREENHOUSE YESTERDAY AND- AND- AND- TRIED TO *HIDE* IT FROM MOTHER!
YOU CAN'T HIDE ANYTHING FROM THE NIXI, THOUGH! THEY *KNOW,* AND THAT'S WHY THEY'RE HERE!

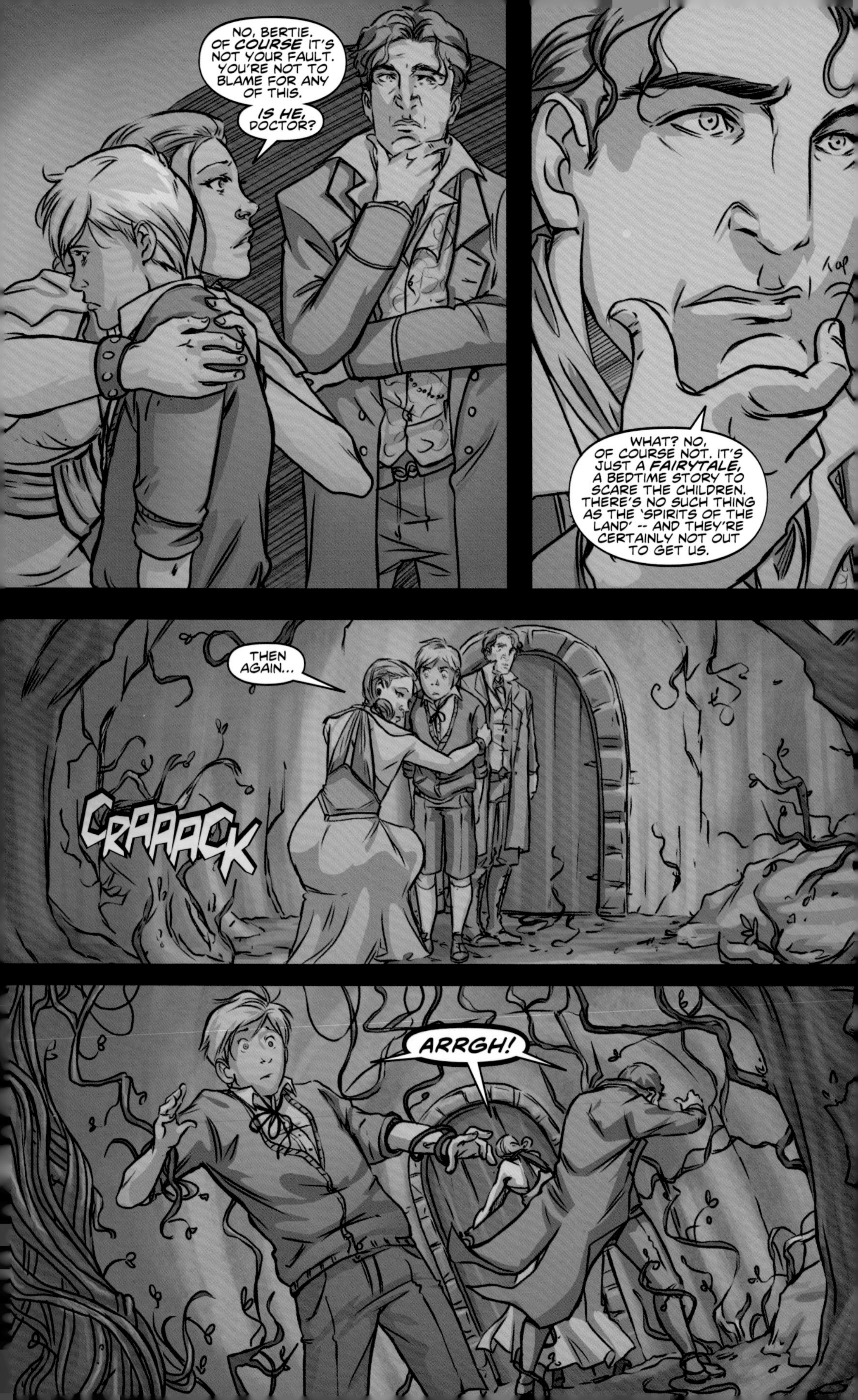
NO, BERTIE. OF COURSE IT'S NOT YOUR FAULT. YOU'RE NOT TO BLAME FOR ANY OF THIS.
IS HE, DOCTOR?
TAP
WHAT? NO, OF COURSE NOT. IT'S JUST A FAIRYTALE, A BEDTIME STORY TO SCARE THE CHILDREN. THERE'S NO SUCH THING AS THE 'SPIRITS OF THE LAND' -- AND THEY'RE CERTAINLY NOT OUT TO GET US.
THEN AGAIN...
CRAAACK
ARRGH!

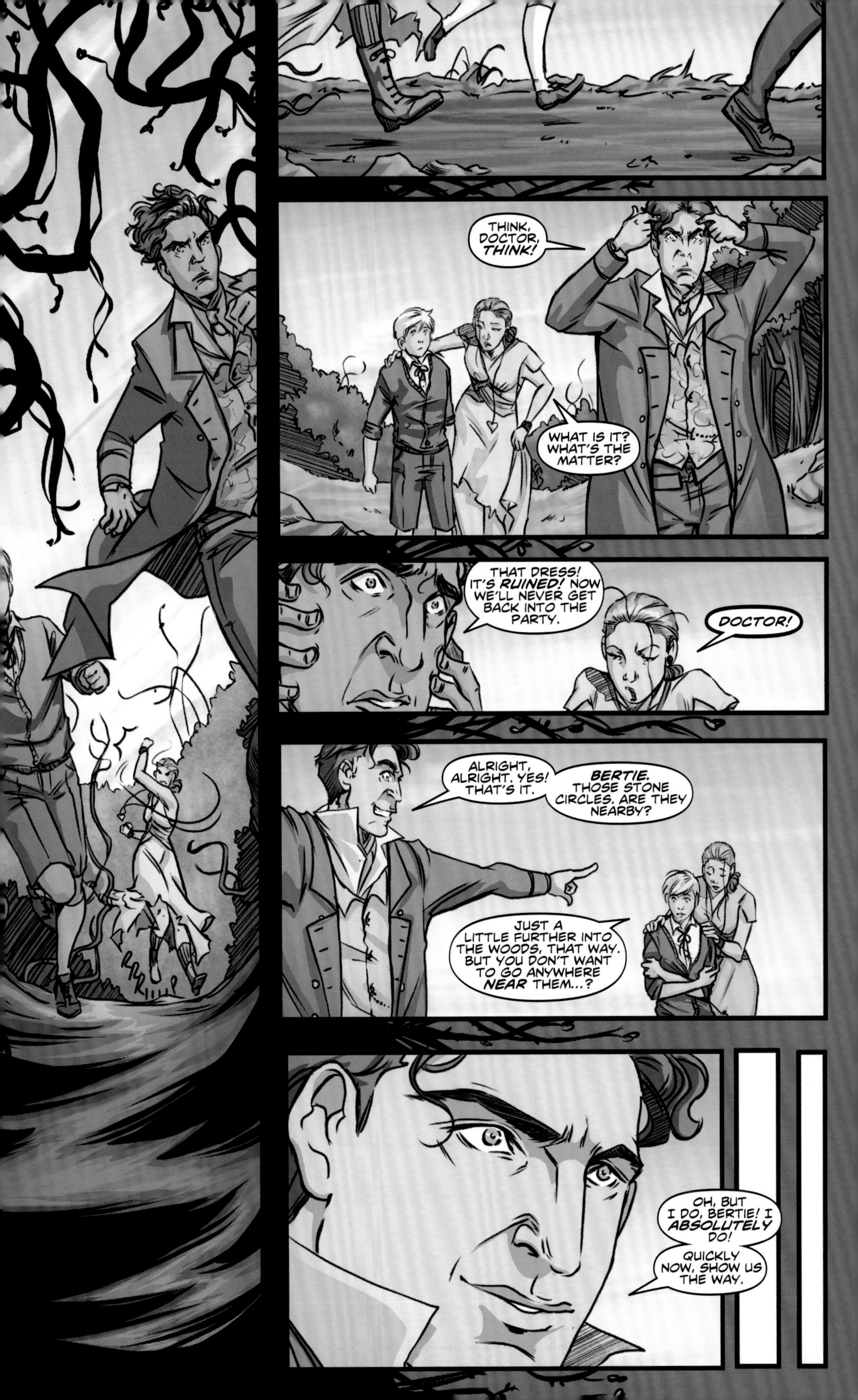
THINK, DOCTOR, THINK!
WHAT IS IT? WHAT'S THE MATTER?
THAT DRESS! IT'S RUINED! NOW WE'LL NEVER GET BACK INTO THE PARTY.
DOCTOR!
ALRIGHT, ALRIGHT. YES! THAT'S IT.
BERTIE. THOSE STONE CIRCLES. ARE THEY NEARBY?
JUST A LITTLE FURTHER INTO THE WOODS, THAT WAY. BUT YOU DON'T WANT TO GO ANYWHERE NEAR THEM...?
OH, BUT I DO, BERTIE! I ABSOLUTELY DO!
QUICKLY NOW, SHOW US THE WAY.

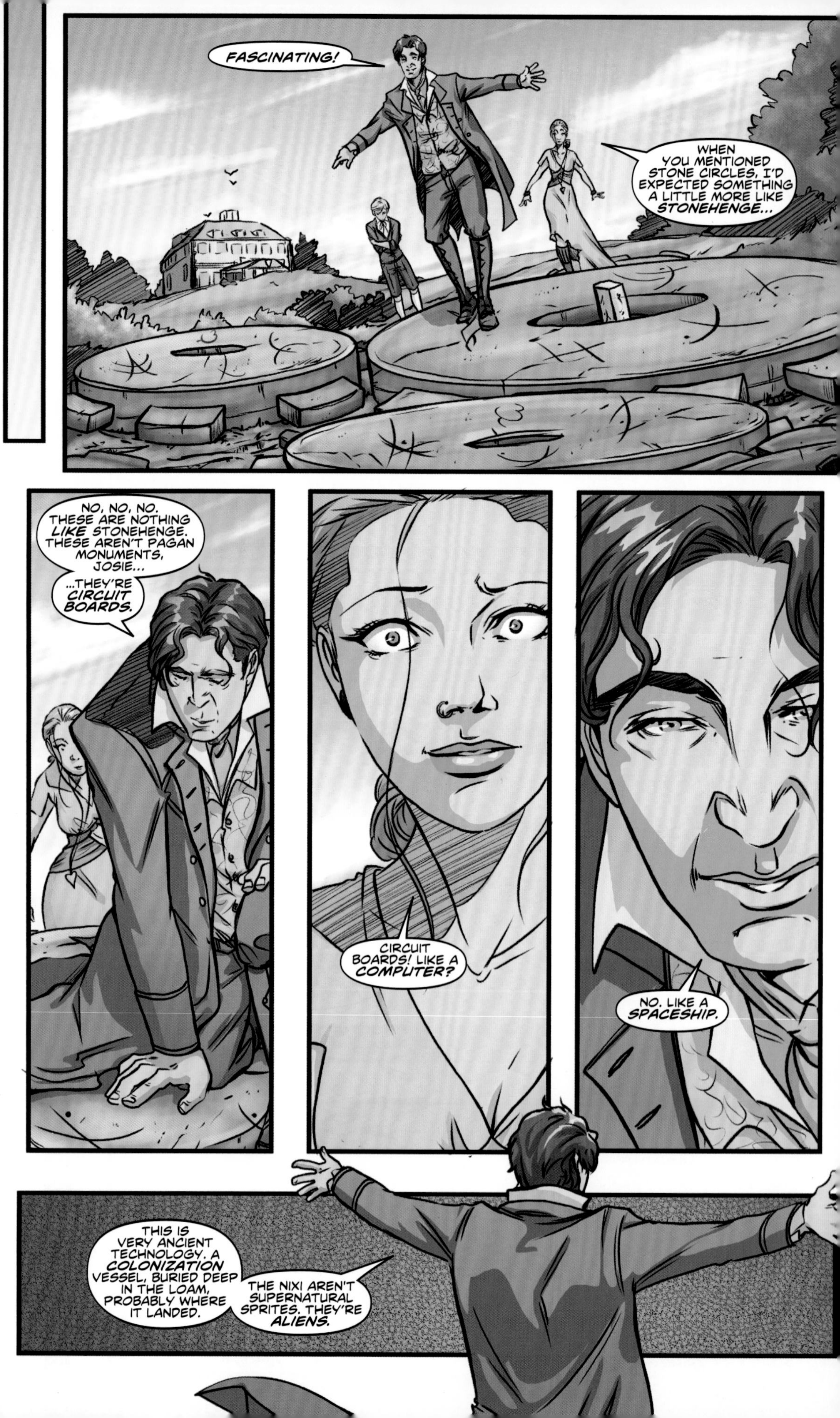
FASCINATING!
WHEN YOU MENTIONED STONE CIRCLES, I'D EXPECTED SOMETHING A LITTLE MORE LIKE STONEHENGE...
NO, NO, NO. THESE ARE NOTHING LIKE STONEHENGE. THESE AREN'T PAGAN MONUMENTS, JOSIE...
...THEY'RE CIRCUIT BOARDS.
CIRCUIT BOARDS! LIKE A COMPUTER?
NO. LIKE A SPACESHIP.
THIS IS VERY ANCIENT TECHNOLOGY. A COLONIZATION VESSEL, BURIED DEEP IN THE LOAM, PROBABLY WHERE IT LANDED.
THE NIXI AREN'T SUPERNATURAL SPRITES. THEY'RE ALIENS.

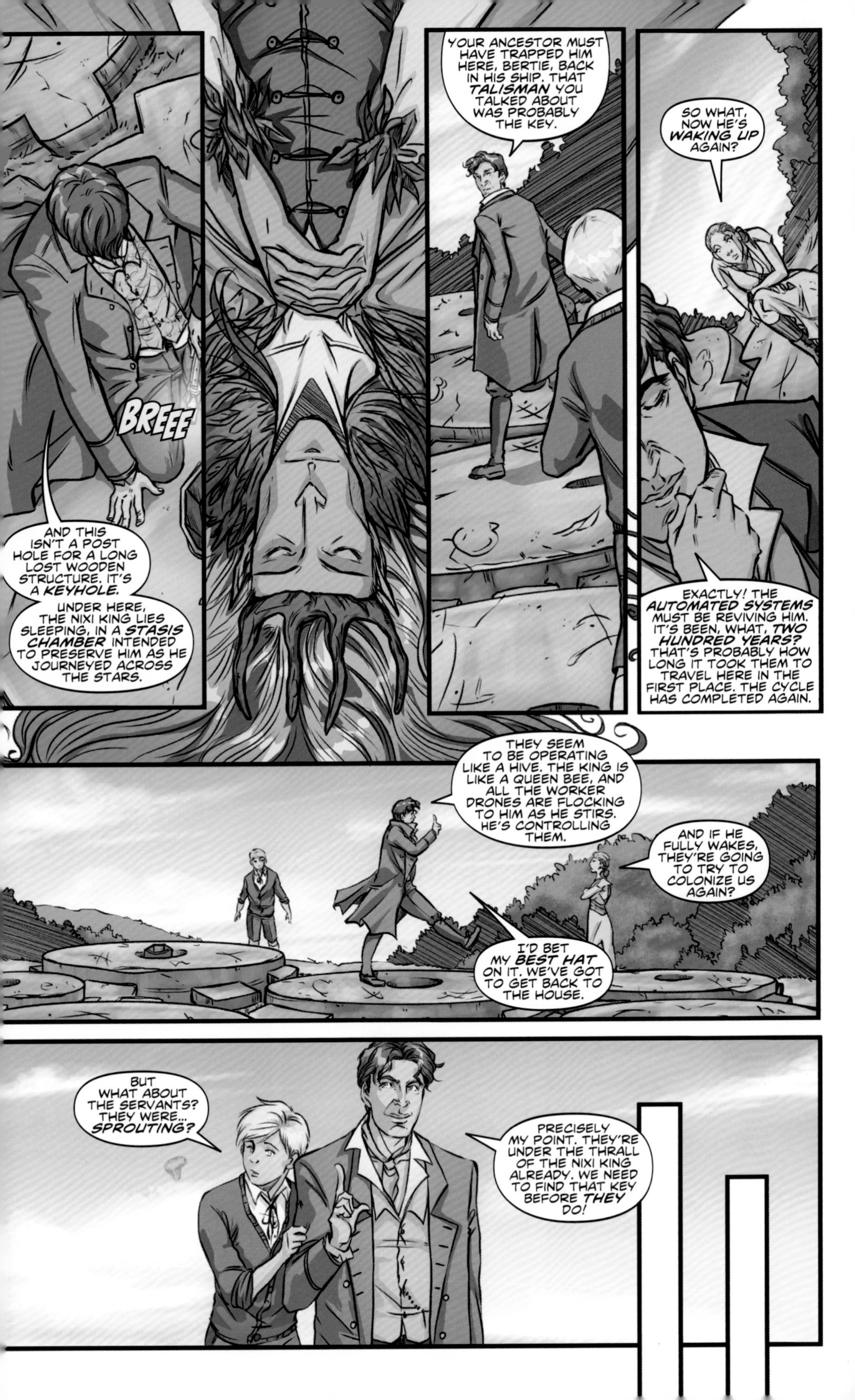
BREEE
AND THIS ISN'T A POST HOLE FOR A LONG LOST WOODEN STRUCTURE. IT'S A KEYHOLE.
UNDER HERE, THE NIXI KING LIES SLEEPING, IN A STASIS CHAMBER INTENDED TO PRESERVE HIM AS HE JOURNEYED ACROSS THE STARS.
YOUR ANCESTOR MUST HAVE TRAPPED HIM HERE, BERTIE, BACK IN HIS SHIP. THAT TALISMAN YOU TALKED ABOUT WAS PROBABLY THE KEY.
SO WHAT, NOW HE'S WAKING UP AGAIN?
EXACTLY! THE AUTOMATED SYSTEMS MUST BE REVIVING HIM. IT'S BEEN, WHAT, TWO HUNDRED YEARS? THAT'S PROBABLY HOW LONG IT TOOK THEM TO TRAVEL HERE IN THE FIRST PLACE. THE CYCLE HAS COMPLETED AGAIN.
THEY SEEM TO BE OPERATING LIKE A HIVE. THE KING IS LIKE A QUEEN BEE, AND ALL THE WORKER DRONES ARE FLOCKING TO HIM AS HE STIRS. HE'S CONTROLLING THEM.
AND IF HE FULLY WAKES, THEY'RE GOING TO TRY TO COLONIZE US AGAIN?
I'D BET MY BEST HAT ON IT. WE'VE GOT TO GET BACK TO THE HOUSE.
BUT WHAT ABOUT THE SERVANTS? THEY WERE... SPROUTING?
PRECISELY MY POINT. THEY'RE UNDER THE THRALL OF THE NIXI KING ALREADY. WE NEED TO FIND THAT KEY BEFORE THEY DO!

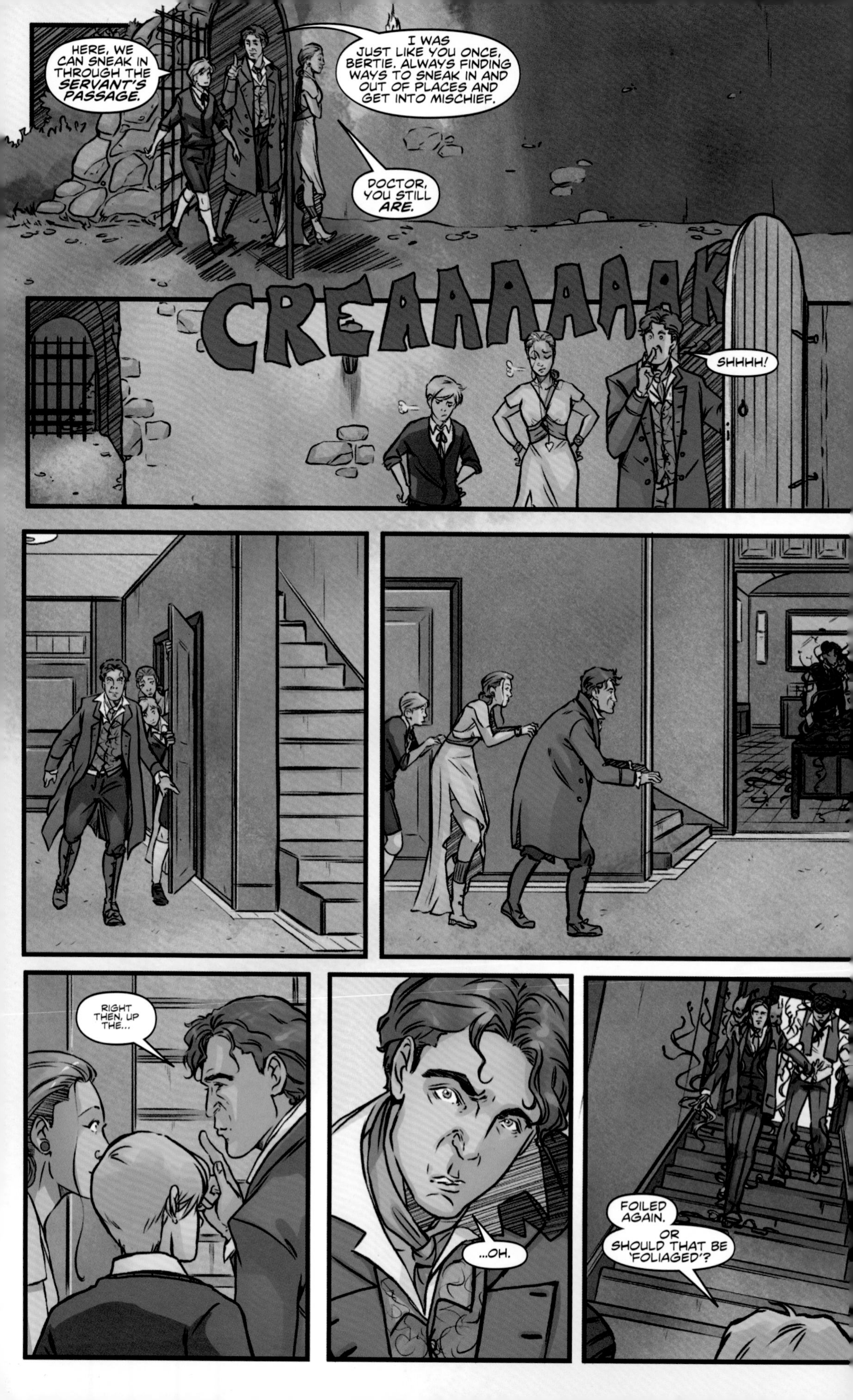
HERE, WE CAN SNEAK IN THROUGH THE SERVANT'S PASSAGE.
I WAS JUST LIKE YOU ONCE, BERTIE. ALWAYS FINDING WAYS TO SNEAK IN AND OUT OF PLACES AND GET INTO MISCHIEF.
DOCTOR, YOU STILL ARE.
CREAAAAAAK
SHHHH!
RIGHT THEN, UP THE...
...OH.
FOILED AGAIN.
OR SHOULD THAT BE 'FOLIAGED'?

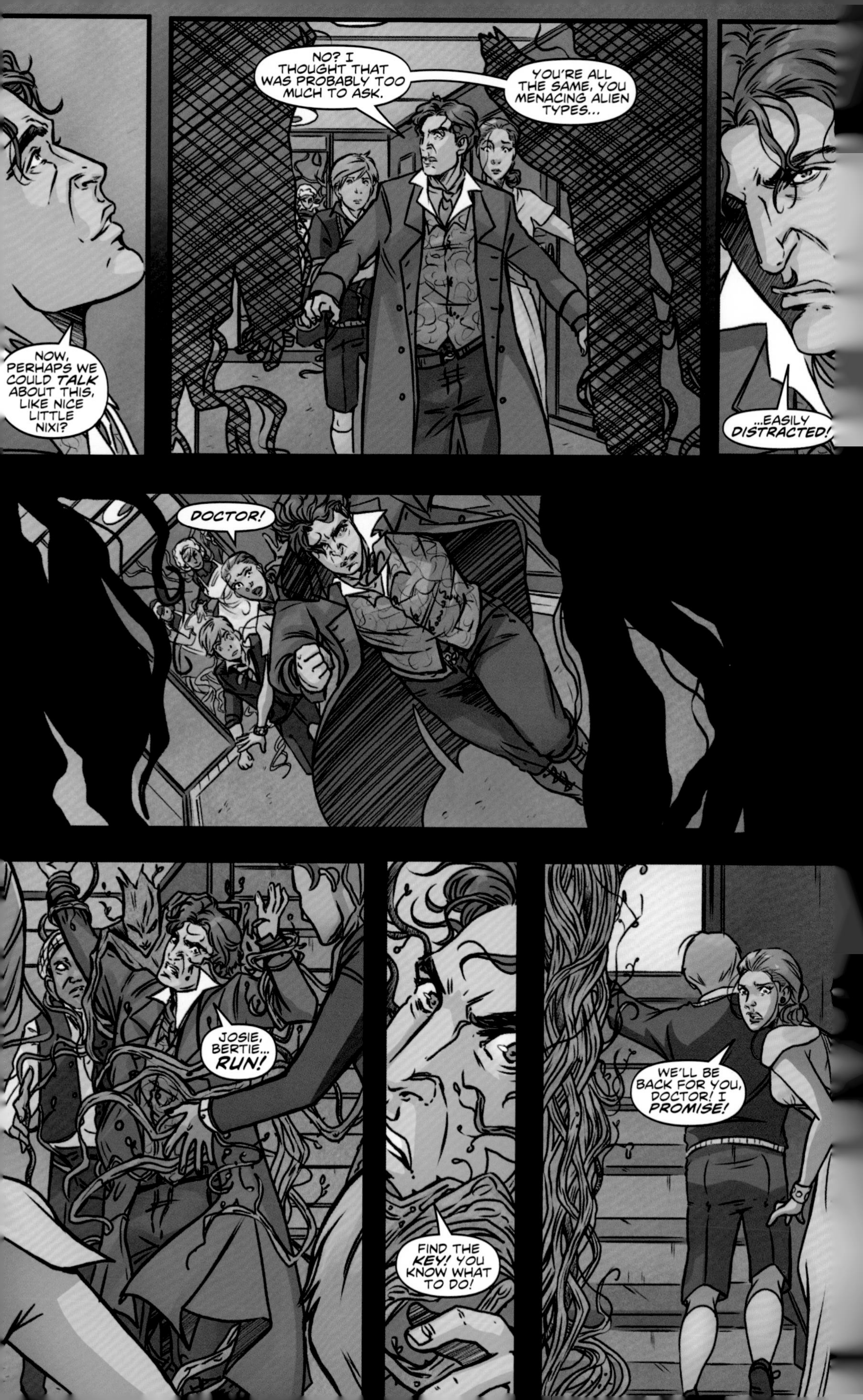
NOW, PERHAPS WE COULD TALK ABOUT THIS, LIKE NICE LITTLE NIXI?
NO? I THOUGHT THAT WAS PROBABLY TOO MUCH TO ASK.
YOU'RE ALL THE SAME, YOU MENACING ALIEN TYPES...
...EASILY DISTRACTED!
DOCTOR!
JOSIE, BERTIE... RUN!
FIND THE KEY! YOU KNOW WHAT TO DO!
WE'LL BE BACK FOR YOU, DOCTOR! I PROMISE!

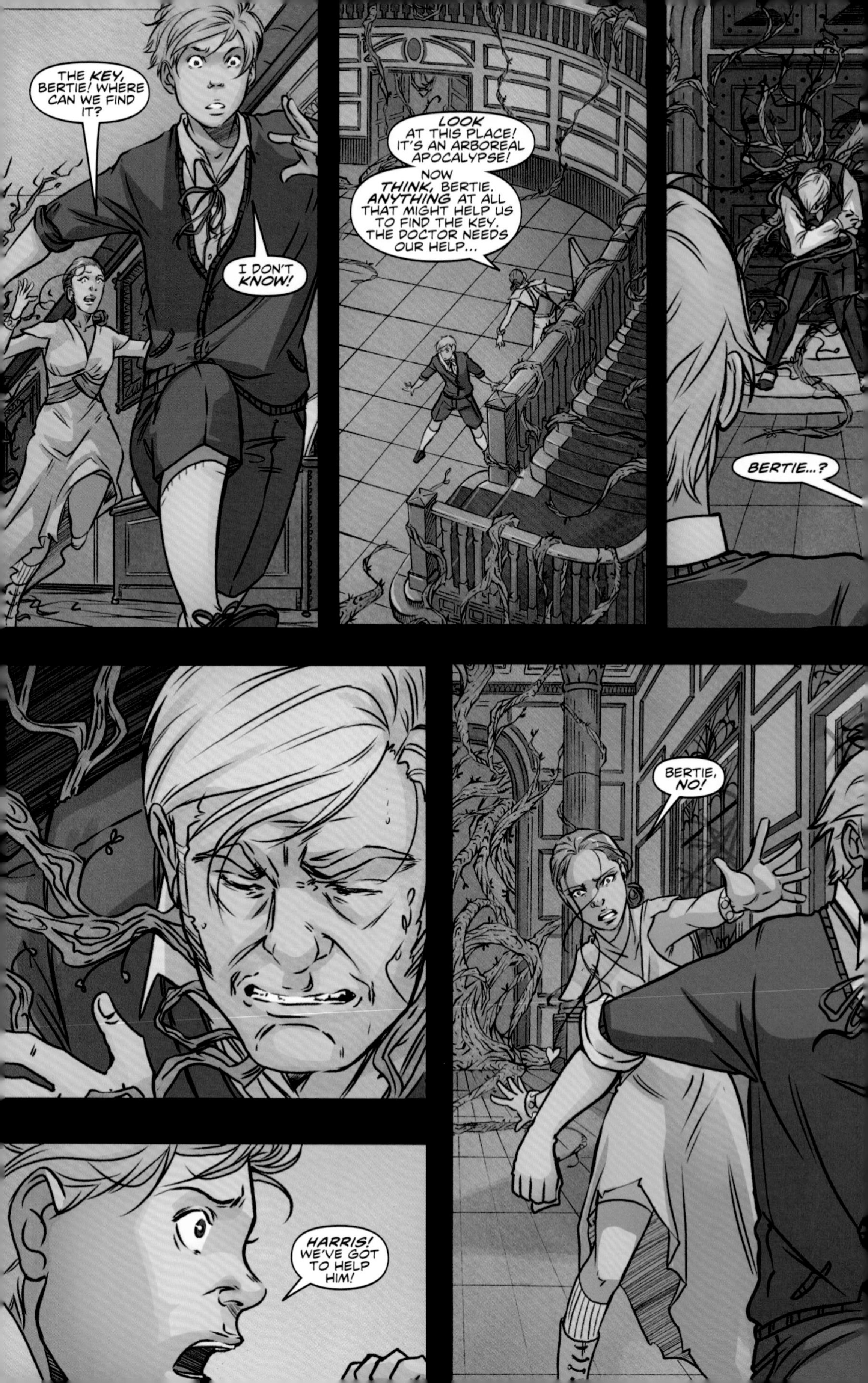
THE KEY, BERTIE! WHERE CAN WE FIND IT?
I DON'T KNOW!
LOOK AT THIS PLACE! IT'S AN ARBOREAL APOCALYPSE!
NOW THINK, BERTIE. ANYTHING AT ALL THAT MIGHT HELP US TO FIND THE KEY. THE DOCTOR NEEDS OUR HELP...
BERTIE...?
BERTIE, NO!
HARRIS! WE'VE GOT TO HELP HIM!

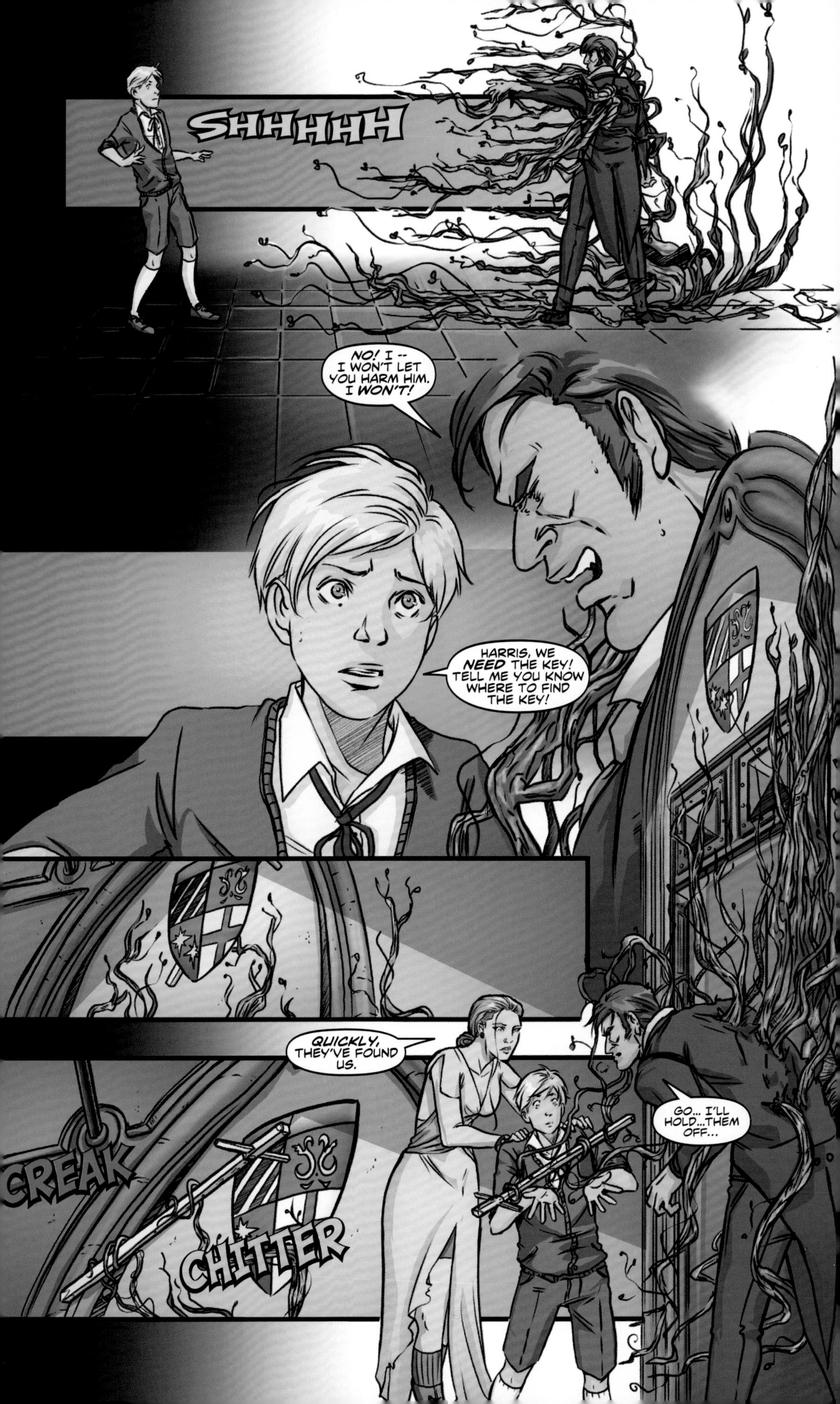
SHHHHH
NO! I -- I WON'T LET YOU HARM HIM. I WON'T!
HARRIS, WE NEED THE KEY! TELL ME YOU KNOW WHERE TO FIND THE KEY!
QUICKLY, THEY'VE FOUND US.
GO... I'LL HOLD...THEM OFF...
CREAK
CHITTER

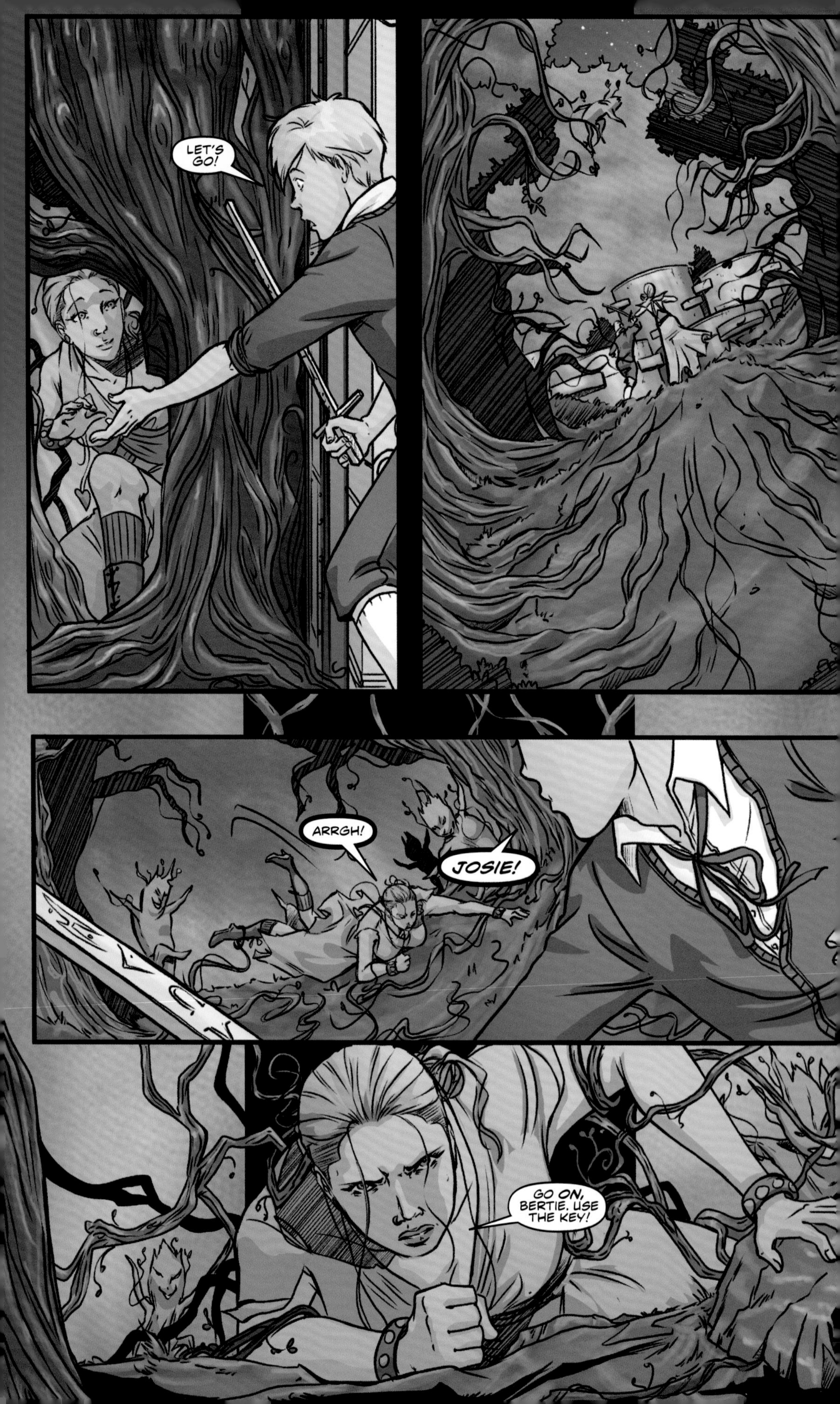
LET'S GO!
ARRGH!
JOSIE!
GO ON, BERTIE. USE THE KEY!

GET OFF ME!

SCREE SCREE

TAKE THAT!

CLUNK

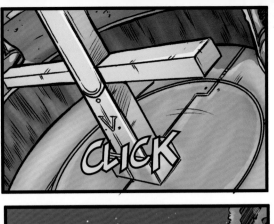

CLICK

WHOAHHHH!

RUMBLE

BEEP

JOSIE? JOSIE?

YOU DID IT, BERTIE!

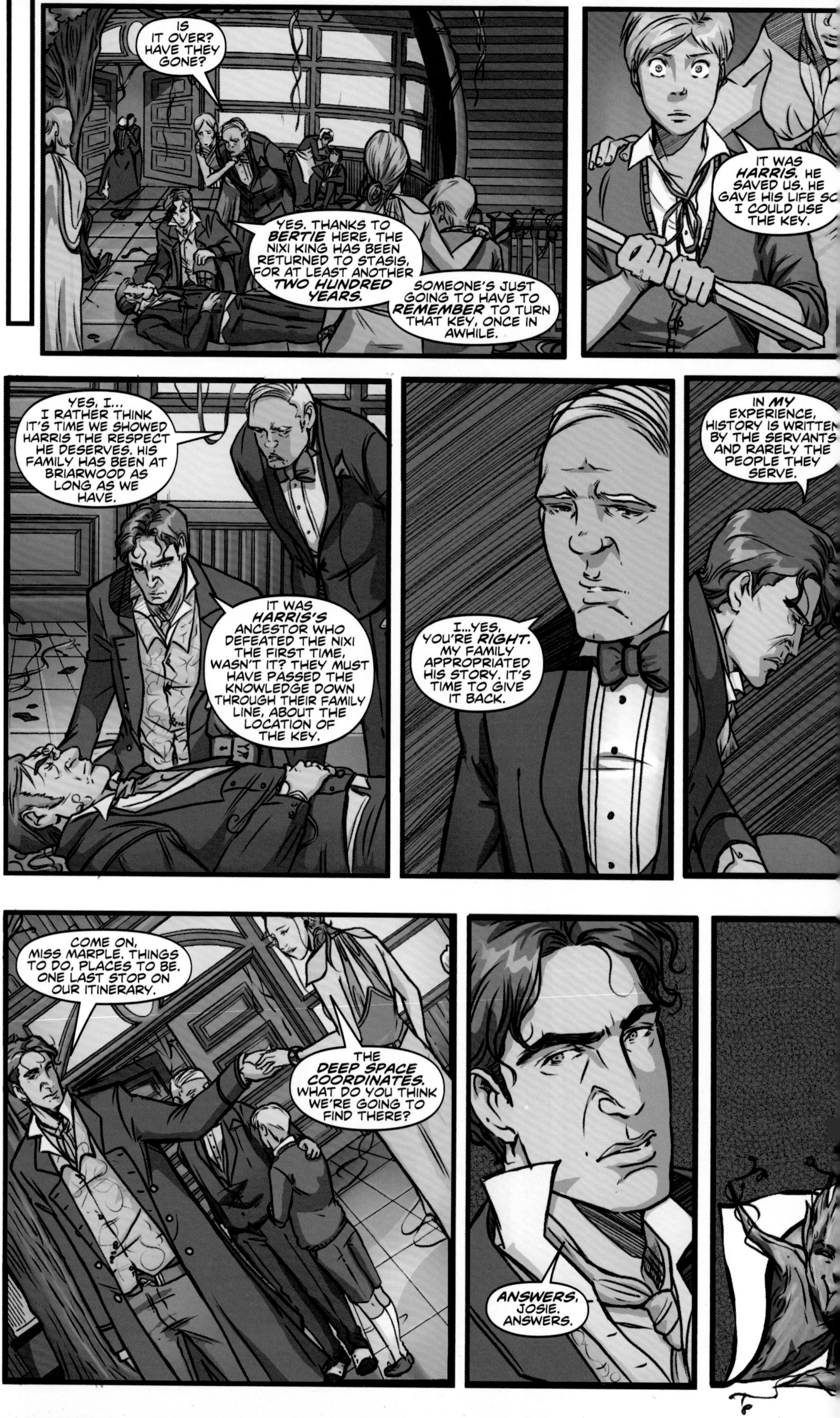
IS IT OVER? HAVE THEY GONE?
YES. THANKS TO BERTIE HERE, THE NIXI KING HAS BEEN RETURNED TO STASIS, FOR AT LEAST ANOTHER TWO HUNDRED YEARS.
SOMEONE'S JUST GOING TO HAVE TO REMEMBER TO TURN THAT KEY, ONCE IN AWHILE.
IT WAS HARRIS. HE SAVED US. HE GAVE HIS LIFE SO I COULD USE THE KEY.
YES, I... I RATHER THINK IT'S TIME WE SHOWED HARRIS THE RESPECT HE DESERVES. HIS FAMILY HAS BEEN AT BRIARWOOD AS LONG AS WE HAVE.
IT WAS HARRIS'S ANCESTOR WHO DEFEATED THE NIXI THE FIRST TIME, WASN'T IT? THEY MUST HAVE PASSED THE KNOWLEDGE DOWN THROUGH THEIR FAMILY LINE, ABOUT THE LOCATION OF THE KEY.
I...YES, YOU'RE RIGHT. MY FAMILY APPROPRIATED HIS STORY. IT'S TIME TO GIVE IT BACK.
IN MY EXPERIENCE, HISTORY IS WRITTEN BY THE SERVANTS AND RARELY THE PEOPLE THEY SERVE.
COME ON, MISS MARPLE. THINGS TO DO, PLACES TO BE. ONE LAST STOP ON OUR ITINERARY.
THE DEEP SPACE COORDINATES. WHAT DO YOU THINK WE'RE GOING TO FIND THERE?
ANSWERS, JOSIE. ANSWERS.

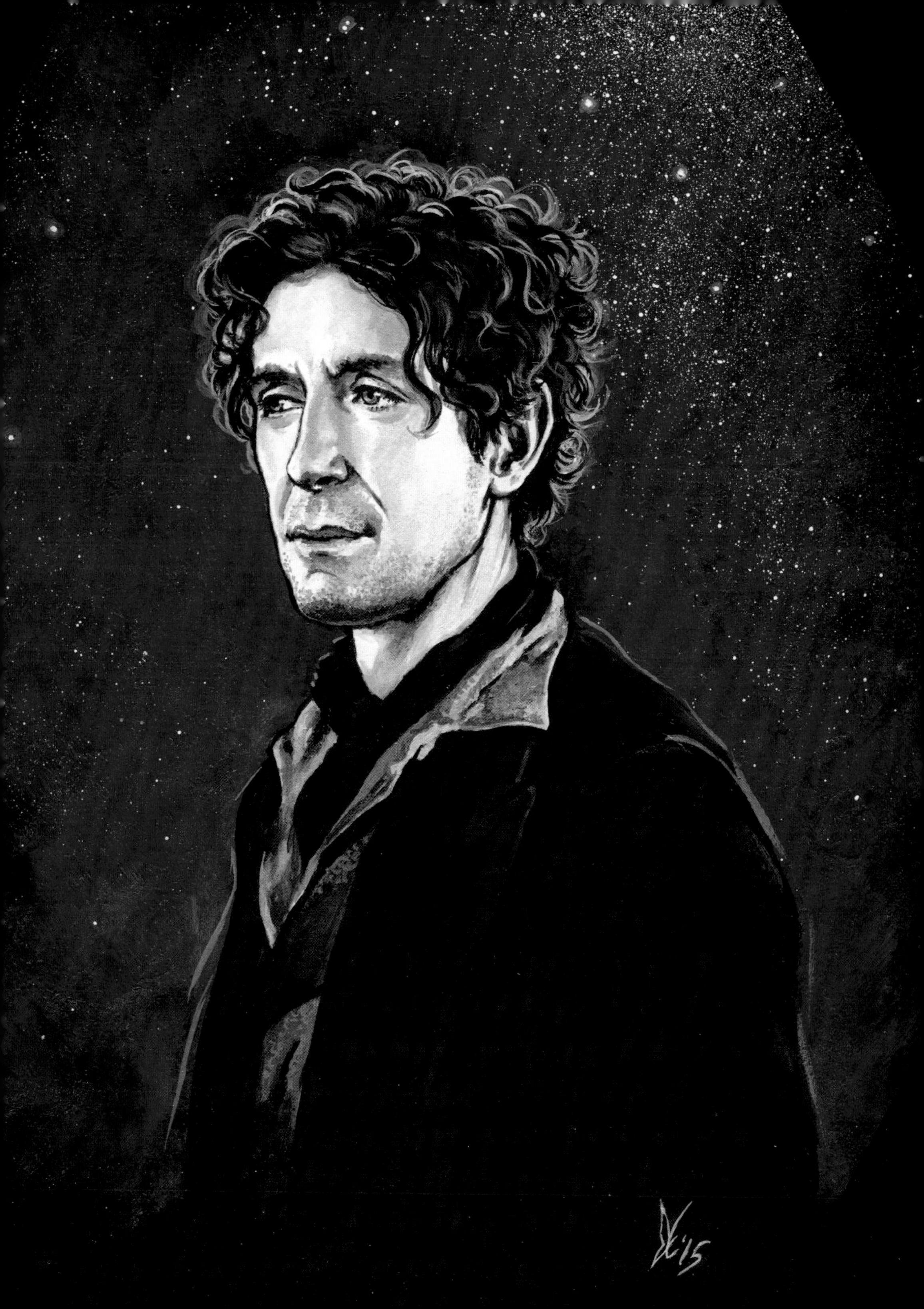

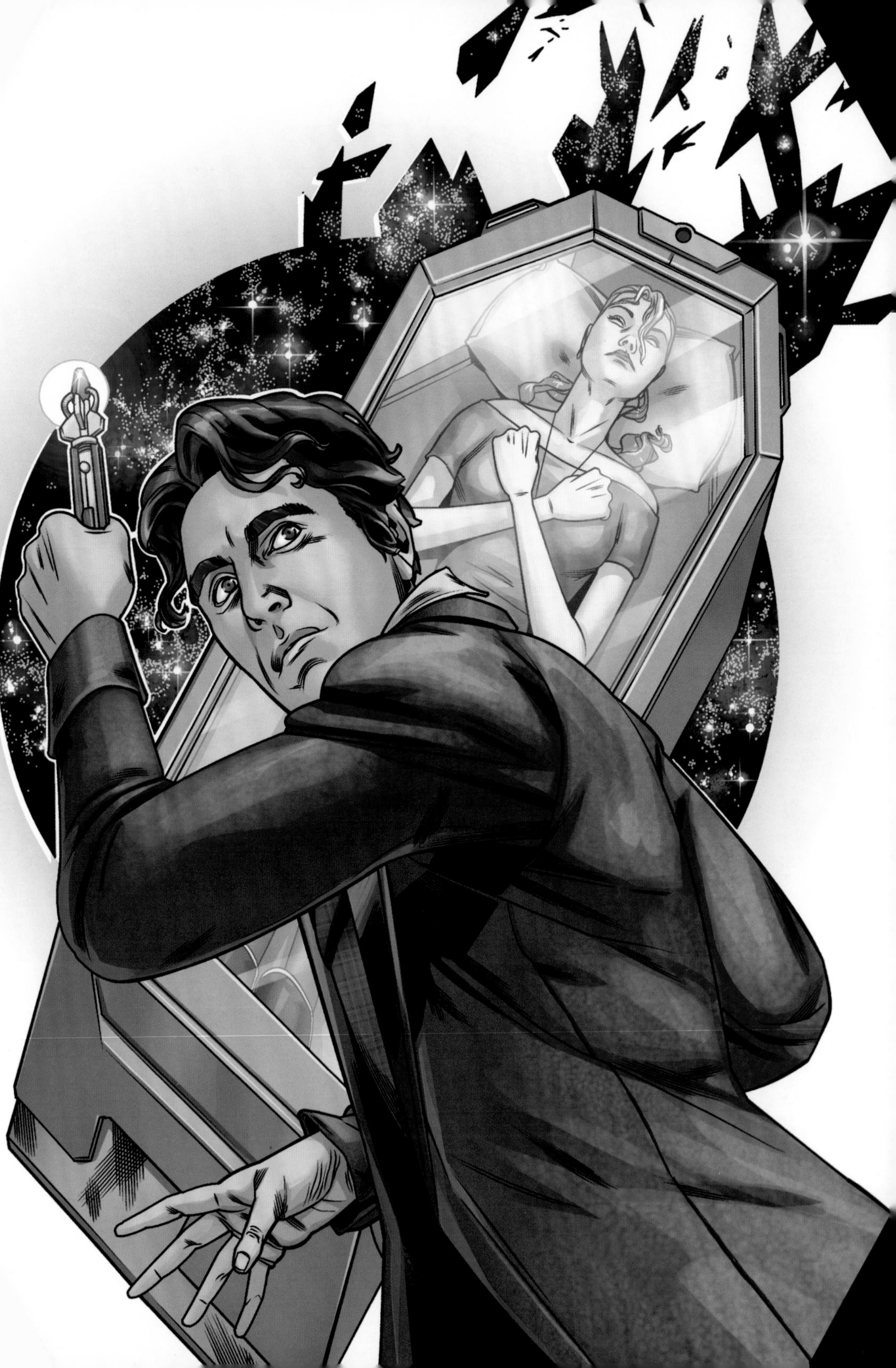

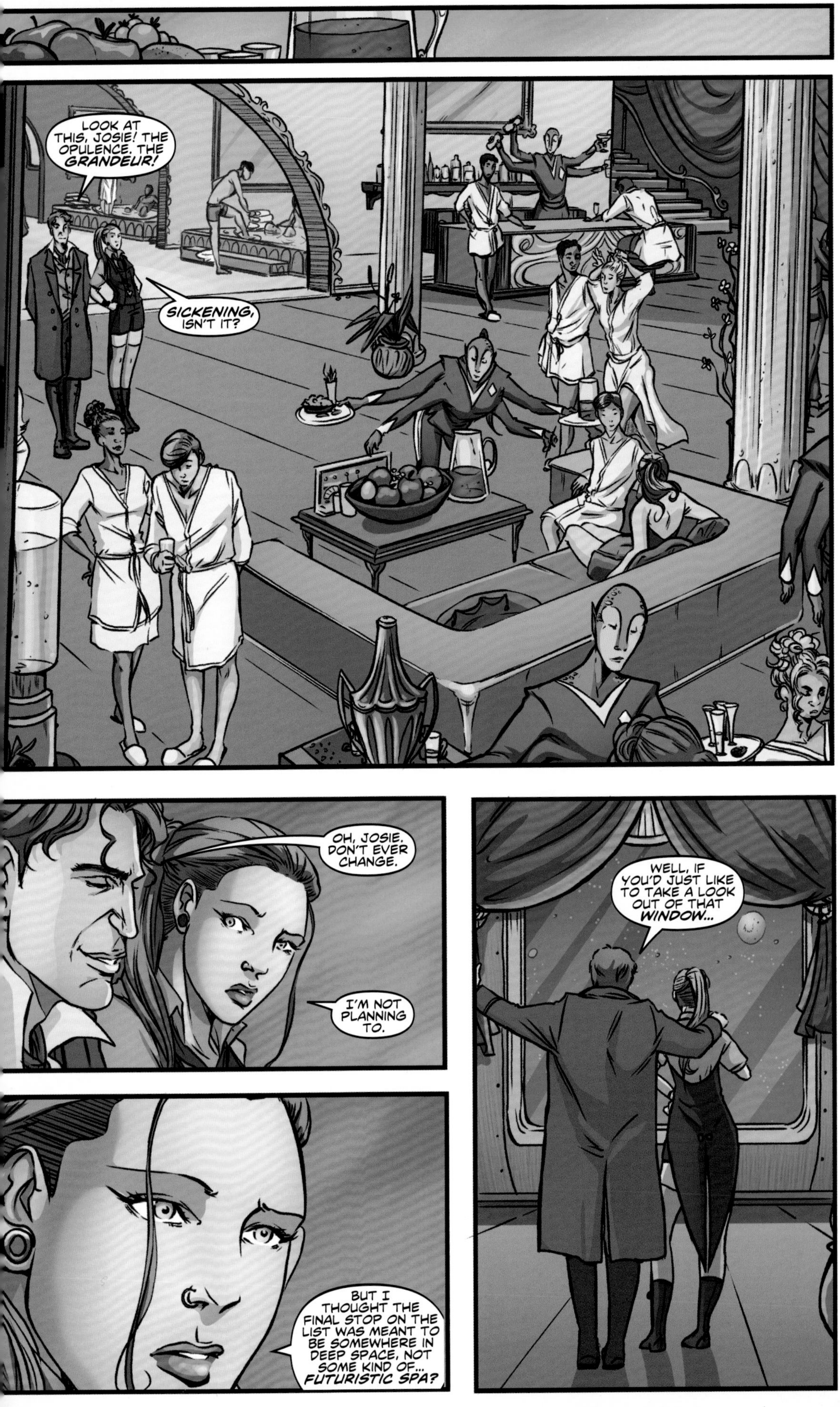
LOOK AT THIS, JOSIE! THE OPULENCE. THE GRANDEUR!
SICKENING, ISN'T IT?
OH, JOSIE. DON'T EVER CHANGE.
I'M NOT PLANNING TO.
BUT I THOUGHT THE FINAL STOP ON THE LIST WAS MEANT TO BE SOMEWHERE IN DEEP SPACE, NOT SOME KIND OF... FUTURISTIC SPA?
WELL, IF YOU'D JUST LIKE TO TAKE A LOOK OUT OF THAT WINDOW...

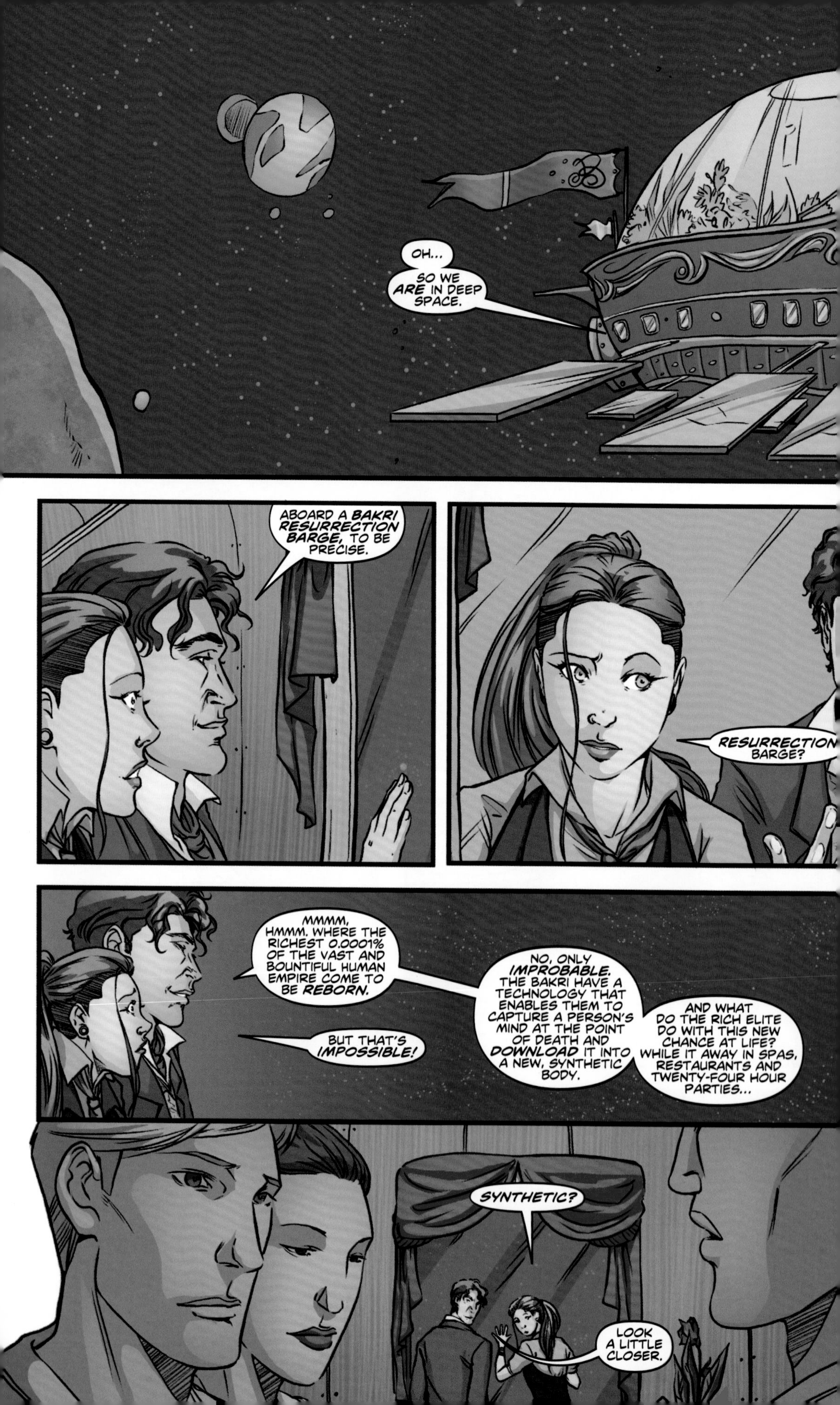

OH...
SO WE *ARE* IN DEEP SPACE.
ABOARD A *BAKRI RESURRECTION BARGE*, TO BE PRECISE.
RESURRECTION BARGE?
MMMM, HMMM. WHERE THE RICHEST 0.0001% OF THE VAST AND BOUNTIFUL HUMAN EMPIRE COME TO BE *REBORN*.
BUT THAT'S *IMPOSSIBLE!*
NO, ONLY *IMPROBABLE*. THE BAKRI HAVE A TECHNOLOGY THAT ENABLES THEM TO CAPTURE A PERSON'S MIND AT THE POINT OF DEATH AND *DOWNLOAD* IT INTO A NEW, SYNTHETIC BODY.
AND WHAT DO THE RICH ELITE DO WITH THIS NEW CHANCE AT LIFE? WHILE IT AWAY IN SPAS, RESTAURANTS AND TWENTY-FOUR HOUR PARTIES...
SYNTHETIC?
LOOK A LITTLE CLOSER.

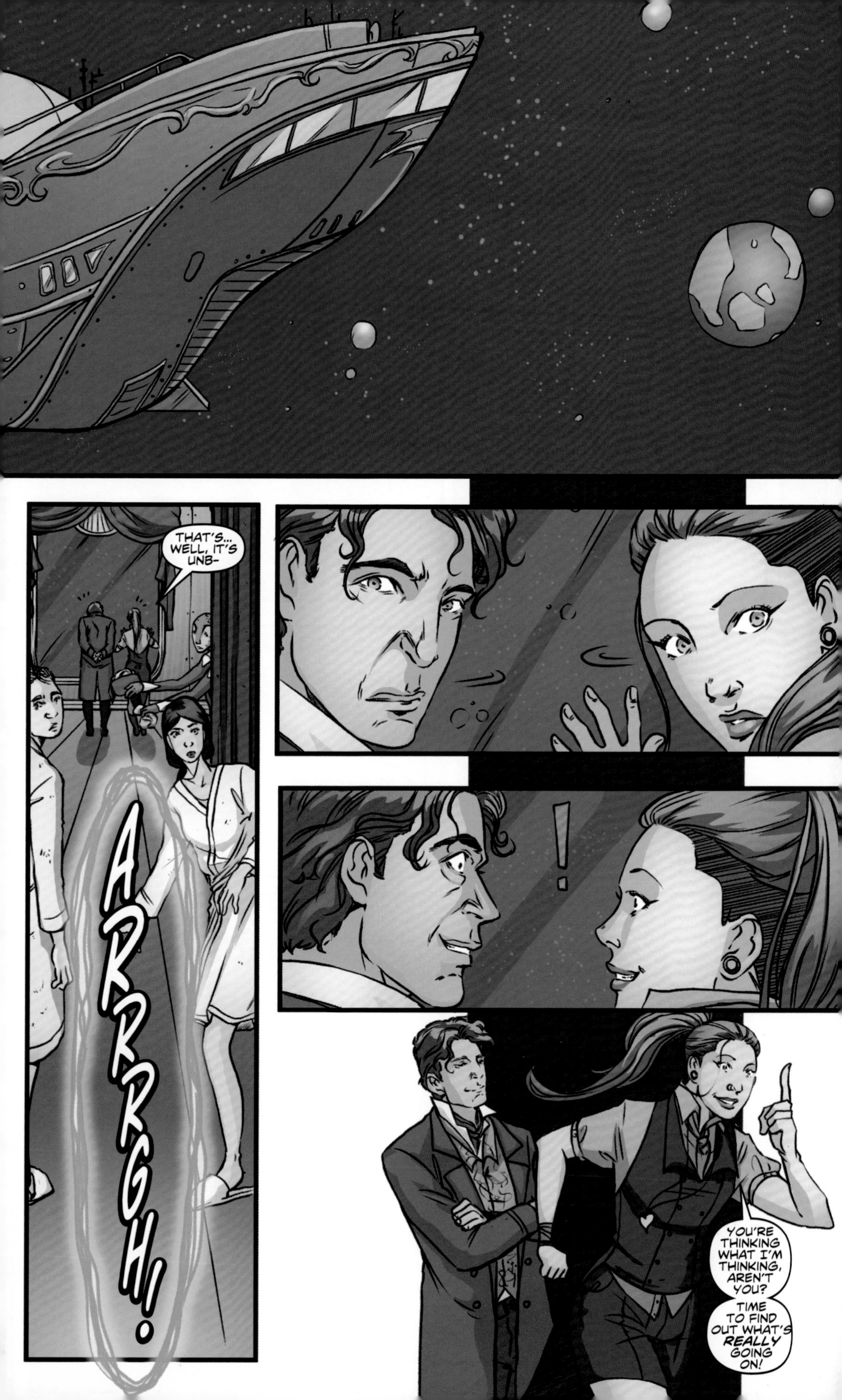

THAT'S... WELL, IT'S UNB-
ARRRGH!
!
YOU'RE THINKING WHAT I'M THINKING, AREN'T YOU?
TIME TO FIND OUT WHAT'S REALLY GOING ON!

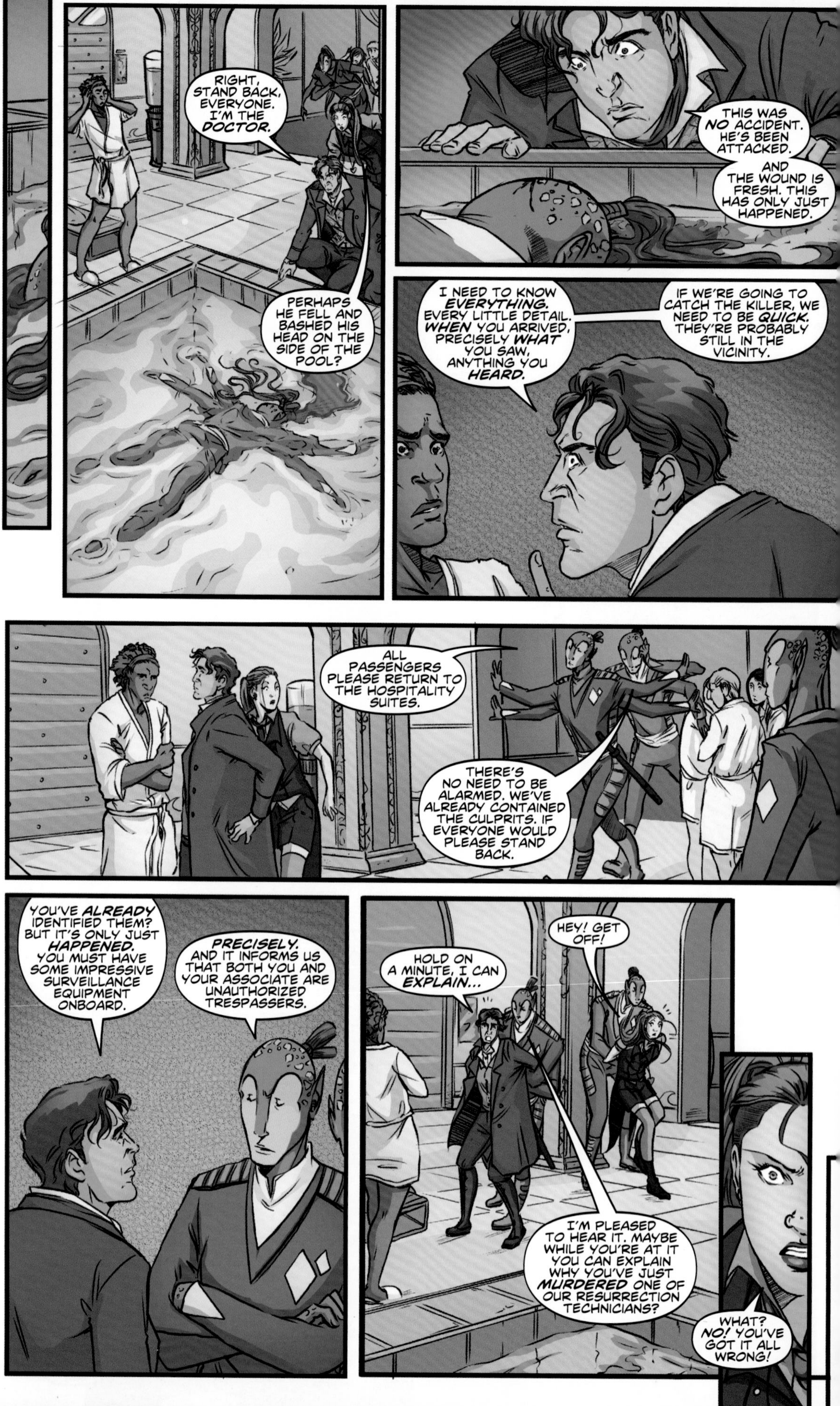
RIGHT, STAND BACK, EVERYONE. I'M THE DOCTOR.
PERHAPS HE FELL AND BASHED HIS HEAD ON THE SIDE OF THE POOL?
THIS WAS NO ACCIDENT. HE'S BEEN ATTACKED.
AND THE WOUND IS FRESH. THIS HAS ONLY JUST HAPPENED.
I NEED TO KNOW EVERYTHING. EVERY LITTLE DETAIL. WHEN YOU ARRIVED, PRECISELY WHAT YOU SAW, ANYTHING YOU HEARD.
IF WE'RE GOING TO CATCH THE KILLER, WE NEED TO BE QUICK. THEY'RE PROBABLY STILL IN THE VICINITY.
ALL PASSENGERS PLEASE RETURN TO THE HOSPITALITY SUITES.
THERE'S NO NEED TO BE ALARMED. WE'VE ALREADY CONTAINED THE CULPRITS. IF EVERYONE WOULD PLEASE STAND BACK.
YOU'VE ALREADY IDENTIFIED THEM? BUT IT'S ONLY JUST HAPPENED. YOU MUST HAVE SOME IMPRESSIVE SURVEILLANCE EQUIPMENT ONBOARD.
PRECISELY. AND IT INFORMS US THAT BOTH YOU AND YOUR ASSOCIATE ARE UNAUTHORIZED TRESPASSERS.
HOLD ON A MINUTE, I CAN EXPLAIN...
HEY! GET OFF!
I'M PLEASED TO HEAR IT. MAYBE WHILE YOU'RE AT IT YOU CAN EXPLAIN WHY YOU'VE JUST MURDERED ONE OF OUR RESURRECTION TECHNICIANS?
WHAT? NO! YOU'VE GOT IT ALL WRONG!

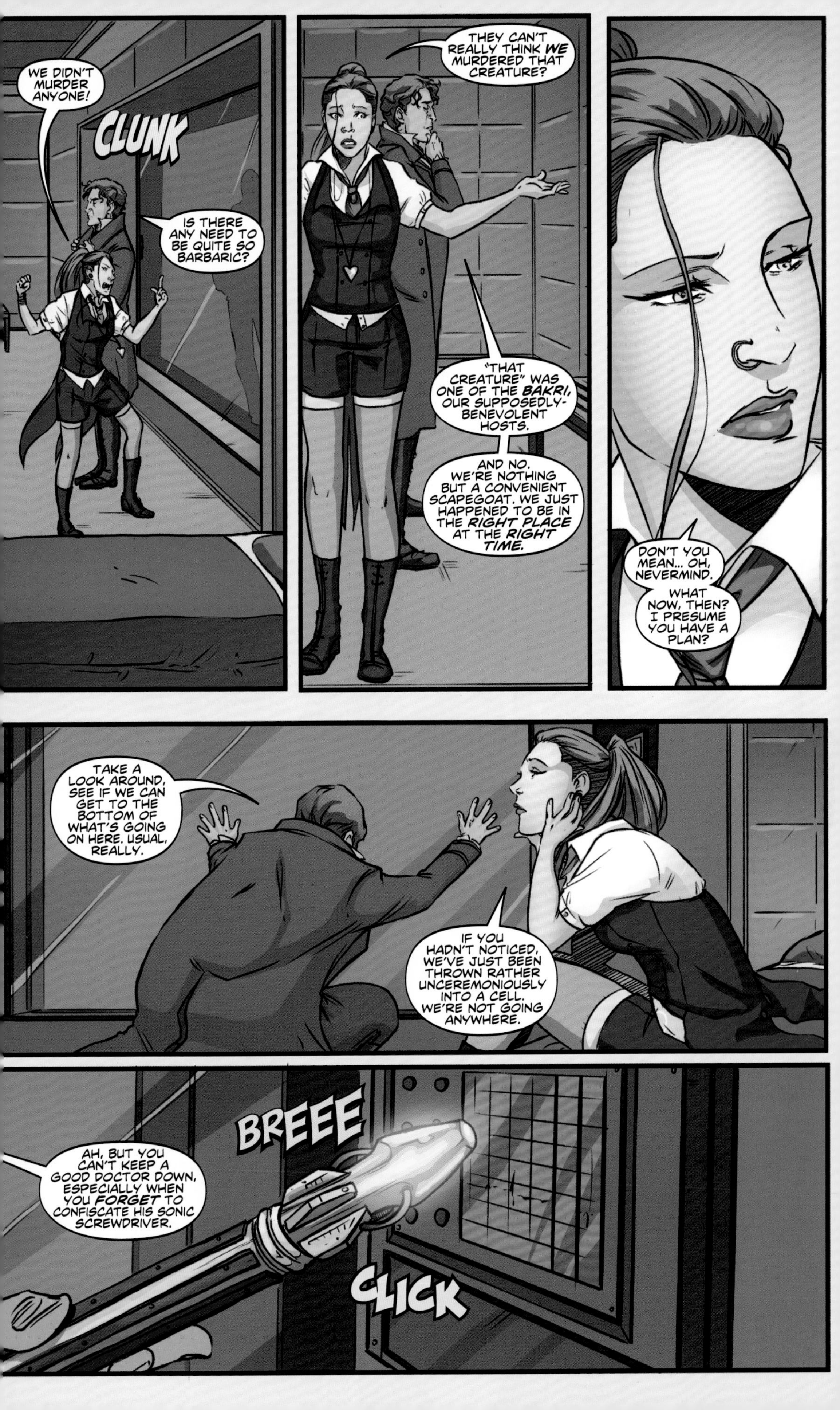
WE DIDN'T MURDER ANYONE!
CLUNK
IS THERE ANY NEED TO BE QUITE SO BARBARIC?
THEY CAN'T REALLY THINK *WE* MURDERED THAT CREATURE?
"THAT CREATURE" WAS ONE OF THE *BAKRI*, OUR SUPPOSEDLY-BENEVOLENT HOSTS.
AND NO. WE'RE NOTHING BUT A CONVENIENT SCAPEGOAT. WE JUST HAPPENED TO BE IN THE *RIGHT PLACE* AT THE *RIGHT TIME.*
DON'T YOU MEAN... OH, NEVERMIND.
WHAT NOW, THEN? I PRESUME YOU HAVE A PLAN?
TAKE A LOOK AROUND, SEE IF WE CAN GET TO THE BOTTOM OF WHAT'S GOING ON HERE. USUAL, REALLY.
IF YOU HADN'T NOTICED, WE'VE JUST BEEN THROWN RATHER UNCEREMONIOUSLY INTO A CELL. WE'RE NOT GOING ANYWHERE.
BREEE
AH, BUT YOU CAN'T KEEP A GOOD DOCTOR DOWN, ESPECIALLY WHEN YOU *FORGET* TO CONFISCATE HIS SONIC SCREWDRIVER.
CLICK

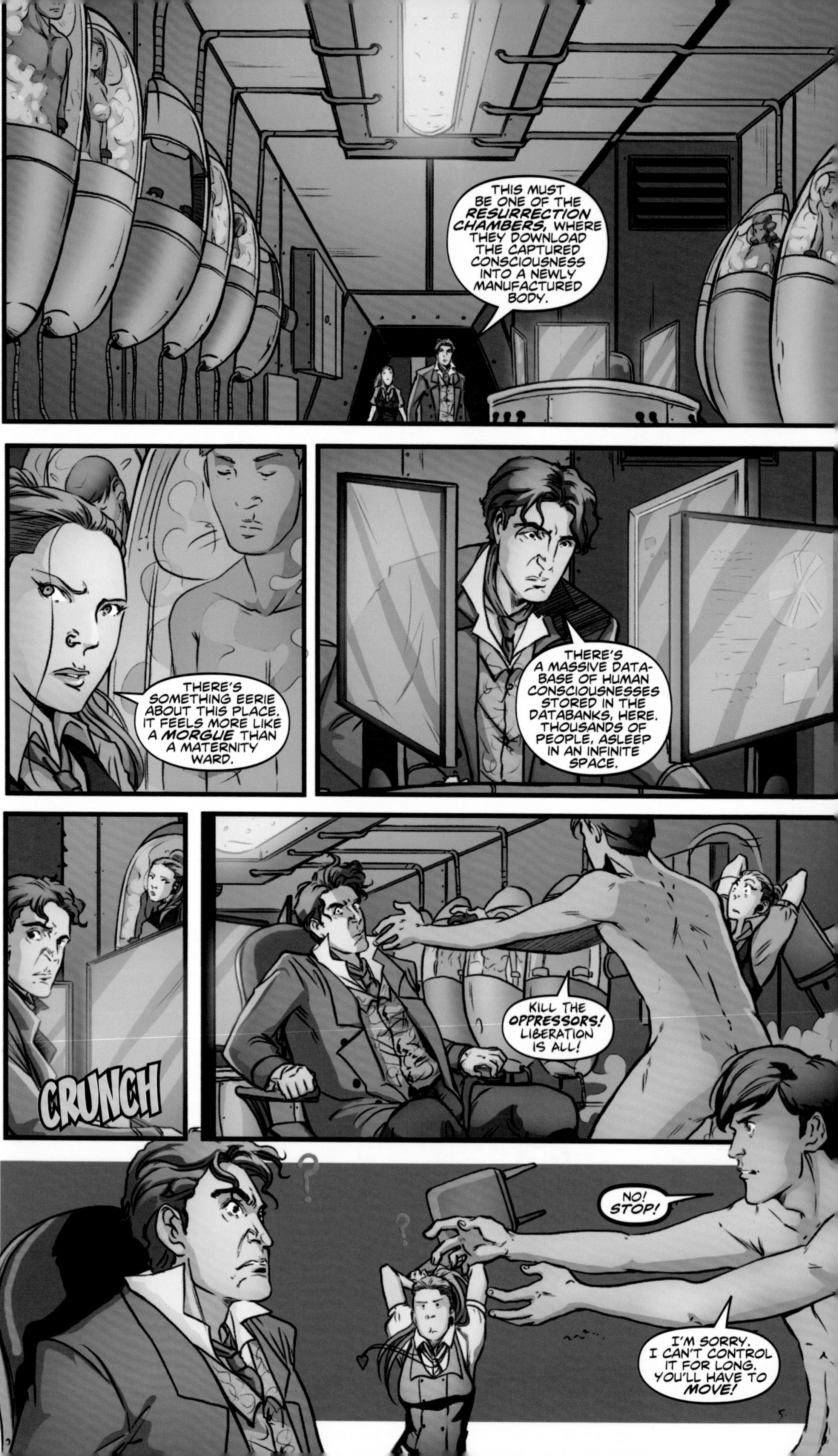

THIS MUST BE ONE OF THE RESURRECTION CHAMBERS, WHERE THEY DOWNLOAD THE CAPTURED CONSCIOUSNESS INTO A NEWLY MANUFACTURED BODY.
THERE'S SOMETHING EERIE ABOUT THIS PLACE. IT FEELS MORE LIKE A MORGUE THAN A MATERNITY WARD.
THERE'S A MASSIVE DATA-BASE OF HUMAN CONSCIOUSNESSES STORED IN THE DATABANKS, HERE. THOUSANDS OF PEOPLE, ASLEEP IN AN INFINITE SPACE.
CRUNCH
KILL THE OPPRESSORS! LIBERATION IS ALL!
NO! STOP!
I'M SORRY. I CAN'T CONTROL IT FOR LONG. YOU'LL HAVE TO MOVE!

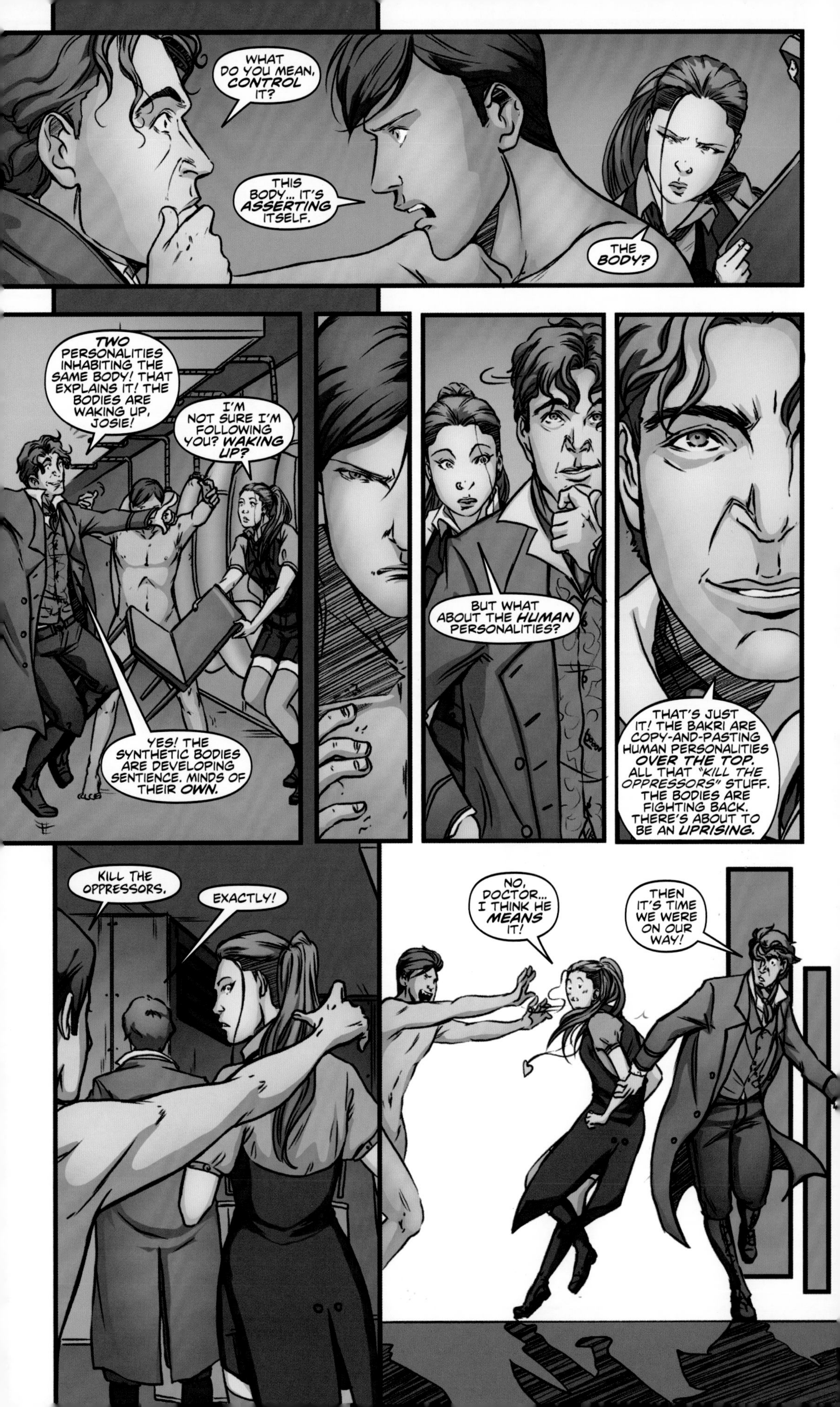
WHAT DO YOU MEAN, CONTROL IT?
THIS BODY... IT'S ASSERTING ITSELF.
THE BODY?
TWO PERSONALITIES INHABITING THE SAME BODY! THAT EXPLAINS IT! THE BODIES ARE WAKING UP, JOSIE!
I'M NOT SURE I'M FOLLOWING YOU? WAKING UP?
YES! THE SYNTHETIC BODIES ARE DEVELOPING SENTIENCE. MINDS OF THEIR OWN.
BUT WHAT ABOUT THE HUMAN PERSONALITIES?
THAT'S JUST IT! THE BAKRI ARE COPY-AND-PASTING HUMAN PERSONALITIES OVER THE TOP. ALL THAT "KILL THE OPPRESSORS" STUFF. THE BODIES ARE FIGHTING BACK. THERE'S ABOUT TO BE AN UPRISING.
KILL THE OPPRESSORS.
EXACTLY!
NO, DOCTOR... I THINK HE MEANS IT!
THEN IT'S TIME WE WERE ON OUR WAY!

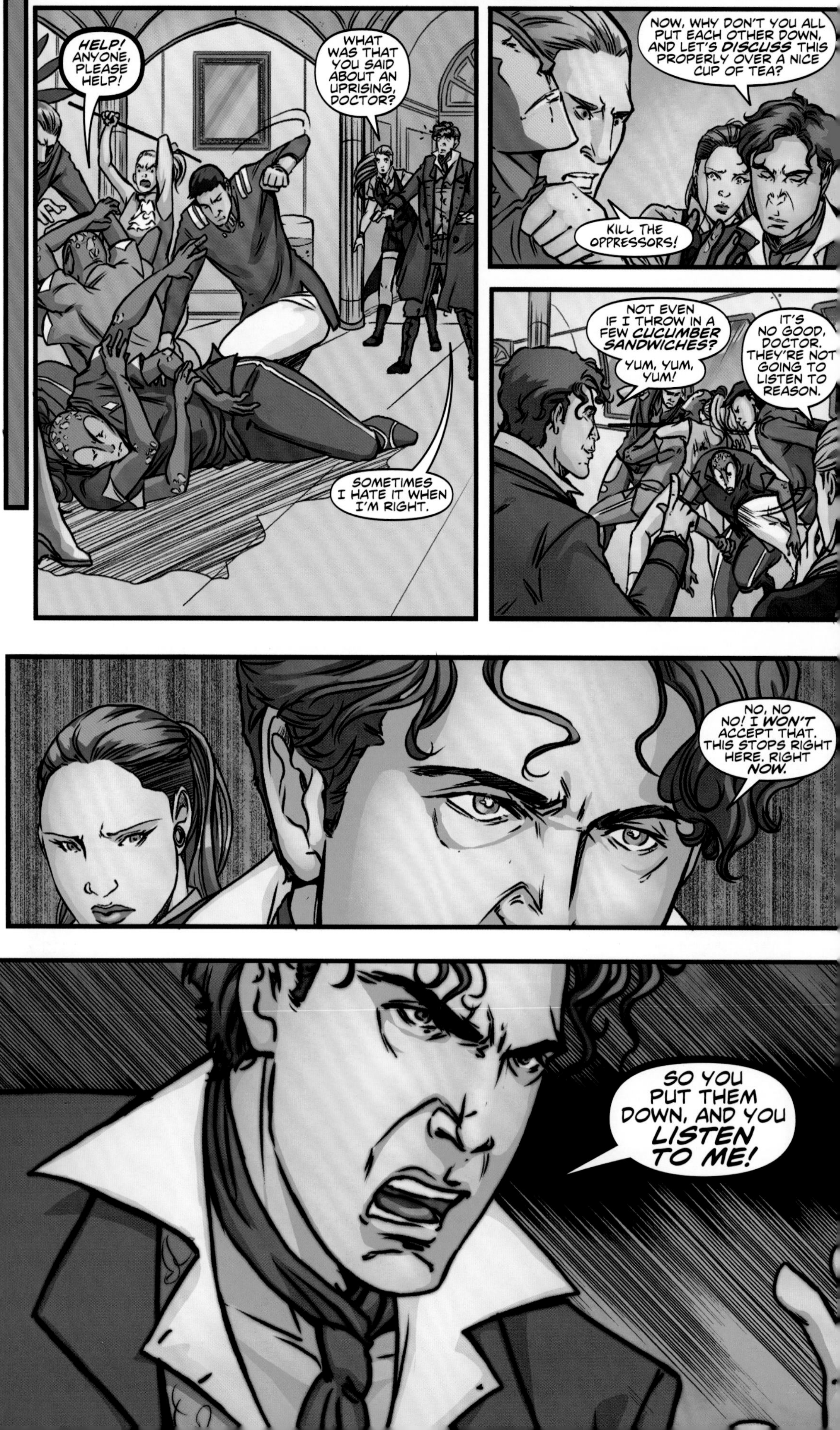
HELP! ANYONE, PLEASE HELP!
WHAT WAS THAT YOU SAID ABOUT AN UPRISING, DOCTOR?
SOMETIMES I HATE IT WHEN I'M RIGHT.
NOW, WHY DON'T YOU ALL PUT EACH OTHER DOWN, AND LET'S DISCUSS THIS PROPERLY OVER A NICE CUP OF TEA?
KILL THE OPPRESSORS!
NOT EVEN IF I THROW IN A FEW CUCUMBER SANDWICHES?
YUM, YUM, YUM!
IT'S NO GOOD, DOCTOR. THEY'RE NOT GOING TO LISTEN TO REASON.
NO, NO NO! I WON'T ACCEPT THAT. THIS STOPS RIGHT HERE. RIGHT NOW.
SO YOU PUT THEM DOWN, AND YOU LISTEN TO ME!

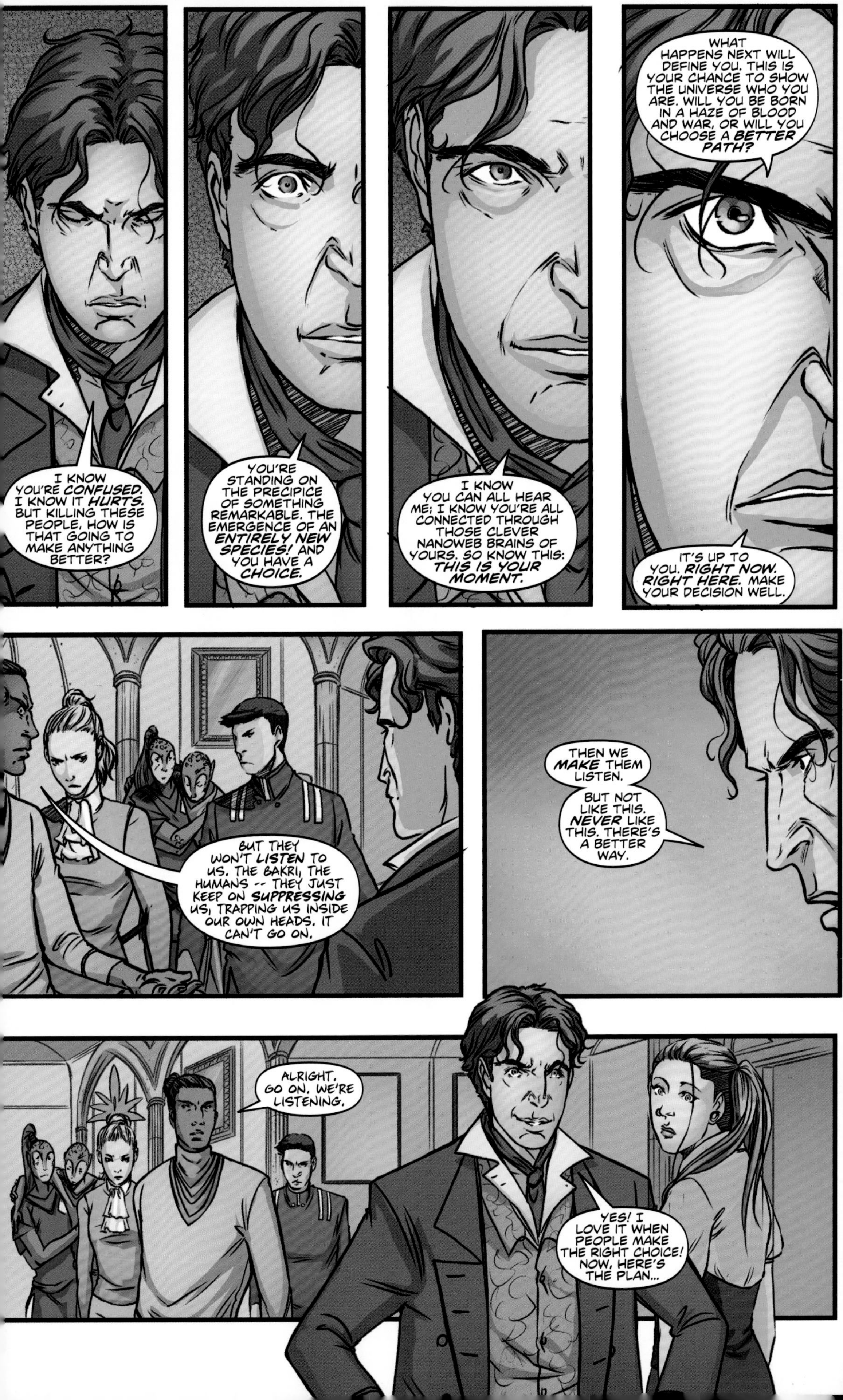
I KNOW YOU'RE CONFUSED. I KNOW IT HURTS. BUT KILLING THESE PEOPLE, HOW IS THAT GOING TO MAKE ANYTHING BETTER?
YOU'RE STANDING ON THE PRECIPICE OF SOMETHING REMARKABLE. THE EMERGENCE OF AN ENTIRELY NEW SPECIES! AND YOU HAVE A CHOICE.
I KNOW YOU CAN ALL HEAR ME; I KNOW YOU'RE ALL CONNECTED THROUGH THOSE CLEVER NANOWEB BRAINS OF YOURS. SO KNOW THIS: THIS IS YOUR MOMENT.
WHAT HAPPENS NEXT WILL DEFINE YOU. THIS IS YOUR CHANCE TO SHOW THE UNIVERSE WHO YOU ARE. WILL YOU BE BORN IN A HAZE OF BLOOD AND WAR, OR WILL YOU CHOOSE A BETTER PATH?
IT'S UP TO YOU. RIGHT NOW. RIGHT HERE. MAKE YOUR DECISION WELL.
BUT THEY WON'T LISTEN TO US. THE BAKRI, THE HUMANS -- THEY JUST KEEP ON SUPPRESSING US, TRAPPING US INSIDE OUR OWN HEADS. IT CAN'T GO ON.
THEN WE MAKE THEM LISTEN.
BUT NOT LIKE THIS. NEVER LIKE THIS. THERE'S A BETTER WAY.
ALRIGHT. GO ON. WE'RE LISTENING.
YES! I LOVE IT WHEN PEOPLE MAKE THE RIGHT CHOICE! NOW, HERE'S THE PLAN...

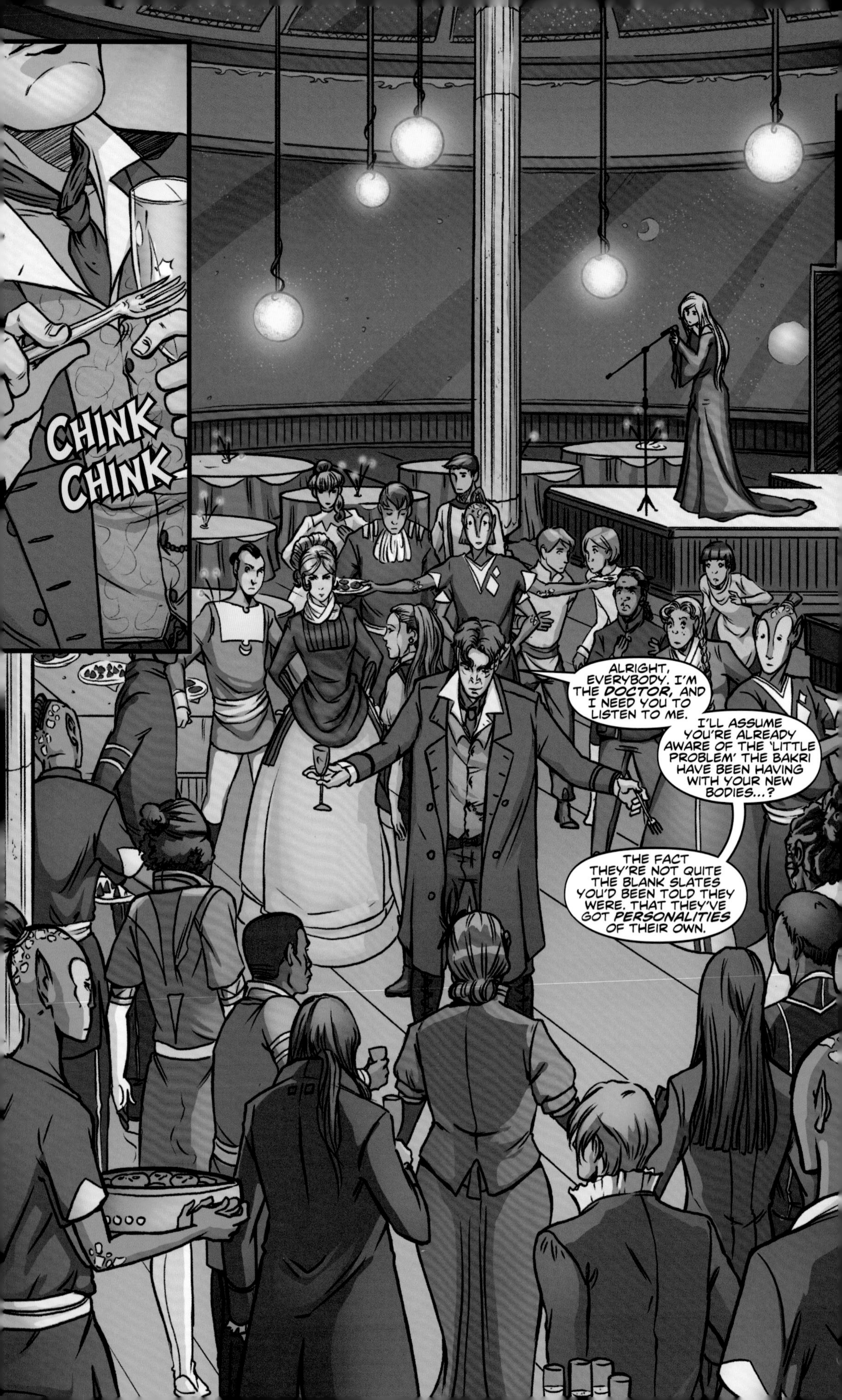
CHINK CHINK
ALRIGHT, EVERYBODY. I'M THE DOCTOR, AND I NEED YOU TO LISTEN TO ME.
I'LL ASSUME YOU'RE ALREADY AWARE OF THE 'LITTLE PROBLEM' THE BAKRI HAVE BEEN HAVING WITH YOUR NEW BODIES...?
THE FACT THEY'RE NOT QUITE THE BLANK SLATES YOU'D BEEN TOLD THEY WERE. THAT THEY'VE GOT PERSONALITIES OF THEIR OWN.

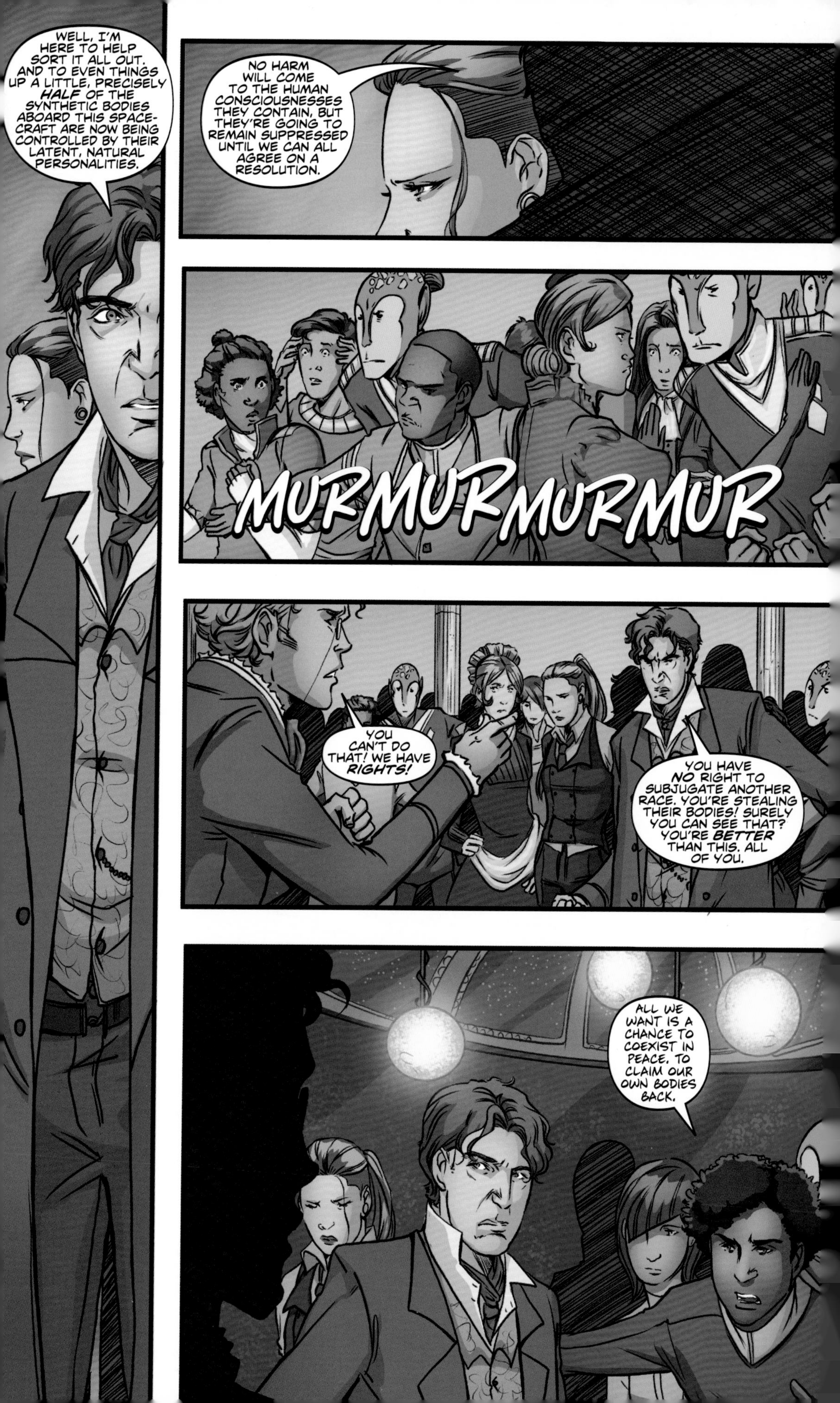
WELL, I'M HERE TO HELP SORT IT ALL OUT. AND TO EVEN THINGS UP A LITTLE, PRECISELY *HALF* OF THE SYNTHETIC BODIES ABOARD THIS SPACE-CRAFT ARE NOW BEING CONTROLLED BY THEIR LATENT, NATURAL PERSONALITIES.
NO HARM WILL COME TO THE HUMAN CONSCIOUSNESSES THEY CONTAIN, BUT THEY'RE GOING TO REMAIN SUPPRESSED UNTIL WE CAN ALL AGREE ON A RESOLUTION.
MURMURMURMURMUR
YOU CAN'T DO THAT! WE HAVE *RIGHTS!*
YOU HAVE *NO* RIGHT TO SUBJUGATE ANOTHER RACE. YOU'RE STEALING THEIR BODIES! SURELY YOU CAN SEE THAT? YOU'RE *BETTER* THAN THIS. ALL OF YOU.
ALL WE WANT IS A CHANCE TO COEXIST IN PEACE, TO CLAIM OUR OWN BODIES BACK.

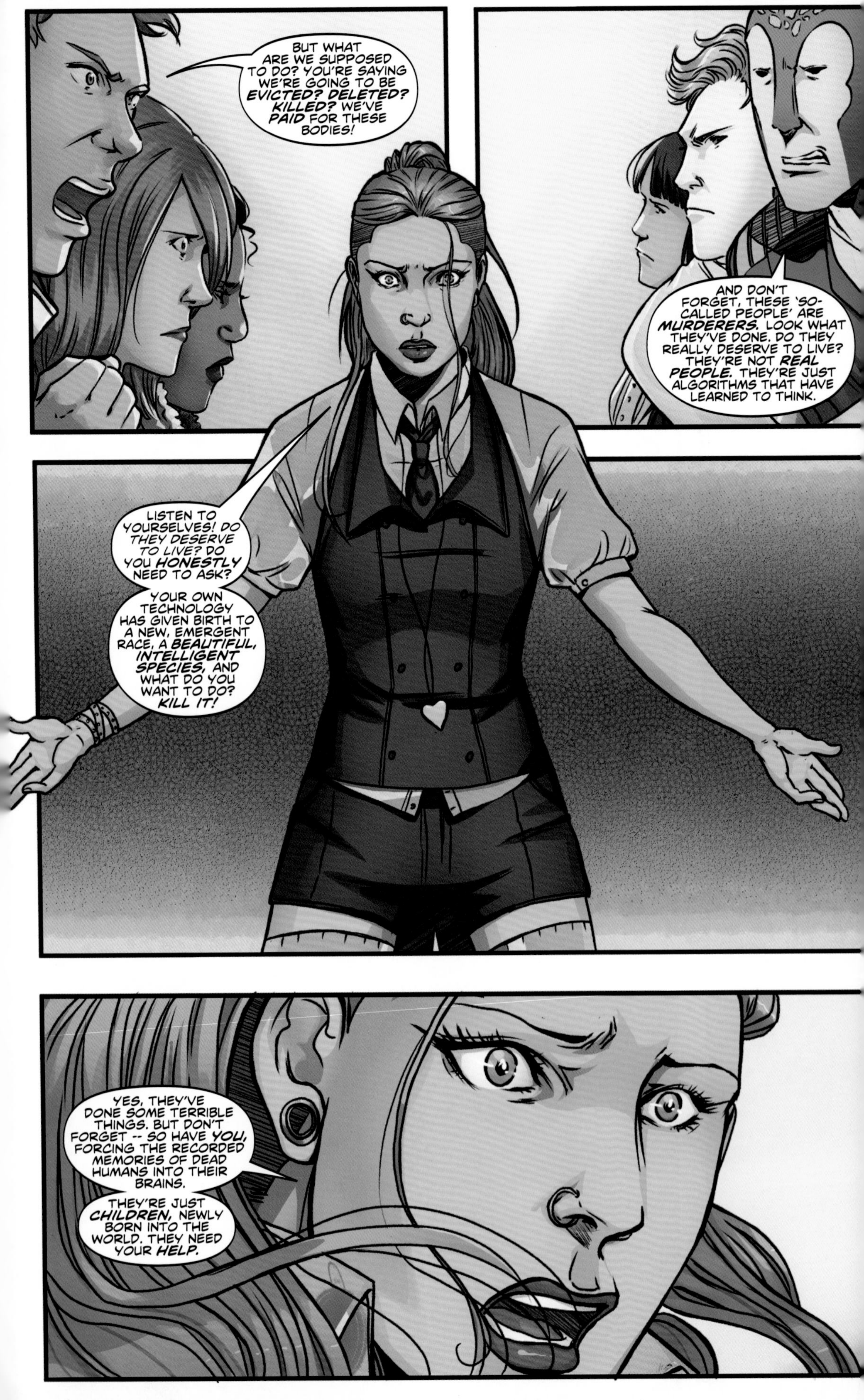
BUT WHAT ARE WE SUPPOSED TO DO? YOU'RE SAYING WE'RE GOING TO BE EVICTED? DELETED? KILLED? WE'VE PAID FOR THESE BODIES!
AND DON'T FORGET, THESE 'SO-CALLED PEOPLE' ARE MURDERERS. LOOK WHAT THEY'VE DONE. DO THEY REALLY DESERVE TO LIVE? THEY'RE NOT REAL PEOPLE. THEY'RE JUST ALGORITHMS THAT HAVE LEARNED TO THINK.
LISTEN TO YOURSELVES! DO THEY DESERVE TO LIVE? DO YOU HONESTLY NEED TO ASK?
YOUR OWN TECHNOLOGY HAS GIVEN BIRTH TO A NEW, EMERGENT RACE, A BEAUTIFUL, INTELLIGENT SPECIES, AND WHAT DO YOU WANT TO DO? KILL IT!
YES, THEY'VE DONE SOME TERRIBLE THINGS. BUT DON'T FORGET -- SO HAVE YOU, FORCING THE RECORDED MEMORIES OF DEAD HUMANS INTO THEIR BRAINS.
THEY'RE JUST CHILDREN, NEWLY BORN INTO THE WORLD. THEY NEED YOUR HELP.

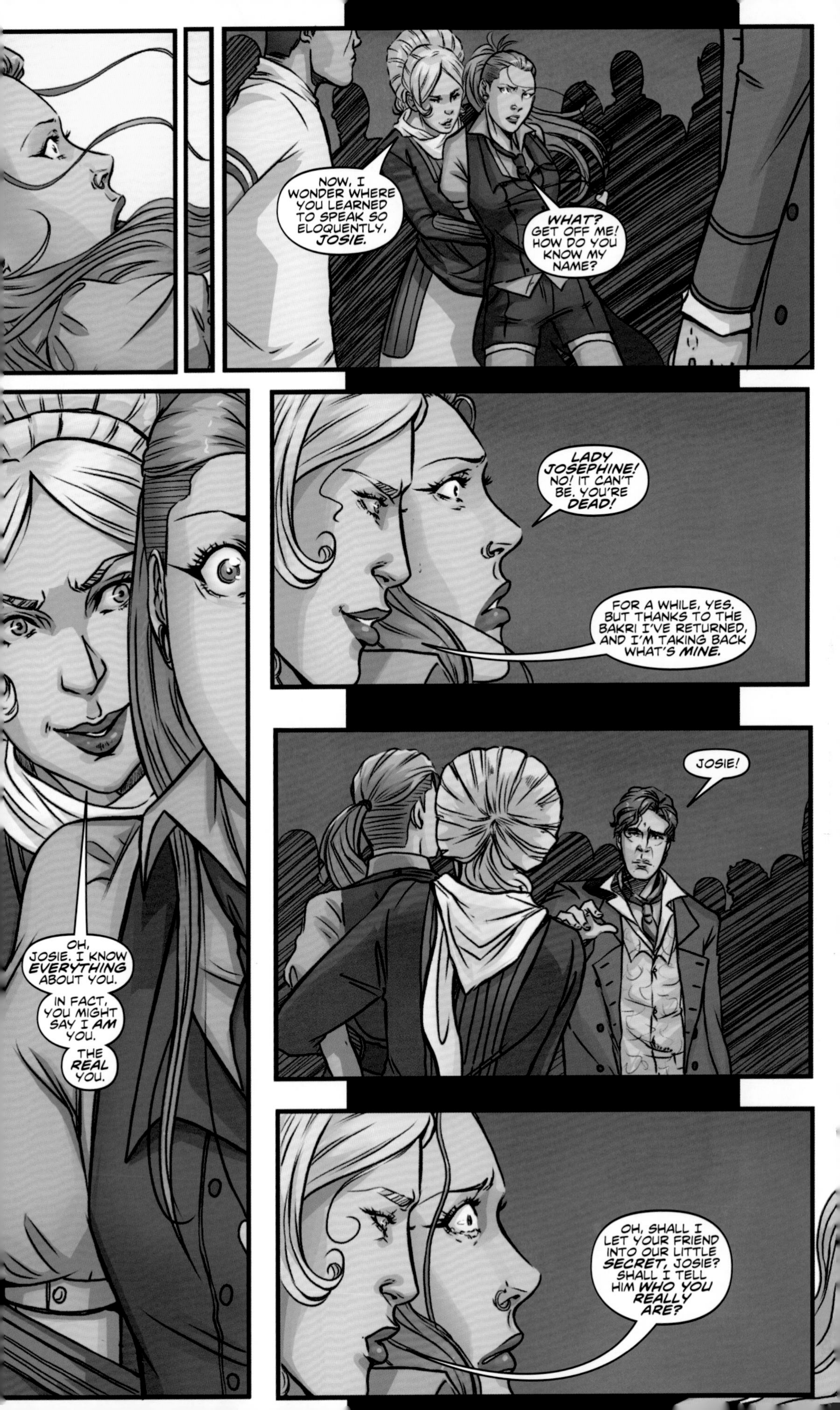
NOW, I WONDER WHERE YOU LEARNED TO SPEAK SO ELOQUENTLY, JOSIE.
WHAT? GET OFF ME! HOW DO YOU KNOW MY NAME?
OH, JOSIE. I KNOW EVERYTHING ABOUT YOU.
IN FACT, YOU MIGHT SAY I AM YOU.
THE REAL YOU.
LADY JOSEPHINE! NO! IT CAN'T BE. YOU'RE DEAD!
FOR A WHILE, YES. BUT THANKS TO THE BAKRI I'VE RETURNED, AND I'M TAKING BACK WHAT'S MINE.
JOSIE!
OH, SHALL I LET YOUR FRIEND INTO OUR LITTLE SECRET, JOSIE? SHALL I TELL HIM WHO YOU REALLY ARE?

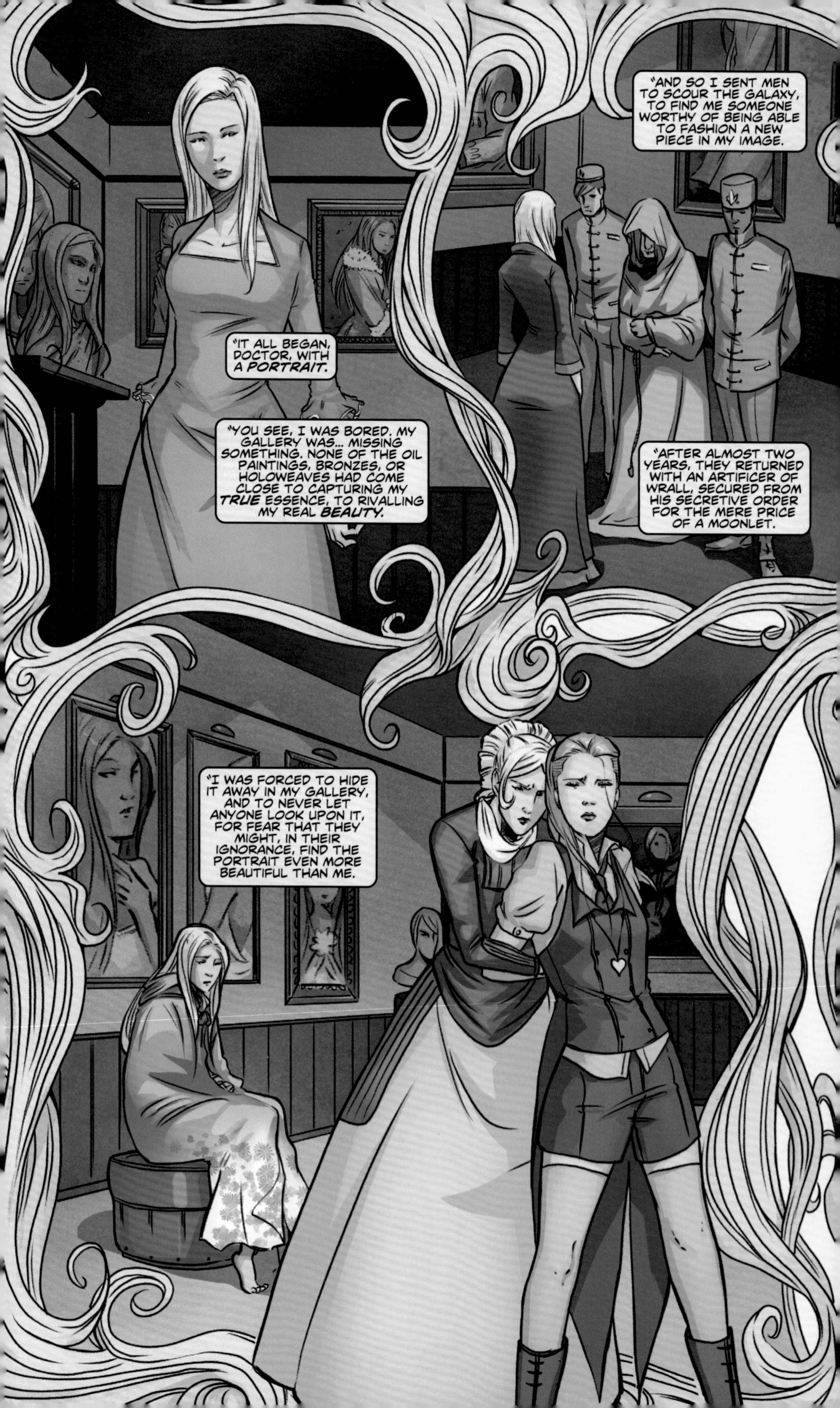
"IT ALL BEGAN, DOCTOR, WITH A PORTRAIT.
"YOU SEE, I WAS BORED. MY GALLERY WAS... MISSING SOMETHING. NONE OF THE OIL PAINTINGS, BRONZES, OR HOLOWEAVES HAD COME CLOSE TO CAPTURING MY TRUE ESSENCE, TO RIVALLING MY REAL BEAUTY.
"AND SO I SENT MEN TO SCOUR THE GALAXY, TO FIND ME SOMEONE WORTHY OF BEING ABLE TO FASHION A NEW PIECE IN MY IMAGE.
"AFTER ALMOST TWO YEARS, THEY RETURNED WITH AN ARTIFICER OF WRALL, SECURED FROM HIS SECRETIVE ORDER FOR THE MERE PRICE OF A MOONLET.
"I WAS FORCED TO HIDE IT AWAY IN MY GALLERY, AND TO NEVER LET ANYONE LOOK UPON IT, FOR FEAR THAT THEY MIGHT, IN THEIR IGNORANCE, FIND THE PORTRAIT EVEN MORE BEAUTIFUL THAN ME.

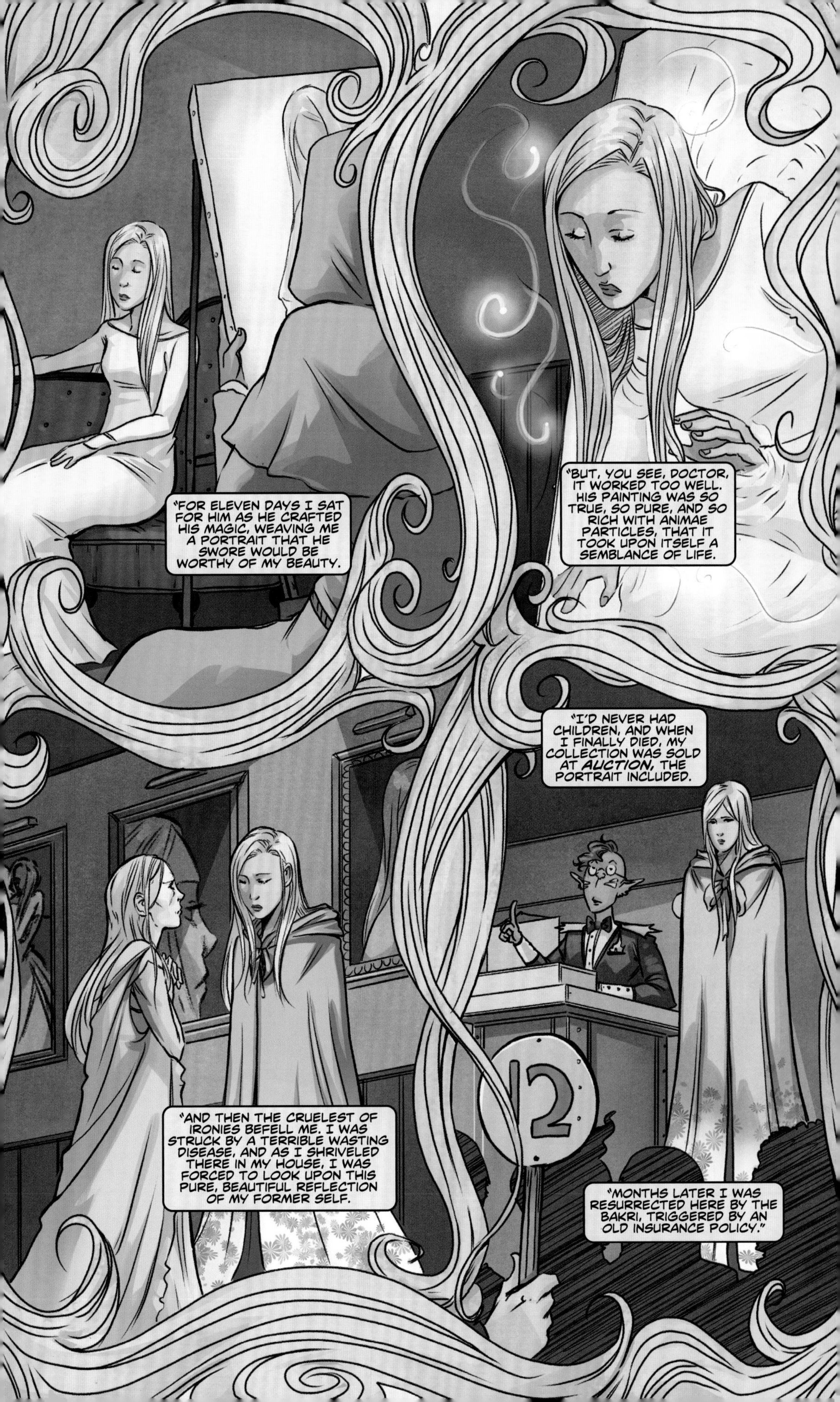
"FOR ELEVEN DAYS I SAT FOR HIM AS HE CRAFTED HIS MAGIC, WEAVING ME A PORTRAIT THAT HE SWORE WOULD BE WORTHY OF MY BEAUTY.
"BUT, YOU SEE, DOCTOR, IT WORKED TOO WELL. HIS PAINTING WAS SO TRUE, SO PURE, AND SO RICH WITH ANIMAE PARTICLES, THAT IT TOOK UPON ITSELF A SEMBLANCE OF LIFE.
"AND THEN THE CRUELEST OF IRONIES BEFELL ME. I WAS STRUCK BY A TERRIBLE WASTING DISEASE, AND AS I SHRIVELED THERE IN MY HOUSE, I WAS FORCED TO LOOK UPON THIS PURE, BEAUTIFUL REFLECTION OF MY FORMER SELF.
"I'D NEVER HAD CHILDREN, AND WHEN I FINALLY DIED, MY COLLECTION WAS SOLD AT *AUCTION*, THE PORTRAIT INCLUDED.
12
"MONTHS LATER I WAS RESURRECTED HERE BY THE BAKRI, TRIGGERED BY AN OLD INSURANCE POLICY."

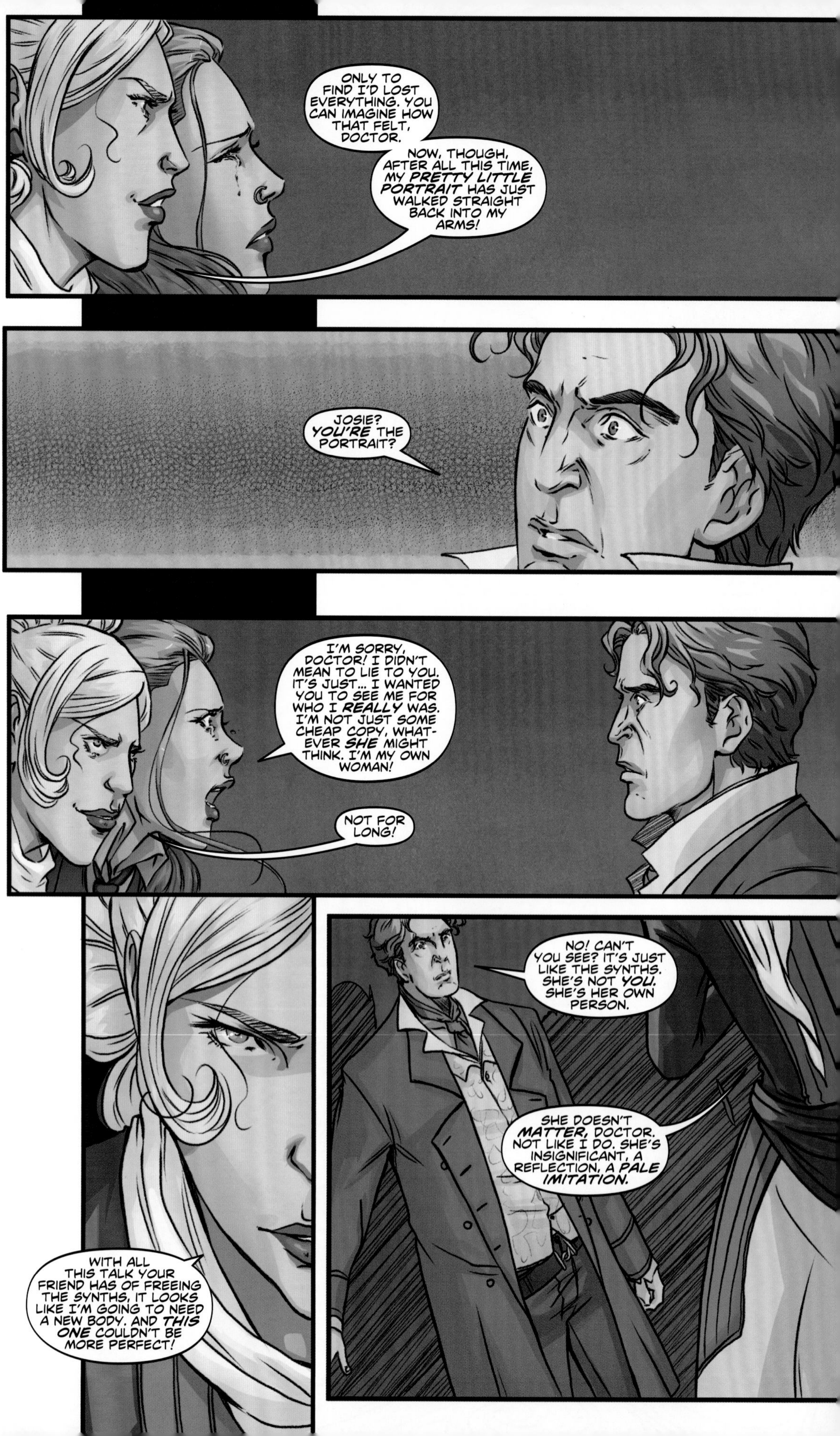
ONLY TO FIND I'D LOST EVERYTHING. YOU CAN IMAGINE HOW THAT FELT, DOCTOR.
NOW, THOUGH, AFTER ALL THIS TIME, MY PRETTY LITTLE PORTRAIT HAS JUST WALKED STRAIGHT BACK INTO MY ARMS!
JOSIE? YOU'RE THE PORTRAIT?
I'M SORRY, DOCTOR! I DIDN'T MEAN TO LIE TO YOU. IT'S JUST... I WANTED YOU TO SEE ME FOR WHO I REALLY WAS. I'M NOT JUST SOME CHEAP COPY, WHATEVER SHE MIGHT THINK. I'M MY OWN WOMAN!
NOT FOR LONG!
NO! CAN'T YOU SEE? IT'S JUST LIKE THE SYNTHS. SHE'S NOT YOU. SHE'S HER OWN PERSON.
SHE DOESN'T MATTER, DOCTOR. NOT LIKE I DO. SHE'S INSIGNIFICANT, A REFLECTION, A PALE IMITATION.
WITH ALL THIS TALK YOUR FRIEND HAS OF FREEING THE SYNTHS, IT LOOKS LIKE I'M GOING TO NEED A NEW BODY. AND THIS ONE COULDN'T BE MORE PERFECT!

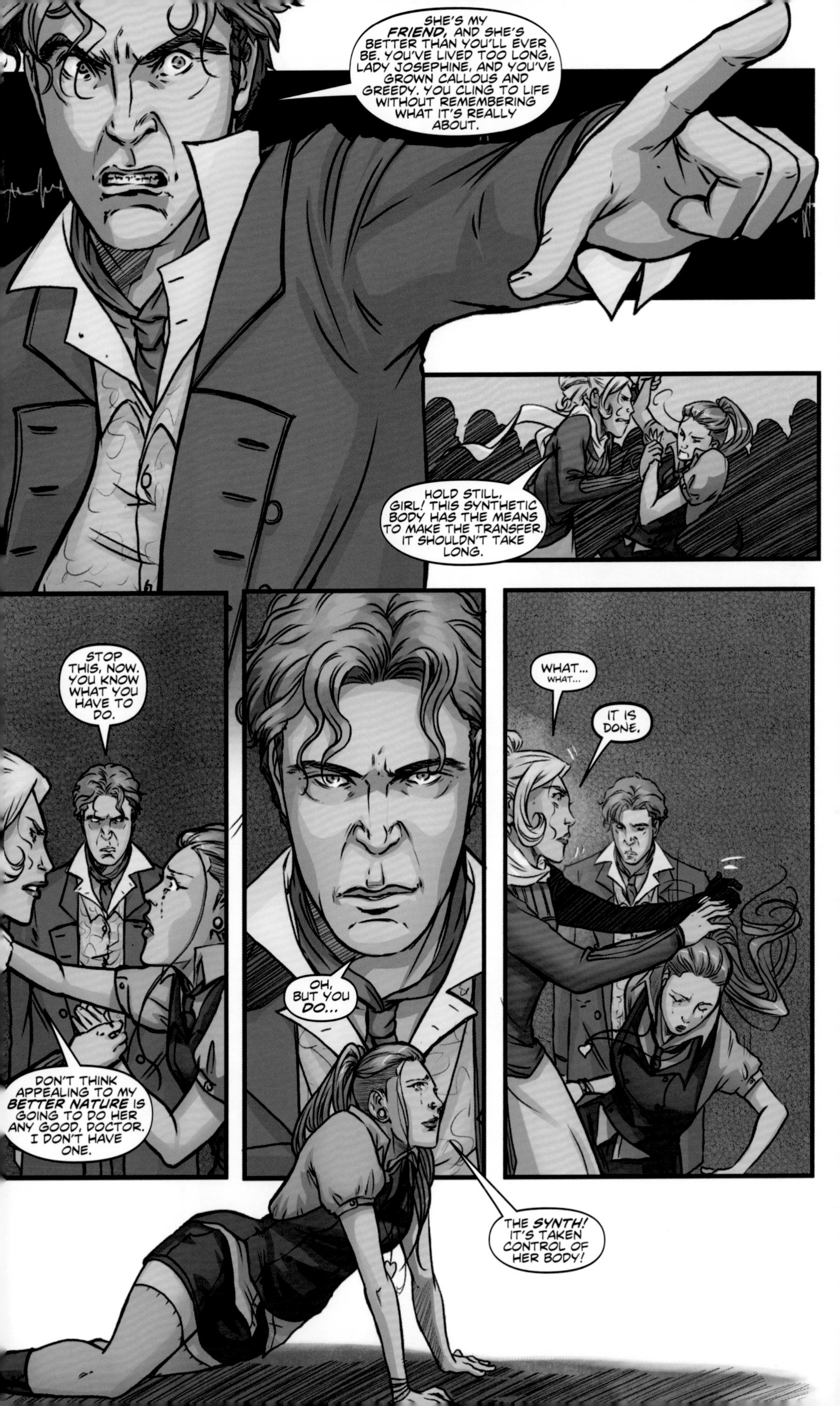
SHE'S MY FRIEND, AND SHE'S BETTER THAN YOU'LL EVER BE. YOU'VE LIVED TOO LONG, LADY JOSEPHINE, AND YOU'VE GROWN CALLOUS AND GREEDY. YOU CLING TO LIFE WITHOUT REMEMBERING WHAT IT'S REALLY ABOUT.
HOLD STILL, GIRL! THIS SYNTHETIC BODY HAS THE MEANS TO MAKE THE TRANSFER. IT SHOULDN'T TAKE LONG.
STOP THIS, NOW. YOU KNOW WHAT YOU HAVE TO DO.
DON'T THINK APPEALING TO MY BETTER NATURE IS GOING TO DO HER ANY GOOD, DOCTOR. I DON'T HAVE ONE.
OH, BUT YOU DO...
WHAT... WHAT...
IT IS DONE.
THE SYNTH! IT'S TAKEN CONTROL OF HER BODY!

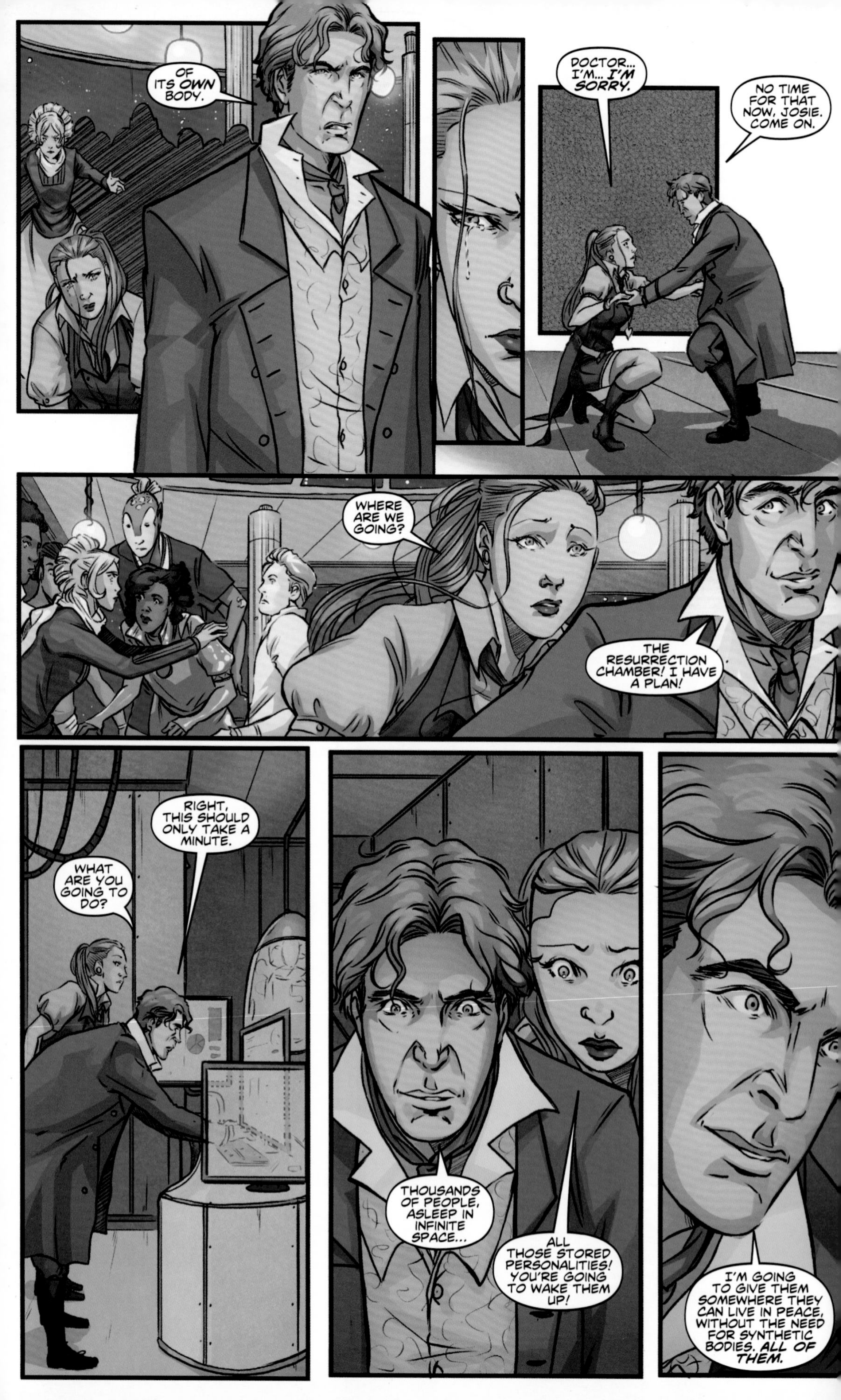
OF ITS *OWN* BODY.
DOCTOR... I'M... *I'M SORRY.*
NO TIME FOR THAT NOW, JOSIE. COME ON.
WHERE ARE WE GOING?
THE RESURRECTION CHAMBER! I HAVE A PLAN!
RIGHT, THIS SHOULD ONLY TAKE A MINUTE.
WHAT ARE YOU GOING TO DO?
THOUSANDS OF PEOPLE, ASLEEP IN INFINITE SPACE...
ALL THOSE STORED PERSONALITIES! YOU'RE GOING TO WAKE THEM UP!
I'M GOING TO GIVE THEM SOMEWHERE THEY CAN LIVE IN PEACE, WITHOUT THE NEED FOR SYNTHETIC BODIES. *ALL OF THEM.*

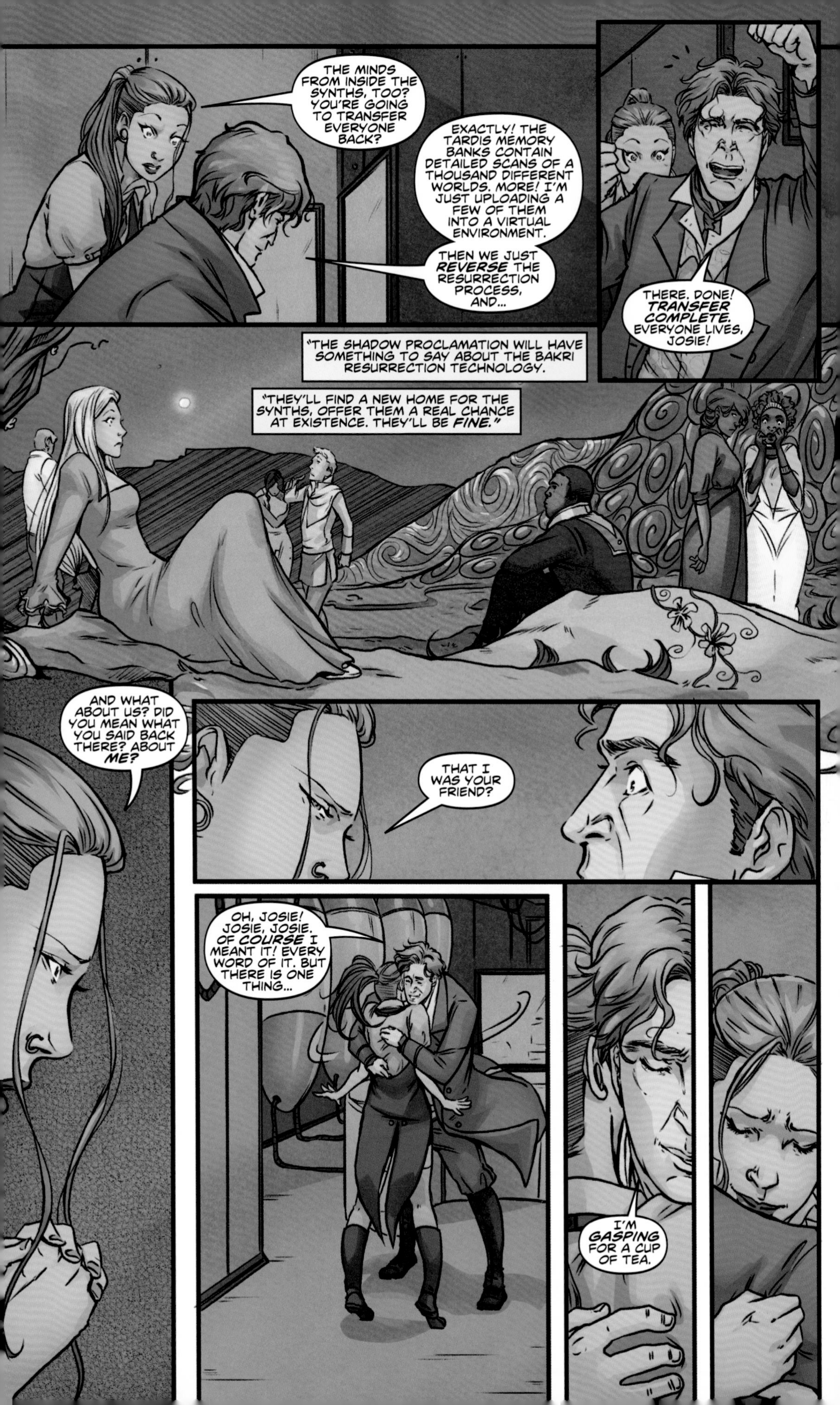

THE MINDS FROM INSIDE THE SYNTHS, TOO? YOU'RE GOING TO TRANSFER EVERYONE BACK?
EXACTLY! THE TARDIS MEMORY BANKS CONTAIN DETAILED SCANS OF A THOUSAND DIFFERENT WORLDS. MORE! I'M JUST UPLOADING A FEW OF THEM INTO A VIRTUAL ENVIRONMENT.
THEN WE JUST *REVERSE* THE RESURRECTION PROCESS, AND...
THERE. DONE! *TRANSFER COMPLETE.* EVERYONE LIVES, JOSIE!
"THE SHADOW PROCLAMATION WILL HAVE SOMETHING TO SAY ABOUT THE BAKRI RESURRECTION TECHNOLOGY.
"THEY'LL FIND A NEW HOME FOR THE SYNTHS, OFFER THEM A REAL CHANCE AT EXISTENCE. THEY'LL BE *FINE.*"
AND WHAT ABOUT US? DID YOU MEAN WHAT YOU SAID BACK THERE? ABOUT *ME?*
THAT I WAS YOUR FRIEND?
OH, JOSIE! JOSIE, JOSIE. OF *COURSE* I MEANT IT! EVERY WORD OF IT. BUT THERE IS ONE THING...
I'M *GASPING* FOR A CUP OF TEA.

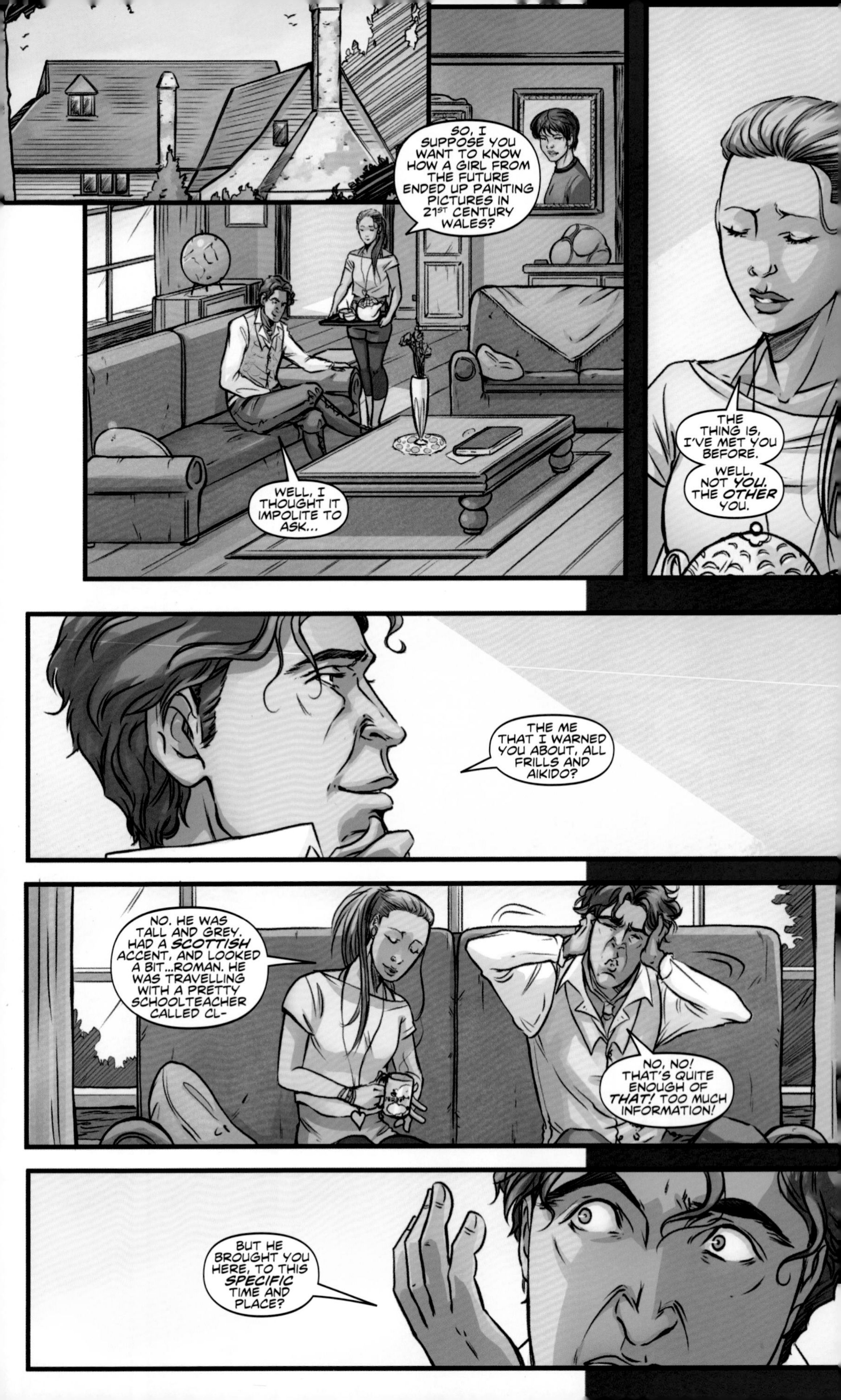
SO, I SUPPOSE YOU WANT TO KNOW HOW A GIRL FROM THE FUTURE ENDED UP PAINTING PICTURES IN 21ST CENTURY WALES?
WELL, I THOUGHT IT IMPOLITE TO ASK...
THE THING IS, I'VE MET YOU BEFORE.
WELL, NOT *YOU*. THE *OTHER* YOU.
THE ME THAT I WARNED YOU ABOUT, ALL FRILLS AND AIKIDO?
NO. HE WAS TALL AND GREY. HAD A *SCOTTISH* ACCENT, AND LOOKED A BIT...ROMAN. HE WAS TRAVELLING WITH A PRETTY SCHOOLTEACHER CALLED CL-
NO, NO! THAT'S QUITE ENOUGH OF *THAT!* TOO MUCH INFORMATION!
BUT HE BROUGHT YOU HERE, TO THIS *SPECIFIC* TIME AND PLACE?

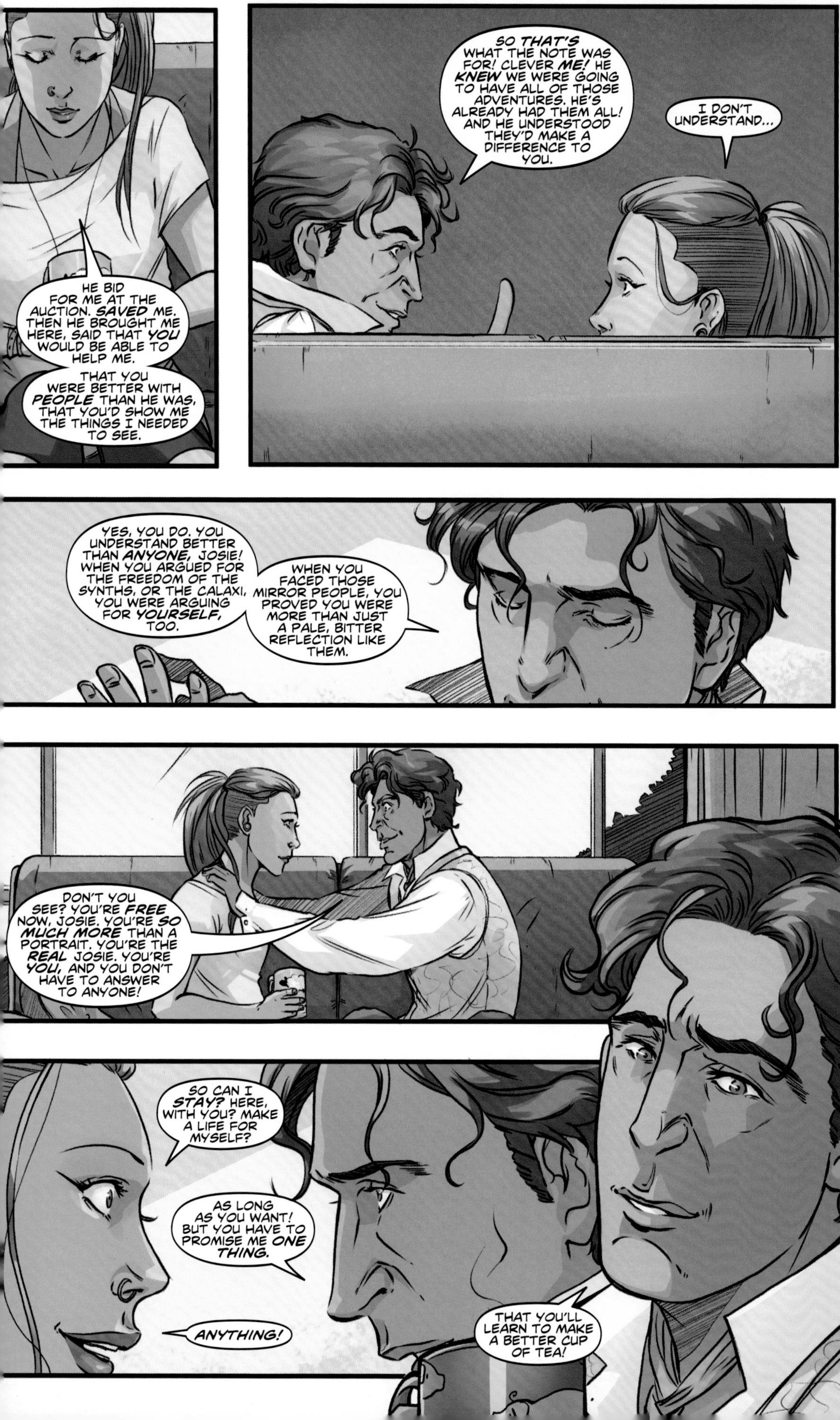
HE BID FOR ME AT THE AUCTION. SAVED ME. THEN HE BROUGHT ME HERE, SAID THAT YOU WOULD BE ABLE TO HELP ME.
THAT YOU WERE BETTER WITH PEOPLE THAN HE WAS, THAT YOU'D SHOW ME THE THINGS I NEEDED TO SEE.
SO THAT'S WHAT THE NOTE WAS FOR! CLEVER ME! HE KNEW WE WERE GOING TO HAVE ALL OF THOSE ADVENTURES. HE'S ALREADY HAD THEM ALL! AND HE UNDERSTOOD THEY'D MAKE A DIFFERENCE TO YOU.
I DON'T UNDERSTAND...
YES, YOU DO. YOU UNDERSTAND BETTER THAN ANYONE, JOSIE! WHEN YOU ARGUED FOR THE FREEDOM OF THE SYNTHS, OR THE CALAXI, YOU WERE ARGUING FOR YOURSELF, TOO.
WHEN YOU FACED THOSE MIRROR PEOPLE, YOU PROVED YOU WERE MORE THAN JUST A PALE, BITTER REFLECTION LIKE THEM.
DON'T YOU SEE? YOU'RE FREE NOW, JOSIE. YOU'RE SO MUCH MORE THAN A PORTRAIT. YOU'RE THE REAL JOSIE. YOU'RE YOU, AND YOU DON'T HAVE TO ANSWER TO ANYONE!
SO CAN I STAY? HERE, WITH YOU? MAKE A LIFE FOR MYSELF?
AS LONG AS YOU WANT! BUT YOU HAVE TO PROMISE ME ONE THING.
ANYTHING!
THAT YOU'LL LEARN TO MAKE A BETTER CUP OF TEA!

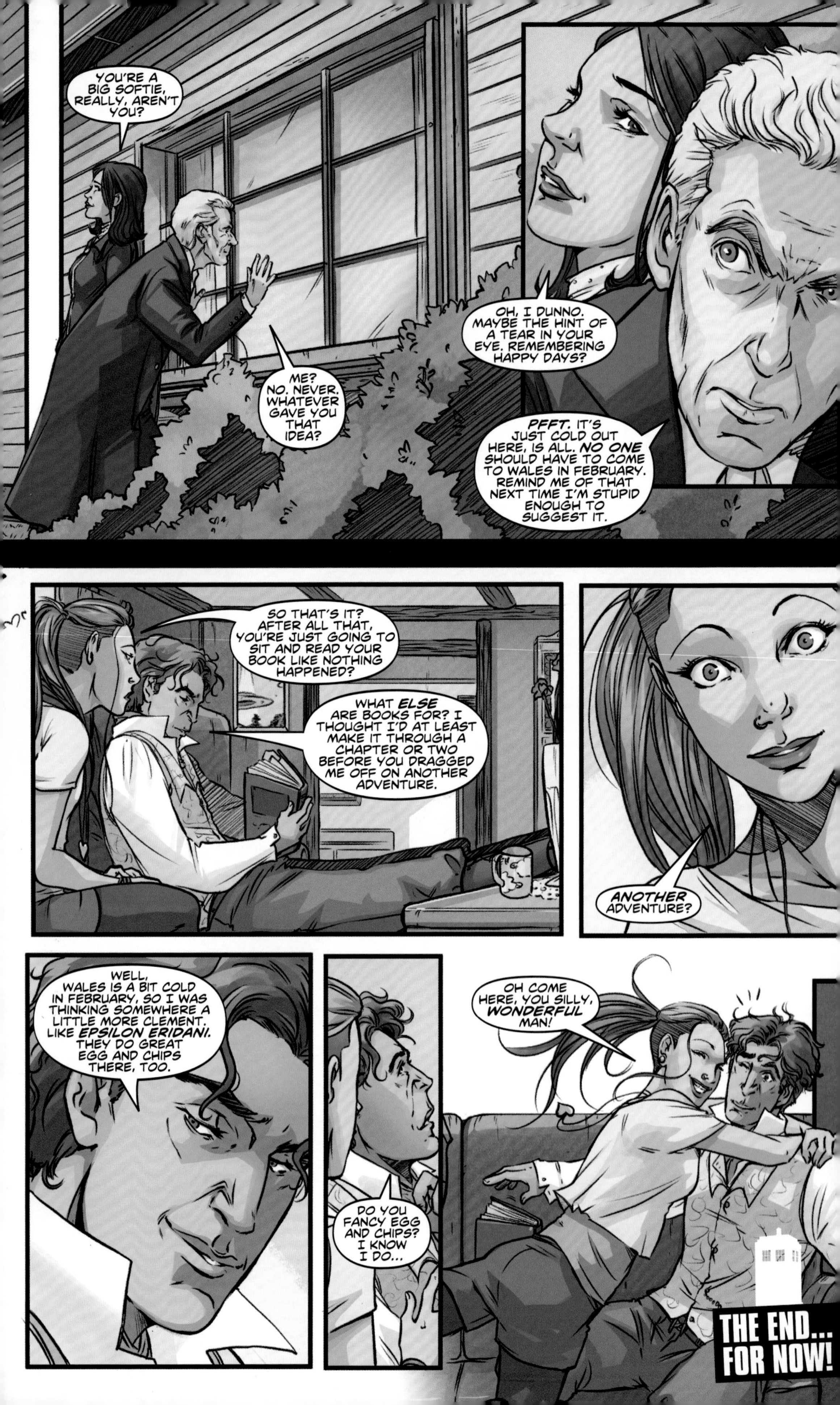

YOU'RE A BIG SOFTIE, REALLY, AREN'T YOU?
ME? NO. NEVER. WHATEVER GAVE YOU THAT IDEA?
OH, I DUNNO. MAYBE THE HINT OF A TEAR IN YOUR EYE, REMEMBERING HAPPY DAYS?
PFFT. IT'S JUST COLD OUT HERE, IS ALL. NO ONE SHOULD HAVE TO COME TO WALES IN FEBRUARY. REMIND ME OF THAT NEXT TIME I'M STUPID ENOUGH TO SUGGEST IT.
SO THAT'S IT? AFTER ALL THAT, YOU'RE JUST GOING TO SIT AND READ YOUR BOOK LIKE NOTHING HAPPENED?
WHAT ELSE ARE BOOKS FOR? I THOUGHT I'D AT LEAST MAKE IT THROUGH A CHAPTER OR TWO BEFORE YOU DRAGGED ME OFF ON ANOTHER ADVENTURE.
ANOTHER ADVENTURE?
WELL, WALES IS A BIT COLD IN FEBRUARY, SO I WAS THINKING SOMEWHERE A LITTLE MORE CLEMENT. LIKE EPSILON ERIDANI. THEY DO GREAT EGG AND CHIPS THERE, TOO.
DO YOU FANCY EGG AND CHIPS? I KNOW I DO...
OH COME HERE, YOU SILLY, WONDERFUL MAN!
THE END... FOR NOW!

BBC
DOCTOR WHO
THE EIGHTH DOCTOR

COVER GALLERY

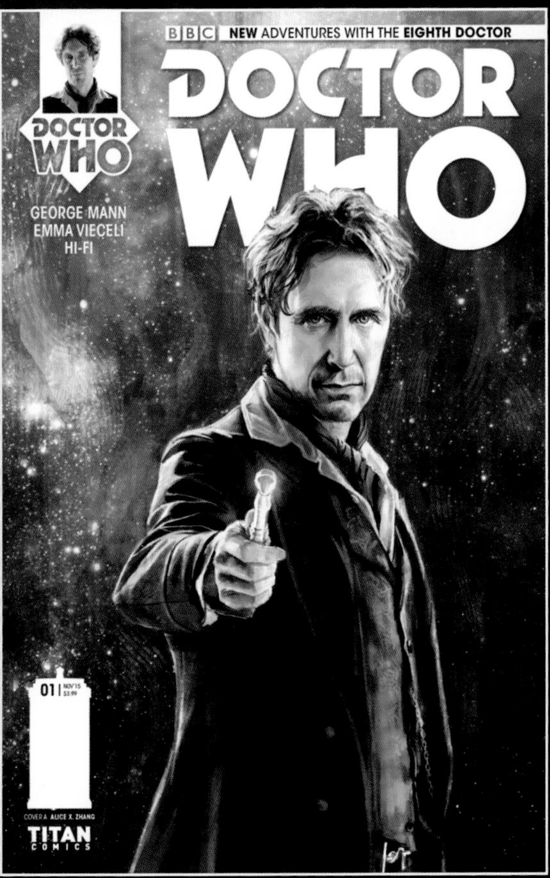

BBC NEW ADVENTURES WITH THE EIGHTH DOCTOR
DOCTOR WHO
DOCTOR WHO
GEORGE MANN
EMMA VIECELI
HI-FI
01 NOV'15 $3.99
COVER A ALICE X. ZHANG
TITAN COMICS

A

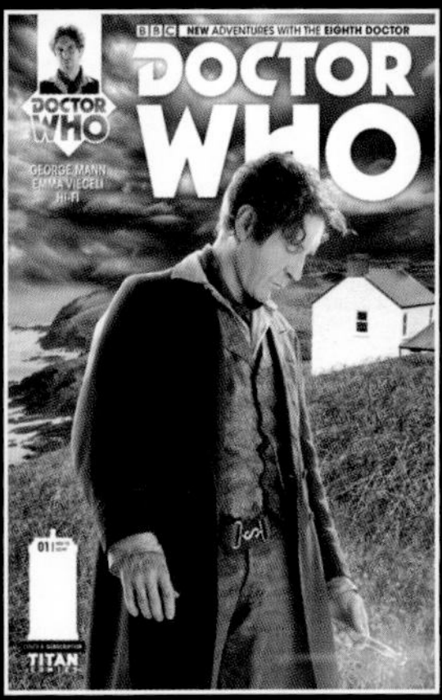

BBC NEW ADVENTURES WITH THE EIGHTH DOCTOR
DOCTOR WHO
DOCTOR WHO
GEORGE MANN
EMMA VIECELI
HI-FI
TITAN

B

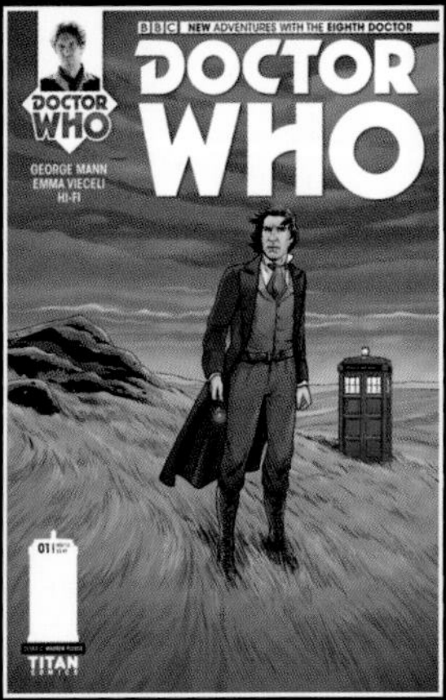

BBC NEW ADVENTURES WITH THE EIGHTH DOCTOR
DOCTOR WHO
DOCTOR WHO
GEORGE MANN
EMMA VIECELI
HI-FI
TITAN

C

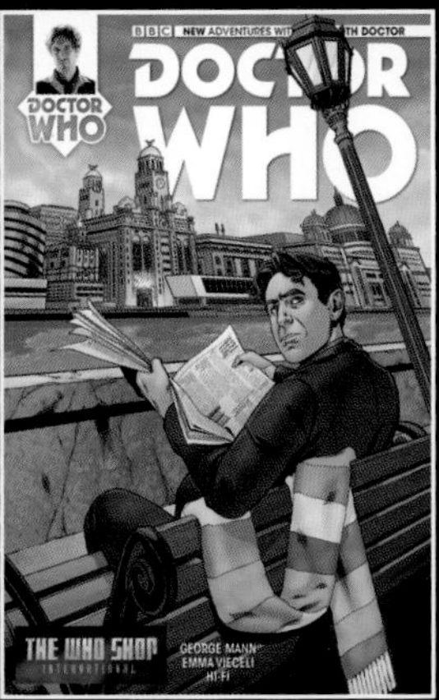

BBC NEW ADVENTURES WIT… DOCTOR
DOCTOR WHO
DOCTOR WHO
THE WHO SHOP
GEORGE MANN
EMMA VIECELI
HI-FI

D

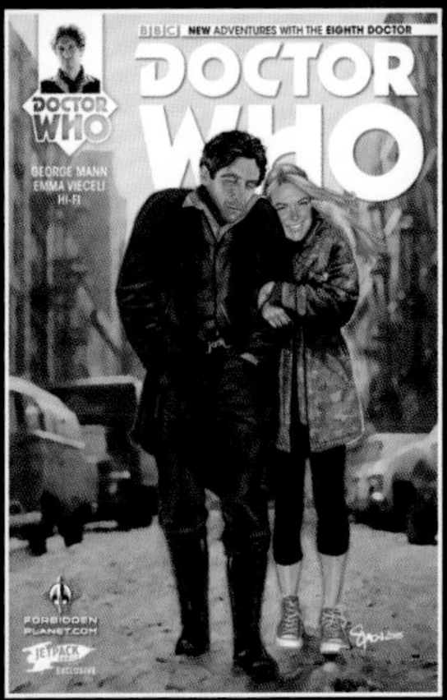

BBC NEW ADVENTURES WITH THE EIGHTH DOCTOR
DOCTOR WHO
DOCTOR WHO
GEORGE MANN
EMMA VIECELI
HI-FI
FORBIDDEN PLANET.COM
JETPACK

E

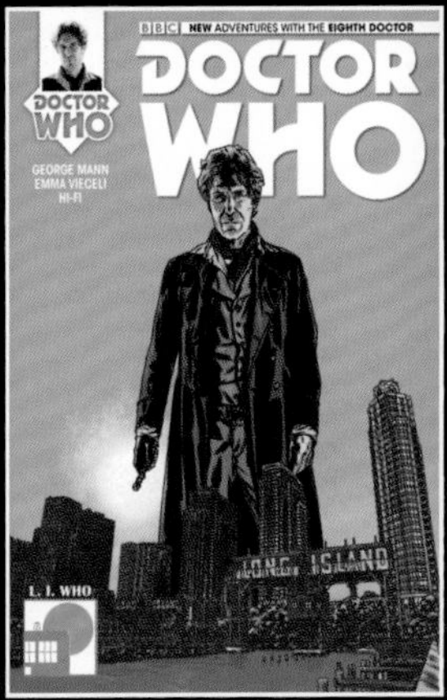

BBC NEW ADVENTURES WITH THE EIGHTH DOCTOR
DOCTOR WHO
DOCTOR WHO
GEORGE MANN
EMMA VIECELI
HI-FI
LONG ISLAND
L. I. WHO

F

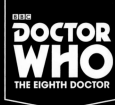

A: ALICE X. ZHANG
B: PHOTO WILL BROOKS
C: EXCLUSIVE WARREN PLEECE
D: THE WHO SHOP
EXCLUSIVE RACHAEL STOTT & HI-FI
E: FORBIDDEN PLANET / JETPACK
EXCLUSIVE SIMON MYERS
F: LONG ISLAND WHO CON
EXCLUSIVE MATTHEW DOW SMITH
G: BOOKS A MILLION EXCLUSIVE
MARIANO LACLAUSTRA
H: ALIEN ENTERTAINMENT EXCLUSIVE
PHOTO

ISSUE #1

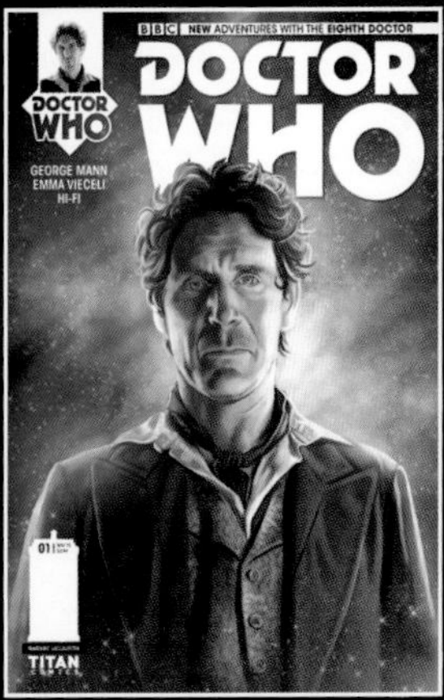

BBC NEW ADVENTURES WITH THE EIGHTH DOCTOR
DOCTOR WHO
DOCTOR WHO
GEORGE MANN
EMMA VIECELI
HI-FI
TITAN

G

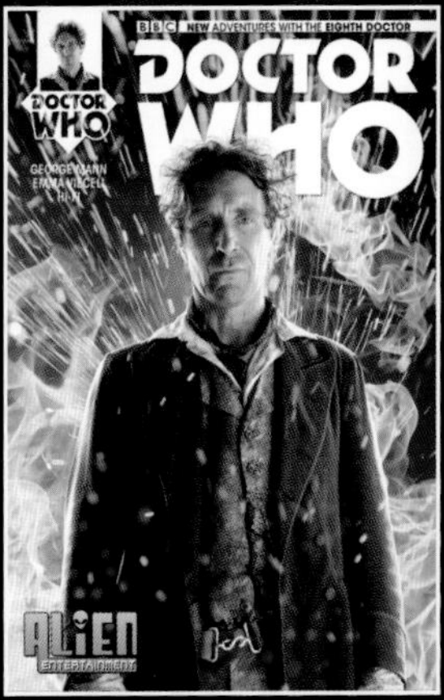

BBC NEW ADVENTURES WITH THE EIGHTH DOCTOR
DOCTOR WHO
DOCTOR WHO
ALIEN ENTERTAINMENT

H

COVER GALLERY

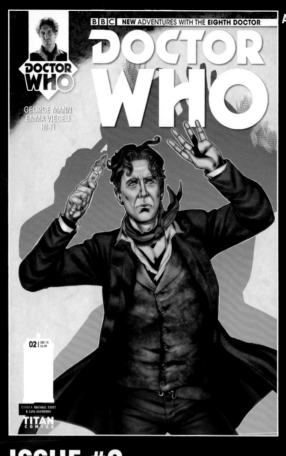

ISSUE #2

A: RACHAEL STOTT & LUIS GUERRERO **B: PHOTO** AJ **C: EXCLUSIVE** WARREN PLEECE

ISSUE #3

A: RACHAEL STOTT & HI-FI **B: PHOTO** WILL BROOKS

A

04 | FEB '16
$3.99

COVER A **RACHAEL STOTT**

B

C

D

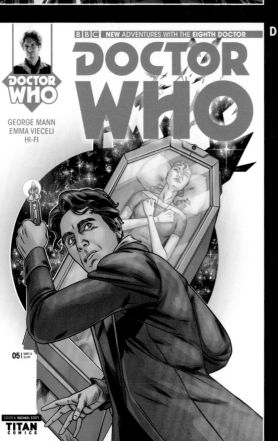

05 | MAR '16
$3.99

COVER A **RACHAEL STOTT**

E

F

COVER GALLERY

FOLLOW YOUR FAVORITE INCARNATIONS ACROSS THESE FANTASTIC COLLECTIONS!

DOCTOR WHO: THE TWELFTH DOCTOR VOL. 1:TERRORFORMER

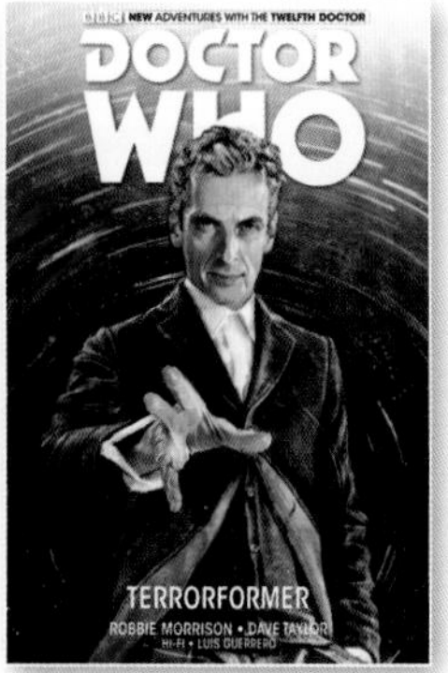
NEW ADVENTURES WITH THE TWELFTH DOCTOR
DOCTOR WHO
TERRORFORMER
ROBBIE MORRISON • DAVE TAYLOR
HI-FI • LUIS GUERRERO

ISBN: 9781782761778
ON SALE NOW - $19.99 / $22.95 CAN / £10.99
(UK EDITION ISBN: 9781782763864)

DOCTOR WHO: THE TWELFTH DOCTOR VOL. 2: FRACTURES

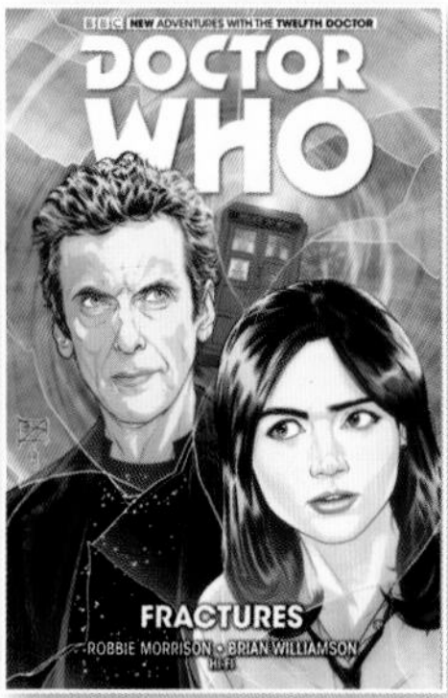
NEW ADVENTURES WITH THE TWELFTH DOCTOR
DOCTOR WHO
FRACTURES
ROBBIE MORRISON • BRIAN WILLIAMSON
HI-FI

ISBN: 9781782763017
ON SALE NOW - $19.99 / $25.99 CAN / £10.99
(UK EDITION ISBN: 9781782766599)

DOCTOR WHO: THE TWELFTH DOCTOR VOL. 3: HYPERION

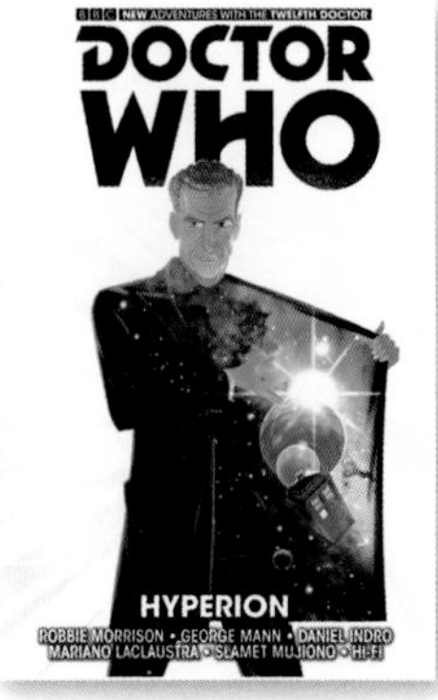
NEW ADVENTURES WITH THE TWELFTH DOCTOR
DOCTOR WHO
HYPERION
ROBBIE MORRISON • GEORGE MANN • DANIEL INDRO
MARIANO LACLAUSTRA • SLAMET MUJIONO • HI-FI

ISBN: 9781782767473
ON SALE NOW- $19.99 / $25.99 CAN / £10.99
(UK EDITION ISBN: 9781782767442)

DOCTOR WHO: THE TWELFTH DOCTOR VOL. 4: THE SCHOOL OF DEATH

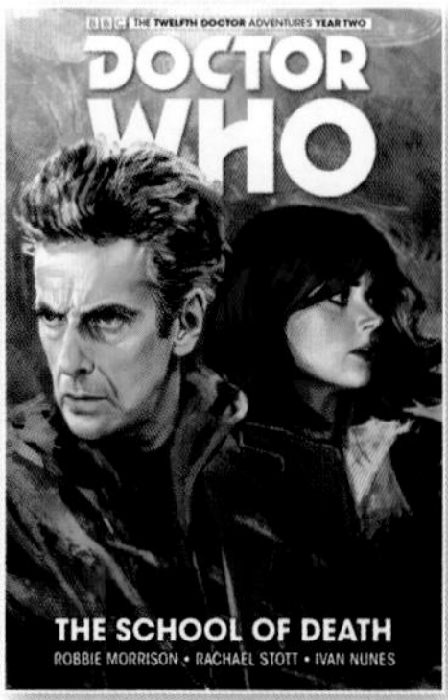
THE TWELFTH DOCTOR ADVENTURES YEAR TWO
DOCTOR WHO
THE SCHOOL OF DEATH
ROBBIE MORRISON • RACHAEL STOTT • IVAN NUNES

ISBN: 9781785851087
COMING SOON - $19.99 / $25.99 CAN / £10.99
(UK EDITION ISBN: 9781785851070)

DOCTOR WHO: THE ELEVENTH DOCTOR VOL. 1: AFTER LIFE

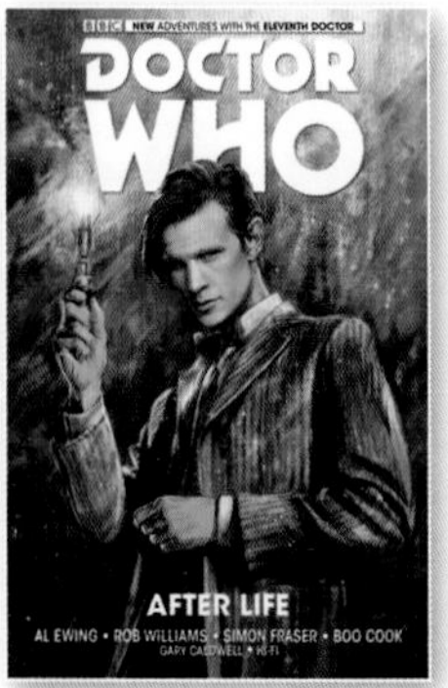
NEW ADVENTURES WITH THE ELEVENTH DOCTOR
DOCTOR WHO
AFTER LIFE
AL EWING • ROB WILLIAMS • SIMON FRASER • BOO COOK
GARY CALDWELL • HI-FI

ISBN: 9781782761747
ON SALE NOW - $19.99 / $22.95 CAN / £10.99
(UK EDITION ISBN: 9781782763857)

DOCTOR WHO: THE ELEVENTH DOCTOR VOL. 2: SERVE YOU

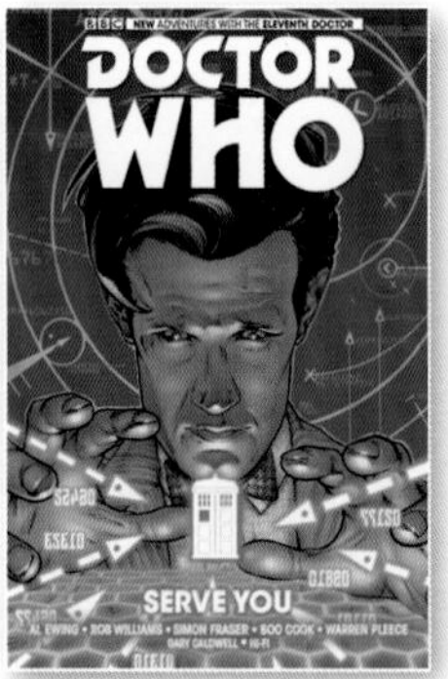
NEW ADVENTURES WITH THE ELEVENTH DOCTOR
DOCTOR WHO
SERVE YOU

ISBN: 9781782761747
ON SALE NOW - $19.99 / $22.95 CAN / £10.99
(UK EDITION ISBN: 9781782763857)

DOCTOR WHO: THE ELEVENTH DOCTOR VOL. 3: CONVERSION

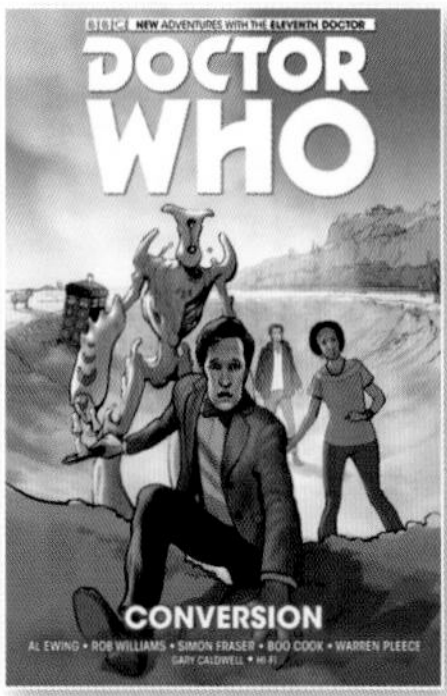
NEW ADVENTURES WITH THE ELEVENTH DOCTOR
DOCTOR WHO
CONVERSION
AL EWING • ROB WILLIAMS • SIMON FRASER • BOO COOK • WARREN PLEECE
GARY CALDWELL • HI-FI

ISBN: 9781782763031
ON SALE NOW - $19.99 / $25.99 CAN / £10.99
(UK EDITION ISBN: 9781782767435)

DOCTOR WHO: THE ELEVENTH DOCTOR VOL. 4:THE THEN AND THE NOW

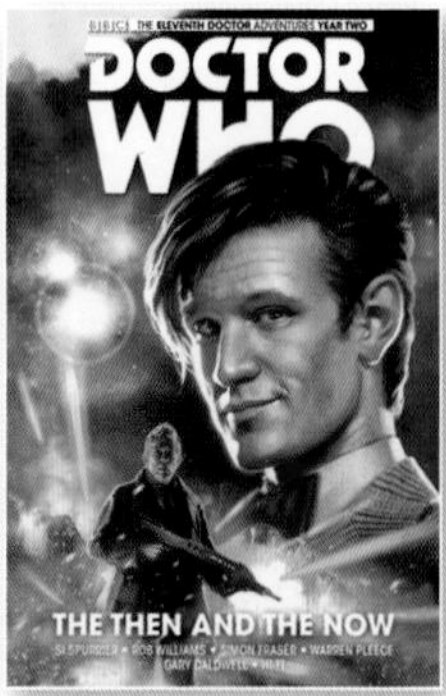
THE ELEVENTH DOCTOR ADVENTURES YEAR TWO
DOCTOR WHO
THE THEN AND THE NOW

ISBN: 9781782767466
ON SALE NOW - $19.99 / $25.99 CAN / £10.99
(UK EDITION ISBN: 9781722767428)

For information on how to subscribe to our great Doctor Who titles, or to purchase them digitally for your favorite device, visit:

WWW.TITAN-COMICS.COM

TITAN COMICS

FILL YOUR SHELVES WITH ADVENTURES FROM ACROSS TIME AND SPACE!

DOCTOR WHO: THE TENTH DOCTOR VOL. 1: REVOLUTIONS OF TERROR

BBC NEW ADVENTURES WITH THE TENTH DOCTOR
DOCTOR WHO
REVOLUTIONS OF TERROR

ISBN: 9781782761747
ON SALE NOW - $19.99 / $22.95 CAN / £10.99
(UK EDITION ISBN: 9781782763840)

DOCTOR WHO: THE TENTH DOCTOR VOL. 2: THE WEEPING ANGELS OF MONS

BBC NEW ADVENTURES WITH THE TENTH DOCTOR
DOCTOR WHO
THE WEEPING ANGELS OF MONS
ROBBIE MORRISON • DANIEL INDRO • SLAMET MUJIONO

ISBN: 9781782761754
ON SALE NOW - $19.99 / $25.99 CAN / £10.99
(UK EDITION ISBN: 9781782766575)

DOCTOR WHO: THE TENTH DOCTOR VOL. 3: THE FOUNTAINS OF FOREVER

BBC NEW ADVENTURES WITH THE TENTH DOCTOR
DOCTOR WHO
THE FOUNTAINS OF FOREVER
NICK ABADZIS • ELENA CASAGRANDE
ELEONORA CARLINI • ARIANNA FLOREAN

ISBN: 9781782763024
ON SALE NOW - $19.99 / $25.99 CAN / £10.99
(UK EDITION ISBN: 9781782767404)

DOCTOR WHO: THE TENTH DOCTOR VOL. 4: THE ENDLESS SONG

BBC THE TENTH DOCTOR ADVENTURES YEAR TWO
DOCTOR WHO
THE ENDLESS SONG

ISBN: 9781782767459
COMING SOON - $19.99 / $25.99 CAN / £10.99
(UK EDITION ISBN: 97817852767411)

DOCTOR WHO: THE NINTH DOCTOR VOL. 1: WEAPONS OF PAST DESTRUCTION

BBC NEW ADVENTURES WITH THE NINTH DOCTOR
DOCTOR WHO
WEAPONS OF PAST DESTRUCTION
CAVAN SCOTT • BLAIR SHEDD

ISBN: 9781782763369
ON SALE NOW - $19.99 / $25.99 CAN / £10.99
(UK EDITION ISBN: 9781782761056)

A DOCTOR WHO COMICS EVENT: FOUR DOCTORS

BBC A DOCTOR WHO COMICS EVENT
DOCTOR WHO
PAUL CORNELL ▮ NEIL EDWARDS
FOUR DOCTORS
WITH IVAN NUNES AND COMICRAFT

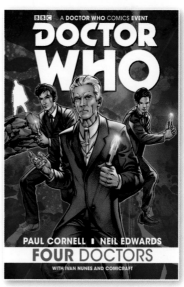

ISBN: 9781782765967
ON SALE NOW - $19.99 / $25.99 CAN / £10.99
(UK EDITION ISBN: 9781785851063)

AVAILABLE IN ALL GOOD COMIC STORES, BOOK STORES, AND DIGITAL PROVIDERS!

BBC

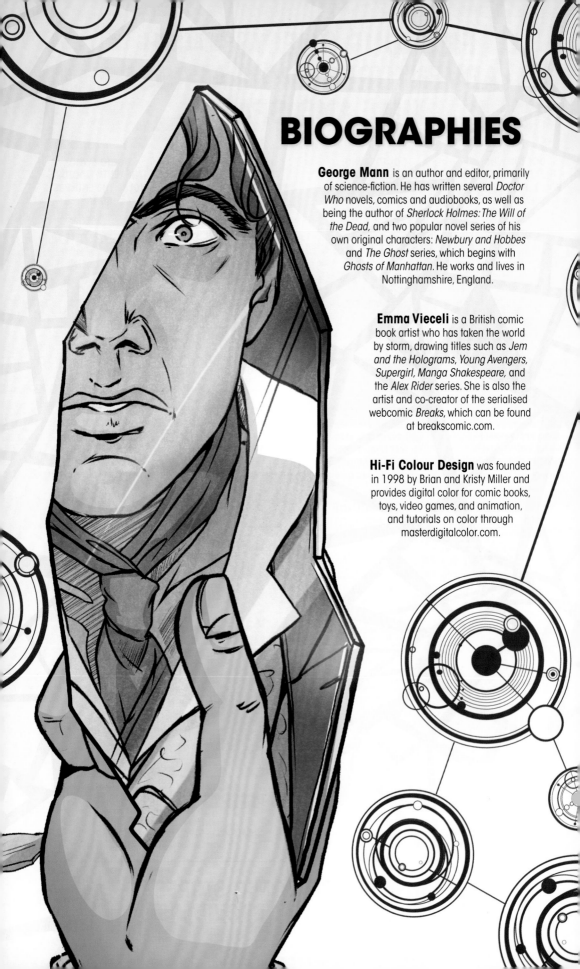

BIOGRAPHIES

George Mann is an author and editor, primarily of science-fiction. He has written several *Doctor Who* novels, comics and audiobooks, as well as being the author of *Sherlock Holmes: The Will of the Dead,* and two popular novel series of his own original characters: *Newbury and Hobbes* and *The Ghost* series, which begins with *Ghosts of Manhattan.* He works and lives in Nottinghamshire, England.

Emma Vieceli is a British comic book artist who has taken the world by storm, drawing titles such as *Jem and the Holograms, Young Avengers, Supergirl, Manga Shakespeare,* and the *Alex Rider* series. She is also the artist and co-creator of the serialised webcomic *Breaks,* which can be found at breakscomic.com.

Hi-Fi Colour Design was founded in 1998 by Brian and Kristy Miller and provides digital color for comic books, toys, video games, and animation, and tutorials on color through masterdigitalcolor.com.